CRITICAL INSIGHTS

The American Thriller

CRITICAL INSIGHTS

The American Thriller

Editor
Gary Hoppenstand
Michigan State University, Lansing Michigan

SALEM PRESS
A Division of EBSCO Information Services, Inc.
Ipswich, Massachusetts

GREY HOUSE PUBLISHING

Library of Congress Cataloging-in-Publication Data

The American thriller / editor, Gary Hoppenstand, Michigan State
   University, Lansing, Michigan. -- [First edition].

    pages ; cm. -- (Critical insights)

   Includes bibliographical references and index.
   ISBN: 978-1-61925-220-2

   1. Suspense fiction, American--History and criticism. 2. Suspense in literature.
I. Hoppenstand, Gary, editor of compilation. II. Series: Critical insights.

PS374.S87 A44 2014
813

First Printing

Contents

About This Volume ————————————

Gary Hoppenstand

The American thriller is a complex and diverse collection of popular fiction categories that rely predominantly on adventure and suspense to propel the story's action, and to elicit a sense of fear or excitement with the reader that obviously lends itself to the descriptive name of this type of fiction. As such, then, to explore all classifications of the American thriller would be a herculean task, one that would fill an encyclopedia-length book, rather than a collection of essays.

An attempt was made, then, to outline four of the more dominant or popular categories of the American thriller. These include the techno thriller, the legal thriller, the crime thriller, and the psychological thriller. John A. Dowell's examination of the techno thriller explores the nineteenth-century science fiction influences on the American thriller, while also providing a broad overview of recent, important authors and novels that have currently made the techno thriller one of the most popular types of popular fiction. Ayoola Onatade's analysis of the legal thriller also charts the history of this type of thriller in American literature, while focusing on several prominent examples of contemporary, bestselling legal thriller writers. Kate Watson defines the literary origins and influences of the crime thriller as well, exploring the tremendous breadth of subject and reach of theme of this memorable literary expression, while Kristopher Mecholsky outlines many of the important motifs and themes that are typically found in examples of the psychological thriller.

Multi-talented writer and director Michael Crichton is discussed by Chris Richardson, who focuses on the novels and films that made Crichton such an important contributor to the development of the American thriller. Crichton's ground-breaking novels, *The Andromeda Strain* (1969) and *Jurassic Park* (1990) remain two of the most important and influential novels to be found in the category of the techno thriller—a type of popular fiction many critics and literary historians claim as being "invented," if not perfected, by Crichton.

The contributions of Tom Clancy are investigated by Helen S. Garson. Clancy, another major contributor to the techno thriller, created one of the more significant American thriller protagonists in his C.I.A. hero, Jack Ryan. Tom Clancy's novels were instrumental in articulating the political paranoia of the later Cold War era, as well as the subsequent threat of terrorism.

Robin Cook took the American thriller in a somewhat different direction than either Cussler or Crichton, as demonstrated by Lorena Laura Stookey. Best known as a master of the tale of medical suspense and intrigue, Cook's novels have entertained readers for over three decades—beginning with his breakthrough novel *Coma* (1977)—with their frightening depiction of medical and biological threats that have gotten out-of-control and have become highly dangerous.

John Grisham is to the legal thriller what Robin Cook is to the medical thriller, that is, Grisham is the reigning master of this type of popular fiction. Susan J. Tyburski offers an informative and comprehensive look at Grisham's work, recognizing his formative influence on the legal thriller in groundbreaking novels, such as *The Firm* (1991). She also scrutinizes Grisham's skills as a top-flight storyteller.

Likewise addressing effective storytelling skills, Abby Bentham gives us a comprehensive review of the darkly disturbing fiction of that master of the psychological thriller, Thomas Harris. Harris' iconic serial killer, Dr. Hannibal Lecter, is part monster and part genius, possessing a strong measure of taste (in both the good and horrible sense) and style. Though limited by the limited number of his published novels, Harris' influence on the contemporary psychological thriller cannot be underestimated.

Garyn G. Roberts also discusses a master of the psychological thriller, perhaps THE master of the serial killer story and the author of the iconic novel, *Psycho* (1959). But, as Roberts notes, Robert Bloch was a talented and highly diverse writer. He was known by his colleagues and his readers as something of a jester, a dark humorist, who effectively employed ironic and horrible twists in his thrillers. *Psycho* itself, seen in this light, becomes a type of twisted joke, on both the characters in the novel and on the reader. Bloch may have exhibited a grisly sense of humor in his work, but there is no denying that he was both one-of-a-kind (in the best sense) and an important pioneer of the psychological thriller.

James Patterson is a prolific and extremely successful writer of the crime thriller. Philip Simpson provides an inclusive look at the extensive contributions of Patterson, including a scrutiny of Patterson's most famous series protagonist, Alex Cross. Patterson has become, in recent years, a one-man publishing industry, releasing numerous books each year, co-authored with a variety of different writers. But such a prodigious output has not diminished Patterson's appeal with his readership, and he continues to be one of the most successful, best-selling crime thriller authors of today.

Though not an American writer, British-born Lee Child is one of the most successful authors of the crime thriller in America. His American vigilante protagonist, Jack Reacher, has ascended to that rarefied pantheon of series heroes that includes Sherlock Holmes and James Bond. Elizabeth Blakesley's analysis of Lee Child's Jack Reacher gives us a comprehensive overview of the character and Child's novels. Her discussion of the Jack Reacher series certainly delivers an intriguing look at one of the crime thriller's most intriguing protagonists and one of its most intense and powerful heroes.

Collectively, the essays in this volume provide an introduction to the American thriller, its major categories, and a number of its most important and influential writers. Though sometimes ignored by the literary establishment, the American thriller has never been ignored by its devoted and widespread readership, and as the contributors discuss in their contributions to this collection, there are ample reasons why the American thriller remains one of the most engaging and entertaining categories of popular fiction today.

On the American Thriller _____

Gary Hoppenstand

From its origin in eighteenth-century England to its evolution in America and Great Britain during the nineteenth and twentieth centuries, fiction experienced exploration, expansion, and solidification of literary genres. Dominated by the adventure story and the Gothic story in the early decades of its evolution, by the twentieth century, popular fiction had seen the creation of science fiction, horror fiction, adventure fiction, detective fiction, romance fiction, frontier fiction (i.e., the western), and modern fantasy fiction. Those critics who study the frame and form of literary genres tend to speak of popular fiction categories as being rigid, or inflexible, and thus are disparaged for their formulaic predictability. Nothing could be further from the truth.

Popular fiction is like a living thing, a symbiotic entity that possesses an intimate and dynamic relationship among author, narrative, publisher, and audience. It is constantly changing to meet (and to help guide) reader expectations for an entertaining story. It persistently articulates new mixtures of formula, while always maintaining that delicate balance between what should be anticipated in the story and what should be unexpected in the story. Economic factors of technology, market, distribution, and culture have driven this incredible narrative ballet over the past several hundred years, ever since the Industrial Revolution facilitated the invention of mass-produced and mass-consumed fiction.

Whereas the critics of popular fiction condemn it for its predictability and easy "access" for a large audience, I would suggest the very opposite: that popular fiction can be highly creative, exceedingly inventive, and quite difficult to pin down with exact definitions. An excellent example of this complexity of popular narrative formula can be found in the development of the thriller.

Indeed, popular narrative formulas, such as the thriller, are "organic" in nature. They grow, shrink, and intersect with other popular narrative formulas in an attempt to better achieve that balance between the predictable and the new, which is the typical recipe for the success of popular fiction storytelling. A good example of this organic elasticity may include urban fantasy and the detective story. Urban fantasy can be defined as contemporary fantasy that usually takes places in a city or modern-day setting. The detective story is usually described as a type of mystery story that features a detective hero who solves a crime. The literary formula crossover between urban fantasy and the detective story resulted in American Jim Butcher's best-selling, hybrid "Dresden Files" series, a collection of novels and shorter fiction featuring a Chicago-based, private-eye wizard named Harry Dresden, who employs his magical talents to solve crimes involving the supernatural. Butcher's series achieved bestseller status and gained a legion of fans.

The thriller is arguably the most obvious example of hybrid literary formula crossovers. The term "thriller" is one commonly used to describe certain popular novels, but it is a term that lacks specific focus or definition in the same way that the term "detective fiction" or "romance fiction" does. Some literary critics may describe certain crime fiction novels as being thrillers. Others may use the term thrillers to categorize horror fiction, romance fiction, science fiction, or espionage fiction. And yet others may list adventure novels as thrillers.

John McCarty identifies the term "thriller" as a narrative that possesses tension. He writes: "What separates the genuine thriller from a novel or film with the odd suspenseful moment or two is the thriller's single minded purpose, which is to put the reader or audience on edge and keep them there" (13). McCarty goes on to state that thrillers can be found in a number of genres other than crime fiction, including westerns, war stories, or romantic comedies. He argues that "This chameleon aspect of the thriller probably accounts for the reason why thrillers not only have enjoyed great popularity with audiences, but also appeal to very broad demographics within those audiences" (13).

I would take issue with McCarty's very broad definition of the thriller, in that a great deal of fiction exhibits "tension" (it's called dramatic conflict), but only a segment of that fiction can properly be categorized as thrillers. What I do not dispute is McCarty's legitimate claim that defends the universal appeal of the thriller across a diverse readership.

There has to be something else other than just narrative "tension" that defines the thriller. In his monograph, *Thrillers: Genesis and Structure of a Popular Genre* (1979), critic Jerry Palmer suggests that thrillers "are about conspiracies" (63), which then place the typical thriller narrative as one in which the story's antagonist attempts to construct a criminal conspiracy, while the protagonist simultaneously attempts to detect (or solve) the villain's conspiracy. In the process, dramatic tension and a sense of unease are created within the reader.

Following Palmer's argument, I would thus place the thriller at the intersecting point of several "sensational" popular fiction genres, including detective fiction, espionage fiction, horror fiction, romance fiction, science fiction, and adventure fiction. Within this intersection point, a given thriller may expand in a particular formulaic direction. For example, some thrillers are closer to the detective story, while others are linked more strongly to the tale of espionage.

Thrillers also embody certain important story traits that underscore and reinforce their widespread popularity with a dedicated readership. First, thrillers feature escapist plots and emphasize narrative action, typically limiting characterization, rather than involving highly realistic plots and deep character development. The audience's interest in thrillers lies more with action and rapid plot development than with the static plotting and introspective nature of realistic, or "slice-of-life" fiction. Second, thrillers are intended to entertain, rather than to instruct. Though many thrillers are well researched by their authors, with interesting facts that are intended to support the verisimilitude of the storytelling, the thriller is not usually meant to be solely didactic in nature (though there are notable exceptions, including popular thriller writer Michael Crichton, who often centered many of his novels around a thesis or argument, such as the dangers of rapid technological growth). Third, thrillers employ protagonists or heroes who are exceptionally brave, exceptionally smart, or exceptionally courageous, as compared to realistic fiction that attempts to mirror "real life" as closely as possible in its character portrayals. A favorite plot technique of the thriller is to place an "average" individual into the middle of an exceptionally dangerous situation, but this type of story often sees the protagonist learn or accomplish unexpectedly heroic behavior during the course of the narrative.

And finally, thrillers are intended to reach as wide a readership as possible, while so-called "highbrow" or "elite" fiction is intended for a very narrow, sophisticated, or highly-educated audience. The predominant function of the thriller is to reach best-seller status by providing a story with heightened danger and excitement, propelled by larger-than-life heroes and villains, and focusing on rapid plotting and unexpected narrative developments, such as "cliffhangers." The realistic story, though perhaps touching on some of these elements, is intended to depict life as accurately as possible, avoiding many of the things that the thriller works very hard to achieve.

The American thriller today will be found closely interconnected with the other major genre categories of popular fiction, and its origins go back as far as the origin of the adventure story, the first major category of popular fiction, whose foundation can be seen in the work of Daniel Defoe (1660–1731). Defoe's *Robinson Crusoe* (1719), based on the real life escapades of castaway Alexander Selkirk, was not only one of the earliest novels published in the English language, it was also the first adventure novel ever published, and a historically remote, yet obvious, source of the American thriller. Crusoe's compelling tale of survival, following his shipwreck, acts as an archetype for the typical thriller hero, in that the thriller plot often follows the protagonist's quest for survival in a dangerous environment. In examining the qualities of the adventure stories over time in both Europe and American, those qualities that made the adventure story so popular with readers for so long also help to make the American thriller popular today. Indeed, the single defining motif of the adventure story—the hero's literal conquest of "Death"—is also the major defining motif of the thriller. In addition, as the typical adventure story possesses nationalistic or imperialistic dimensions (especially during the nineteenth century, as seen in the work of British writers, such as H. Rider Haggard and Rudyard Kipling), the American thriller also possesses these similar dimensions. As the typical adventure story is set in exotic lands or locations, the American thriller is also frequently set in comparable settings. Author Clive Cussler probably best represents the contemporary American thriller writers who employ robust doses of non-stop adventure in their fiction.

Along with adventure, a variety of American thrillers successfully employs elements of the horror story. The horror story can be defined simply as a narrative in which fright and the development of fear are the desired responses. The origin of the horror story can be found in British writer Horace Walpole's short novel, *The Castle of Otranto* (1764), which many literary critics and historians have also defined as the first Gothic novel. The popularity and longevity of the horror story can be seen throughout the nineteenth century in Britain, as best illustrated by Mary Shelley's *Frankenstein; or, The Modern Prometheus* (1818), Robert Louis Stevenson's *The Strange Case of Dr. Jekyll and Mr. Hyde* (1886), and Bram Stoker's *Dracula* (1897). The popularity of the horror story can also be found in America, especially in the tales of Edgar Allan Poe in the nineteenth century, in the work of Ambrose Bierce in the late nineteenth- and early twentieth century, in the tales of H.P. Lovecraft in the early twentieth century, and in the work of Robert Bloch in the second half of the twentieth century. Today, a number of American thriller writers base a significant amount of their literary efforts in horror, including Stephen King, Dean Koontz, and Thomas Harris. These writers, among many others, have efficaciously blended narrative elements of adventure and horror in such a fashion as to generate pleasurable shudders when reading their novels and short fiction.

Romance, specifically romantic suspense, falls under the umbrella of the American thriller. The traditional romance can be defined as an evolving love relationship, which typically (but not always) ends in marriage, and the origins of the romance story can be traced to the work of British authors Samuel Richardson and Jane Austen, as well as to the efforts of a number of female Gothic writers, including the nineteenth-century English writers, Ann Radcliffe and the Brontë sisters, and twentieth-century writer, Daphne du Maurier. Romantic suspense merges adventure with romance, and this type of thriller most often features strong women protagonists, who demonstrate heroic or persevering aspects in solving a crime or mystery that cannot only threaten their lives but also poses substantial obstacles to consummating a romantic relationship. Important American writers of romantic suspense in the category of the American thriller include Nora Roberts (along with her J.D. Robb pseudonym) and Karen Rose, among a number of others.

As Mary Shelley's *Frankenstein* was an important novel in the evolution of the Gothic horror tale, many literary historians also see it as the beginning of modern science fiction, as illustrated by Victor Frankenstein's ill-fated attempt to play God by employing technology to create an artificial human life form from the corpses of the dead. As difficult as it has become to accurately describe science fiction, it may be defined as a narrative category of speculative fiction, supported by scientific fact or theory, which employs past, present, or future societies as settings, and that anticipates future technologies which often explore alien places and people. Science fiction went on to experience substantial popularity in the early twentieth-century American pulp magazines with the publication of Hugo Gernsback's *Amazing Stories* in 1926, commonly regarded as the first pulp science fiction magazine. The category of science fiction thus enjoyed a long and fruitful run in the American pulps through the 1930s and 1940s, and then with the development of the paperback book in America in the decades after World War II.

However, it was the development of the techno thriller in the mid-to-late twentieth century that merged science fiction with the thriller, especially as seen in the bestselling novels of American author and film director, Michael Crichton. In many ways, the techno thriller has come to dominate the American thriller in the last few decades, and many authors, including the writing team of Douglas Preston and Lincoln Child, have published best-selling and critically admired novels in this area.

The American poet and short story writer Edgar Allan Poe has often been cited as the inventor of the modern detective story, with his tale "The Murders in the Rue Morgue" (1841) and with the two subsequent stories that feature his brilliant detective C. Auguste Dupin. Certainly, Poe established the single, paramount principle of the detective story: the narrative must involve a recounting of the exploits of an exceptionally gifted protagonist detective, who investigates and solve otherwise baffling crimes. However, it was the British who borrowed, refined, and perfected this category of fiction in the late nineteenth- and early twentieth-century with Sir Arthur Conan Doyle's Sherlock Holmes stories and with the work of Agatha Christie and Dorothy L. Sayers in the decades following World War I. Many genre historians argue that the hard-boiled detective fiction of American pulp magazines in the 1920s and 1930s (such as *Black Mask*)—best exemplified by the stories of Carroll John Daly, Dashiell Hammett, and Raymond Chandler—feature fictionalized criminal behavior that is more gritty and realistic than what was appearing in stories by the major British writers. This model of hard-boiled detective character later became an important protagonist in the American thrillers of the past several decades, most notably as seen in the many adventures of James Patterson's Alex Cross and especially in British author Lee Child's high-octane series featuring the American ex-military vigilante, Jack Reacher.

The offshoot of the detective story, the spy story (or tale of espionage) also figures proximately in the American thriller. Some critics cite James Fenimore Cooper's novel *The Spy; A Tale of the Neutral Ground* (1821) as one of the earliest examples of the popular tale of espionage, but, as with the detective story, it was the British who perfected this category of fiction, as illustrated by Erskine Childers' 1903 novel *The Riddle of the Sands; A Record of Secret Service* and W. Somerset Maugham's *Ashenden; or The British Agent*, a collection of loosely-related short stories first published in book form in 1928. The most famous British writers of the spy story in the mid-to-late twentieth century include John le Carré, whose stories feature George Smiley, as well as Ian Fleming and his iconic James Bond adventures. The spy story can be defined as a tale of political espionage, featuring a spy protagonist who seeks to uncover the secrets of the nefarious ambitions of political adversaries, while trying not to get caught or killed in the process. The contemporary American thriller features a variety of authors who combine heavy doses of thriller adventure with elements of espionage. A sampling of these writers includes Robert Ludlum and his Jason Bourne series and Tom Clancy and his Jack Ryan novels.

The single most important characteristic of the thriller formula is its ability to conform to changing tastes of new generations of consumers, while maintaining the basic archetypal appeal of its original narrative structures that include the adventure story, the horror story, the romantic suspense story, the technological thriller story, the detective story, or the spy story. The American thriller, in particular, is flexible enough to incorporate the dramatic and formulaic conventions of the various popular literary genres listed above, while also retaining the skeletal structure of conspiracy-based plotting that frequently and clearly separates this type of story from the literary offshoots of popular fiction that feed it. Many sub-categories of the American thriller exist, in addition to the major genre sources, including the legal thriller, the medical thriller, and the historical thriller, to name but a few examples. Some of the kaleidoscopic, formulaic representations of the American thriller, in fact, are discussed in this collection.

Beginning in the late 1960s, with the publication of Michael Crichton's landmark 1969 bestseller, *The Andromeda Strain*, the American thriller has become one of the most important and influential categories of contemporary popular fiction. Perhaps the rudimentary appeal of the American thriller ultimately has to do with the profound storytelling appeal of its writers. In addition, the basic dramatic conflict of the thriller is not too difficult to discover: at its heart, the American thriller outlines that ancient moral conflict between the forces of good and evil. Yet the thriller is not quite that simple to pin down. In its numerous varieties of expression, the American thriller deftly explores the subtle and complex nature of our oftentimes problematic relationship with morality and with the basic nature of good and evil itself.

The very uncertainty of the life-or-death outcome for the protagonist (and antagonist) of the American thriller is what has given the thriller its vicarious "thrill" for readers, and this, no doubt, will continue to do so for many years to come.

Works Cited

McCarty, John. *Thrillers: Seven Decades of Classic Film Suspense.* New York: Citadel Press, 1992.

Palmer, Jerry. *Thrillers: Genesis and Structure of a Popular Genre.* New York: St. Martin's Press, 1979.

CRITICAL
CONTEXTS

The Crime Thriller in Context _____

Kate Watson

As this book collection attests, the thriller is a wide-ranging category. As this chapter will show (and summarize), the sub-genre of the crime thriller has a large corpus and different national traditions, and, consequently, it does not have a singular literary or national history. Crime thriller narratives can be found across many mediums, including literature, television, graphic novels, and film. Added to this, there are many sub-genres of the thriller that incorporate narratives of crime/s. These are: legal thrillers (and the earlier police procedural), spy thrillers, futuristic thrillers, psychological thrillers, political thrillers, racing thrillers, heist thrillers, cyberpunk thrillers, the 'troubling' thriller, and the faction thriller, among others (Scaggs 108). Martin Priestman groups these versions of the crime thriller into the noir thriller and the anti-conspiracy thriller (34).[1] In fact, there is a continual revision and evolution of the crime thriller over time.

To begin: what does it mean exactly to 'thrill'? Typically, a thriller is connected with a visceral response and frisson. A 'thrill' is connected to emotion: it can incite excitement, be suspenseful, salacious, and sensational. It can also be pleasurable, chilling, and terrifying or invoke anxiety, ambiguity, and fear. For these reasons, the crime thriller is closely connected to and has a crossover with the psychological thriller.

So, how can the popular sub-genre of the crime thriller be defined? This chapter will consider the definitions of the 'crime novel/thriller' and 'detective fiction.' Indeed, each of these terms are broad and encompass many sub-genres in each. There are ongoing debates surrounding such classifications and critics do not always agree or see the thriller as a separate sub-genre of crime fiction. In fact, genre boundaries are not rigidly fixed and often cross over one another, sharing common features: David Glover has identified how the thriller has often been subsumed under the umbrella terms of 'crime,' 'detective,' 'mystery,' 'suspense,' and 'horror' (73). Tzvetan Todorov sees the thriller (the *Série noire*) as distinct from the whodunnit and the suspense novel; he writes that: "in other words, its constitutive character is in its themes ... it is around these few constants that the thriller is constituted: violence, generally sordid crime, [and] the amorality of the characters" (162). As Glover, Todorov, and others have indicated, there are many differences between these terms.

Julian Symons has defined the crime novel as distinct from the classic detective story. To summarize Symons, its characteristics are: it does not often have a detective (and when there is one, he or she plays a secondary role); it is based on the psychology of characters or "an intolerable situation that must end in violence;" the setting is often central to the setting and atmosphere of the story (and is inextricably bound up with the nature of the crime itself); "the social perspective of the story is often radical, and questions some aspect of society, law, or justice," and "[t]he lives of characters are shown continuing after the crime, and often their subsequent behaviour is important to the story's effect" (193). The crime and the criminal are central to the crime thriller. The term 'crime novel' has been used interchangeably with the 'thriller' or the 'crime thriller' (such as Lee Horsley and John Scaggs, respectively). This chapter will follow this terminology.

While detective fiction differs from the crime novel, elements from each can be found in the other. The key in detective fiction is the investigation. Traditionally, the Golden Age of crime fiction (generally considered to be between the two World Wars)[2] famously set rules for the detective story, such as Ronald Knox's 'Ten Commandments of Detection' (or 'Decalogue,' 1928). Knox's commandments stipulated that detective fiction should have no supernatural occurrences, that the crime must happen early on in the narrative, the detective must not commit the crime, and no accident or correct intuition must enable the detective to solve the case. 'S. S. Van Dine' (Willard Huntington Wright) has written 'Twenty Rules for Writing Detective Stories' (1928), stating that:

> The detective story is a kind of intellectual game. It is more—it is a sporting event. And for the writing of detective stories there are very definite laws—unwritten, perhaps, but nonetheless binding; and every respectable and self-respecting concocter of literary mysteries lives up to them. Herewith, then, is a sort of credo, based partly on the practice of all the great writers of detective stories, and partly on the promptings of the honest author's inner conscience. (Wright)

Ultimately, the crime is solved, the criminal is removed, and along with this narrative closure, order and safety are restored.

Priestman highlights the difference between the crime thriller and detective story, between emotion versus reason: "the crime thriller emphasizes present danger rather than reflecting on, or investigating, past action and that to create this danger in the present the protagonist of the crime thriller must be threatened, or believe him/herself to be threatened, by powerful external forces in some form" (43). The crime thriller also differs from the rationality of the classic detective story in its narrative form and structure: the crime thriller utilizes a cliff-hanger technique, building on the action (comparable to a modern-day soap opera); this is why these types of texts are commonly referred to as 'page turners.'

This description reinforces the popularity and longevity of the crime thriller; it signifies the public's need to consume these texts, to literally turn their pages. Indeed, Jerry Palmer has indicated that "[t]hrillers are a commercial product, made to be marketed" (69). It is due to this commercial nature, thrilling content, and the attendant class distinction between higher, 'intelligent' literature and 'lower,' popular fiction that has paradoxically led the crime thriller to also have long-standing critical, often negative responses. These include Margaret Oliphant's famous commentaries on sensation fiction in the mid-nineteenth century and Dorothy L. Sayers' discussions. For example, in an essay in 1929, Sayers was disparaging of the thriller, saying that "nothing is explained, " and that this went against "that quiet enjoyment of the logical which we look for in our detective reading." Here, Sayers aligns the thriller with 'the uncritical,' compared to "the modern educated public" (59–73).

The origins and lineage of the crime thriller are important. It is debatable how far back you can trace this and where exactly to draw the line. For example, a case could be made for William Shakespeare's *Titus Andronicus* (1594) as a proto-crime thriller: the tragedy includes rape, violence, and murder and culminates with two sons being killed, cooked in a pie, and fed to their own mother. Initially, the sub-genre of the crime thriller was not fully formed and was a blend of the picaresque, the *Newgate Calendars*, the Gothic, and sensation fiction.

The *Newgate Calendar* takes its name from the famous Newgate prison in London. These were originally broadsheets of *Accounts of the Ordinary at Newgate*, sold at public executions in the eighteenth century. Stephen Knight terms these as 'parables of shocking aberration' (*Crime Fiction* 4). The sale and consumption of the (often sensationalized) details of criminals, their crimes, trials, and their deaths attests to their thrilling nature, spectacle, and popularity. These tales were then collected in book form; Knight has written that *The Newgate Calendar* (1773) was the first major collection of crime without detectives.

This focus on criminals continued in the eighteenth century. Daniel Defoe's *Moll Flanders* (1722) included sensational and thrilling elements, indicated by the novel's full title, 'The Fortunes and Misfortunes of the Famous Moll Flanders, Etc. Who was born in Newgate, and during a life of continu'd Variety for Threescore Years, besides her Childhood, was Twelve Year a Whore, five times a Wife (whereof once to her own brother), Twelve Year a Thief, Eight Year a Transported Felon in Virginia, at last, grew Rich, liv'd Honest, and died a Penitent.' Henry Fielding's tale of the 'thief taker general', Jonathan Wild, in *The Life of Mr. Jonathan Wild, the Great* (1743) points to the later crime thrillers with their 'heroic' figures. The Newgate novel sub-genre (1820–1850) again picks up this picaresque notion, with novels that focused on the criminal protagonist. These could be based on real offenders and include titles, such as Edward Bulwer Lytton's *Paul Clifford* (1830) and *Eugene Aram* (1832); William Harrison Ainsworth's *Rookwood* (1834) and

Jack Sheppard (1839); and Charles Dickens' *Oliver Twist* (1838) and *Martin Chuzzlewit* (1844).

The Gothic inheritance of the crime thriller is also significant. In Britain (1750–1820), the tropes of the Gothic body of writing included secrets, the supernatural, vulnerable, and imprisoned heroines, male villains, ghostly *Doppelgängers*/doublings, foreign mansions and castles, and exotic landscapes. *Blackwood's Edinburgh Magazine's* 'Tales of Terror' were popular, as was the works of E.T.A. Hoffmann and also the Schauerroman ('shudder novel') in Germany in the late eighteenth century, specifically the 1780s and 1790s. Famous British Gothic texts are Horace Walpole's *The Castle of Otranto* (1764), Matthew Lewis' *The Monk* (1796), James Hogg's *The Private Memoirs and Confessions of a Justified Sinner* (1824), and Ann Radcliffe's *A Sicilian Romance* (1792), *The Mysteries of Udolpho* (1794), and *The Italian* (1797). The Gothic was reworked in the nineteenth century, with novels, such as Maria Edgeworth's *Castle Rackrent* (1800); Jane Austen's parody, *Northanger Abbey* (1818); and Mary Shelley's *Frankenstein* (1818). Indeed, Shelley's 1831 Introduction to *Frankenstein* makes clear the intended bodily response of the reader: 'to make the reader dread to look around, to curdle the blood, and quicken the beatings of the heart' (7–8).

The American Gothic also deals with dangerous landscapes, but these are distinctly American with American concerns. Important figures are Charles Brockden Brown, with his novels *Wieland: or, The Transformation: An American Tale* (1798); *Arthur Mervyn; or, Memoirs of the Year 1793* (1799); *Edgar Huntly; or The Memoirs of a Sleep-Walker* (1799); and James Fenimore Cooper's 'Leatherstocking Tales,' featuring frontiersman Natty Bumppo and including *The Pioneers, or, The Sources of the Susquehanna* (1823); *The Last of the Mohicans* (1826); *The Prairie: A Tale* (1827); *The Pathfinder; or, The Inland Sea* (1840); and *The Deerslayer: or The First Warpath* (1841). Robert E. Spiller has coined Brockden Brown's *Edgar Huntly* as the first American detective novel (1). Of course, to this list should be added Edgar Allan Poe (1809–1849), with his celebrated tales of ratiocination, featuring the French detective,

C. Auguste Dupin: 'The Murders in the Rue Morgue' (*Graham's Magazine*, 1841), 'The Mystery of Marie Rogêt' (*Snowden's Lady's Companion*, 1842–3), 'The Gold Bug', 'Thou Art the Man' and 'The Purloined Letter' (*The Gift*, 1845). The locked-room mystery utilized by Poe is revisited in later crime thrillers, such as those written by Sax Rohmer and Edgar Wallace.

Sensation fiction of the 1860s and 1870s provided further thrills and crime content for the reading public. The rise in literacy and cheap production of these tales meant that crime thrillers were accessible to all: the British 'penny dreadfuls' and dime novels in the second half of the nineteenth century in the United States attest to this. Edmund Pearson defines this cheap criminography (dime novels) as 'tales of dread suspense' dealing in 'violent action; in sudden death and its terrors' (13–14). Equally, the serialization of sensation fiction in weekly or monthly magazines and periodicals left the reader wanting more. As the name suggests, sensation fiction's purpose was to shock, to produce bodily sensations. Often, it featured deviant women and crime within the domestic arena. In 1863, Henry Mansel described the sensation novel as:

> a tale which aims at electrifying the nerves of the reader is never thoroughly effective unless the scene be laid in our own days and among the people we are in the habit of meeting [....] The man who shook our hand with a hearty English grasp half an hour ago – the woman whose beauty and grace were the charm of last night [...]— how exciting to think that under these pleasing outsides may be concealed some demon in human shape (495–496).

While there was a wealth of writers contributing to this sub-genre— such as Wilkie Collins, Ellen Price (Mrs. Henry Wood), Charles Reade, and Ouida—Mary Elizabeth Braddon's *Lady Audley's Secret* (1862) is one of the best-known exponents of sensation fiction, as is her oeuvre more generally. Wilkie Collins' *The Woman in White* (1860) has been described by John Scraggs as helping the twentieth-crime thriller develop, with 'its sensational, and often shockingly frank, depictions of sex and violent death' (107). In America, Louisa

May Alcott's pseudonymously and anonymously written, lesser-known 'thrilling' novelettes, written between 1863 and 1869, also contributed to the crime thriller. There is also an Australian tradition that is not often discussed in critical accounts. Stephen Knight has identified sub genres of Australian crime fiction that came into being in the nineteenth-century, including 'Squatter Thrillers.' Knight writes that:

> If convicts and diggers are two central elements in the development of Australian crime fiction, there is a third point to the triangle, namely the squatters—those who owned the land that was at first worked by convicts and later dug for gold. Squatter fictions that deal with crime tended to be in novel rather than short story or fugitive novella form, and often run to several volumes. Both the characters and the form are substantial (*Continent* 38).[3]

Authors in this form include Charles Rowcroft's *Tales of the Colonies, or The Adventures of an Emigrant* (1843) and *The Bushranger of Van Diemen's Land* (1846), Henry Kingsley's *The Recollections of Geoffry Hamlyn* (1859), George Walstab's *Looking Back* (1864), Ellen Davitt's *Force and Fraud* (1865), William Howitt's *Tallangetta: The Squatter's Home* (1857), A. H. Lambton's *From Prison to Power* (1893), and Mary Gaunt's *Deadman's* (1898). Knight also identifies a psycho thriller: Mary Fortune's story, 'Werrimut: A Tale' (1866).

It is in the twentieth century that the crime thriller begins to take a defined shape, drawing from its previous iterations. Erskine Childers' popular novels are significant, with *The Riddle of the Sands* (1903) championed as a founding text of the thriller genre. Rudyard Kipling's *Kim* (1901) and John Buchan's *The Thirty-Nine Steps* (1915) are also important. The espionage central to these novels is seen later in Ian Fleming's popular James Bond novels and short story collections and in John le Carré's *The Spy Who Came in from the Cold* (1963). Marty Roth has commented that the threat of the enemy is what distinguishes the thriller from the adventure story (226).

In Australia, Knight has recognized the tourist crime thriller, which depicts the country as a coterminous spectacle and threat. Knight has written that "the Australian thriller exhibits strongly the double action of receiving from the strange sight both the pleasant and the disturbing meaning of the word 'thrill'" (*Continent* 158). Arthur Upfield is a central writer in this form, with his Australian aboriginal detective, Napoleon Bonaparte. Titles include *Murder Down Under* (1943), *No Footprints in the Bush* (1944), and *Death of a Swagman* (1945). Earlier, in 1933, Miles Franklin's feminist crime pastiche, *Bring the Monkey*, has been described by Marjorie Barnard as "a satire of a satire of a satire, a thriller to end all thrillers" (106).

In Britain, Sax Rohmer's many Dr. Fu-Manchu crime thrillers, beginning with *The Insidious Fu Manchu* (1913), display colonial attitudes towards the 'yellow peril' from the East. The concerns of class and race in the British thriller are again seen with H. C. McNeile's Bulldog Drummond books with his gentleman protagonist. Again, in Britain, Edgar Wallace (titled the 'King of Thrillers') considerably contributed to the sub-genre, with his novels *The Four Just Men* (1905), *Sanders of the River* (1911), *The Man at the Carlton* (1931) and *The Daffodil Mystery* (1920), among others.

Across the Atlantic, the American hard-boiled crime thriller (which overlaps with the noir thriller) was central to the shaping of what was to come in the sub genre. Dime novels, already mentioned, were published in titles as the *New York Detective Library* (1882–1899) and *Secret Service* (1899–1912). The American popular pulp magazines, such as the *Black Mask* in the 1920s, focused on detection and moved away from adventure stories and Westerns with the change of editorship to Joseph Shaw. *Black Mask* authors included Raoul Whitfield, Dashiell Hammett, McCoy, and Carroll John Daly. Shaw described his approach to hard-boiled crime fiction:

> The formula or pattern emphasizes character and the problems inherent in human behaviour over crime solution. In other words, in this new pattern, character conflict is the main theme; the ensuing crime, or its threat, is incidental. . . . Such distinctive treatment comprises a hard, brittle style (2).

This style and the contents of such narratives are inextricably linked to the socio-economic context in which they were written: the Depression Era. Indeed, W. R. Burnett's influential early gangster story, *Little Caesar* (1929), was published in the year of the Wall Street Crash. Raymond Chandler—whose hard-boiled novels include *The Big Sleep* (1939), *Farewell, My Lovely* (1940) and *The Long Goodbye* (1954)—has described this corrupt and violent world:

> It was the smell of fear which these stories managed to generate. Their characters lived in a world gone wrong, a world in which, long before the atom bomb, civilization had created the machinery for its own destruction and was learning to use it with all the moronic delight of a gangster trying out his first machine-gun. The law was something to be manipulated for profit and power. The streets were dark with something more than the night (7).

A key shift is personified in the hard-boiled private eye; as Lee Horsley states, there is an "involvement of the protagonist in menacing events (in contrast to the detachment of the traditional detective)" (8). Gary Hoppenstand has also written that the hard-boiled detective is "an emblem of personal honor, a knight operating within a social structure of civic corruption, decadence and dishonesty" (119). These narratives incorporated lower-class (main) characters and also has a (male) working-class readership, as discussed by Sean McCann. This male dominance is often depicted as misogynistic in these crime thrillers and racism also abounds.

Sexuality, violence, and the hard-boiled thriller are central to William Faulkner's *Sanctuary* (1931) and James M. Cain's *The Postman Always Rings Twice* (1934) and *Double Indemnity* (1936). The former Cain novel is original, as it is retrospectively narrated from the criminal's perspective. This conflation of sex and violence is evident on the second page of the text when Frank describes Cora: "Then I saw her. [...] she had a sulky look to her, and her lips stuck out in a way that made me want to mash them in for her" (*The Postman* 2). Richard Bradbury has indicated how the Depression Era setting and history is connected with suspense: "[t]he urge for financial gain, for access to the means of acquiring material fulfillment, is welded to the urge for sexual fulfillment" (90).

Later, feminist appropriations of the form challenge previous masculine ideologies, such as Sara Paretsky's private detective (V. I. Warshawski) series, beginning with *Indemnity Only* (1982). Other variants of the sub-genre include the neo-*noir* novels of James Ellroy, specifically his 'L. A. Quartet' novels: *The Black Dahlia* (1987), *The Big Nowhere* (1988), *L. A. Confidential* (1990), and *White Jazz* (1992). The comic crime thriller has also appeared, with the city of Los Angeles transposed to Wales. Malcolm Pryce's Aberystwyth *Noir* (Louie Knight mystery) series, beginning with *Aberystwyth Mon Amour* (2001), self-consciously employs pastiche and satire. Knight also discusses the contemporary Australian sub-genre of the private-eye thriller: "the increasing number of these novels and stories—especially in Sydney—have developed from the impact of American private eye novels in recent decades. These have been part of the self-conscious development of Eastern Australia as part of the Pacific rim" (*Continent* 57). Peter Corris—called 'the godfather of Australian crime writing'—is a main player in this form (some of Corris' titles include *The Dying Trade* [1980], *The Marvellous Boy* [1981], *The Empty Beach* [1983]).

This violence inherent in these narratives is developed—and heightened—with psycho crime thrillers. Psycho thrillers include psychopathology, crime, detectives and, often, serial killers. As this article will show, the serial killer figure (or figures) are prevalent in contemporary crime thrillers. Examples include Margaret Millar's *Wall of Eyes* (1943) and Patricia Highsmith's debut, *Strangers on a Train* (1949; adapted by Alfred Hitchcock in 1951), and her Tom Ripley novels, starting with *The Talented Mr. Ripley* (1956). Knight has stated that the Ripley novels can be read as "a conscious rejection of the simplistic Christie-esque notion that murderers were essentially evil" (*Crime Fiction* 150). Jim Thompson's popular novel, *The Killer Inside Me* (1952; film adaptation 2010) again emphasizes violence and the workings of those who "started the game with a crooked cue" (248).

Robert Bloch's well-known crime thriller, *Psycho* (1959), is primarily told through the eyes of Norman Bates, owner of the motel. Bates commits murders under the identity of his mother; this duality and doubling again harks back to the earlier Gothic beginnings of the sub genre. Alfred Hitchcock's film adaptation, *Psycho* (1960), and the recent television series adaptation/prequel, *Bates Motel*, attests to its enduring popularity and also the public's interest in such narratives. Bloch also wrote other psycho thrillers: *American Gothic* (1974), *Psycho II* (1982), *Night of the Ripper* (1984), and *Psycho House* (1990).

The seminal psycho thrillers of Thomas Harris again present the famous cannibal psychiatrist and serial killer, Doctor Hannibal Lecter. *Red Dragon* (1981) introduces Lecter and also the central criminal, Francis Dolarhyde, who murders families. Philip Simpson, writing on *Red Dragon*, states that "[w]hile other authors over the years had written tales of characters who commit multiple murders for reasons rooted in their trauma-ridden pasts, Harris in *Red Dragon* merged the forms of the police procedural, detective fiction, and psycho thriller to produce a hybrid that both terrified readers and appealed to their intellects" (195). The bestseller, *The Silence of the Lambs*, presents a suspenseful interaction and mind play between FBI student Clarice Starling and Lecter (1988). Early on, the novel states that "Clarice Starling was excited, depleted, running on her will. Some of the things Lecter had said about her were true, and some only clanged on the truth" (30). This novel was later followed by *Hannibal* (1999) and *Hannibal Rising* (2006). Again, the 2013 television series, *Hannibal*, demonstrates the longevity of these texts.

Moving forward in time, the crime thriller in contemporary times is truly transnational and diverse. The historical crime thriller is self-referential in both its incorporation and questioning of the past. Caleb Carr's *The Alienist* (1994) is a prime example: it is a thriller with a serial killer and is set in the nineteenth century. Italian Umberto Eco's *The Name of the Rose* (1980; English 1983), is an historical murder thriller set in a fourteenth-century medieval monastery. Other main texts include the works of James Ellroy, such as *Because the Night* (1984), *Blood on the Moon* (1984), *White Jazz* (1992), and *American Tabloid* (1995).

The excess of the thriller of violence is still evident, as seen in Brett Easton Ellis' *American Psycho* (1991), with its noir concerns and monstrous criminal. However, this excess has also been challenged in terms of its sexuality and violence. Examples include Val McDermid's violent postmodern thriller, *The Mermaids Singing* (1995), as well as Stella Duffy's feminist *Fresh Flesh* (1999), Joyce Carol Oates' *Zombie* (1995), Poppy Z. Brite's *Exquisite Corpse* (1996), Susanna Moore's *In the Cut* (1995), and Jake Arnott's *The Long Firm* (1999).

The forensic thriller is also significant. Patricia Cornwell's Dr. Kay Scarpetta novels (introducing the iconic medical examiner in Postmortem, 1990) signify another branch in the sub genre of the crime thriller. Val McDermid has stated that Cornwell's first three novels:

> did something nobody had really done before in books - she used the forensic practitioner as detective. Highsmith and Rendell had shown what you could do with suspense; Cornwell added the extra dimension of a sleuth who could literally look inside the victim.[... She was unafraid to make the] bizzare and the extraordinary centre stage in her work...she combined the fascination of the science, suspense that makes you go "just one more chapter", and that voyeuristic pleasure at horrors you're just glad you're never going to have to confront (Kidd 391).

The crime thrillers' ongoing geographic diversity is again evidenced by China Miéville's existential thriller, science fantasy, murder mystery, and crime procedural, *The City and the City* (2009), which blends crime and urban writing/psychogeography. Other writers and texts include: Mo Hayder's (British) Jack Caffery series of thrillers (beginning with *Birdman* [2000]); Lee Child's Jack Reacher (American hero) thrillers, starting with *Killing Floor* (1997) and the 2012 movie adapted from *One Shot* (2005); and best-selling French author Caryl Férey's 'New Zealand' thrillers, *Haka* (1998) and *Utu* (2004; English translation, 2011). Popular Scandinavian crime thrillers/Nordic noir include Jo Nesbø's Harry Hole thrillers (beginning with *The Bat* [1997]) and Stieg Larsson's immensely successful Millennium trilogy. In Australia, Peter Temple has written both stand-alone novels and Jack Irish thrillers (beginning with *Bad Debts* [1996]). No doubt, this diversity will continue in years to come.

Equally, the popularity of the crime thriller, and the reactions that this creates/incites will continue and evolve. As Christiana Gregoriou and Mike Presdee have both recognized, crime fiction can be seen as a version of the 'carnival'; Gregoriou writes that "[t] he fascination with and crime experienced in contemporary popular culture reveals the potential entertainment value to be realized from such acts" (100).

Notes

1. The *noir* thriller has at its center a protagonist who 'consciously exceeds the law'; in the anti-conspiracy thriller, the protagonist is pitched against a powerful conspiracy without recourse to the forces of law and order (34).

2. See Julian Symons' *Bloody Murder*.

3. The sub genres are: 'Convict Stories,' 'The Goldfields Mystery,' 'Squatter Thrillers,' and 'The Criminal Saga.'

Works Cited

Barnard, Marjorie. *Miles Franklin*. Melbourne: Hill of Content, 1967.

Bradbury, Richard. "Sexuality, Guilt and Detection: Tension between History and Suspense." *American Crime Fiction: Studies in the Genre*. Ed. Brian Docherty. Basingstoke: Macmillan,1988: 88–99.

Cain, James M. *The Postman Always Rings Twice*. 1934. London: Orion, 2005.

Chandler, Raymond. "The Simple Art of Murder." *Saturday Review of Literature*. 15 Apr. 1950: 13–14.

Glover, David. "The Stuff that Dreams Are Made Of: Masculinity, Femininity and the Thriller." *Reading Popular Fiction: Gender, Genre and Narrative Pleasure*. Ed. Derek Longhurst. London: Unwin Hyman, 1989: 67–83.

Gregoriou, Christiana. *Deviance in Contemporary Crime Fiction.* Basingstoke: Palgrave, 2007.

Harris, Thomas. *The Silence of the Lambs.* 1988. London: Arrow Books, 2002.

Horsley, Lee. *The Noir Thriller.* Basingstoke: Palgrave Macmillan, 2009.

Hoppenstand, Gary. *In Search of the Paper Tiger: A Sociological Perspective of Myth, Formula and the Mystery Genre in the Entertainment Print Mass Medium.* Bowling Green, OH: Bowling Green State U Popular P, 1987.

Kidd, James. "A Background to Patricia Cornwell's *Postmortem*—Platinum Edition," *Postmortem.* London: Sphere, 2010: 389–415.

Knight, Stephen. *Continent of Mystery: A Thematic History of Australian Crime Fiction.* Carlton South, Australia: Melbourne UP, 1997.

Landrum, Larry. *American Mystery and Detective Novels: A Reference Guide.* Westport, CT: Greenwood, 1999.

_____. *Crime Fiction 1800-2000: Detection, Death, Diversity.* Basingstoke: Palgrave, 2004.

Mansel, Henry. "Sensation Novels." *Quarterly Review* 113 (1863): 481–514.

McCann, Sean. *Gumshoe America: Hardboiled Crime Fiction and the Rise and Fall of New Deal Liberalism.* Durham, NC & London: Duke UP, 2000.

Palmer, Jerry. *Thrillers: Genesis and Structure of a Popular Genre.* London: Edward Arnold, 1978.

Pearson, Edmund. *Dime Novels; or, Following an Old Trail in Popular Literature.* Boston: Little Brown, 1929.

Presdee, Mike. *Cultural Criminology and the Carnival of Crime.* London: Routledge, 2000.

Priestman, Martin. *Crime Fiction: From Poe to the Present.* Plymouth: Northcote House in Association with the British Council, 1998.

Roth, Marty. *Fair and Foul Play: Reading Genre in Classic Detective Fiction.* Athens: U of Georgia P, 1995.

Sayers, Dorothy L. "The Omnibus of Crime." 1929. *Detective Fiction: A Collection of Critical Essays.* Ed. R. Winks. Englewood Cliffs, NJ: Prentice-Hall, 1980.

Scaggs, John. *Crime Fiction.* London & New York: Routledge, 2005.

Shelley, Mary. *Frankenstein; Or, The Modern Prometheus*. 1831. Harmondsworth: Penguin, 1994.

Simpson, Philip. "Noir and the Psycho Thriller." *A Companion to Crime Fiction*. Eds. Charles Rzepka & Lee Horsley. Chichester: Wiley-Blackwell, 2010: 187–197.

Symons, Julian. *Bloody Murder: from the Detective Story to the Crime Novel*. 3rd ed. New York: Warner Books, 1993.

Thompson, Jim. *The Killer Inside Me*. 1952. London: Zomba Books, 1983.

Todorov, Tzvetan. "The Typology of Detective Fiction". 1966. *Modern Criticism and Theory: A Reader*. Eds. David Lodge & Nigel Wood. London: Longman, 1988: 161–63.

Wilt, David. *Hardboiled in Hollywood*. Madison, WI: U of Wisconsin P, 1991.

Wright, Willard Huntington ('S. S. Van Dine'). "Twenty Rules for Writing Detective Stories." *American Magazine* September 1928. 10 Jan. 2009. Web. 23 Oct. 2013. <http://gaslight.mtroyal.ca/vandine.htm>.

The Legal Thriller in Context _____

Ayoola Onatade

How best to define a legal thriller? The legal thriller is a sub-genre of thrillers in general and crime novels in particular, where main characters are members of the legal profession and most of the proceedings take place within a legal setting. One could also suggest that courtroom dramas might come under the aegis of legal thrillers, even though there is a slight but notable difference. In a legal thriller, there is much more action, but the law is still an important part of the storyline. With a courtroom drama, a majority of the action takes place in a courtroom and is comprised of a judge, the prosecution, the defense lawyers, and the opposing parties. For the purpose of this essay, courtroom dramas have been included as well. Simply put, legal thrillers are novels whose storylines revolve around lawyers, legal cases, or the moral environment of the law, and they generally tend to have an element of social commentary.

In her article for the *American Bar Association Journal*, Adrienne Drell states that "once lawyers wrote airtight contracts and cogent Supreme Court briefs. Now they try to write best sellers" (Drell 46). This is indeed the case. Many have succeeded well in this endeavor.

According to Ray B. Browne, "The lawyer occupies a unique position in society to witness and influence popular culture" (Browne 7). It is clear that legal thrillers have been around for quite some time and, in fact, one can acknowledge that William Shakespeare's *The Merchant of Venice*—where the whole plot hinges on a breach of contract dispute—was among the earliest. Nothing astonishes readers more than recognizing the number of references to the law found in the works of William Shakespeare. For example, *Measure for Measure* is about the tension between the letter of the law and the spirit of the law. *Hamlet*, on the other hand, covers evidence and justification. The nature of legal thrillers changed in the late eighties with the rise of the modern legal thriller and its two main proponents: Scott Turow and John Grisham. However, to gain a good grasp of the genre, its historical significance, and the way in which the writing of legal thrillers evolved over time, one has to take a step back and consider some earlier writers of the genre.

Agatha Christie, known as the Queen of Crime, wrote her legal thriller, *The Witness for the Prosecution*, as a play and subsequently a short story, which was originally published as *Traitor's Hands* in 1925. It is best known through the 1957 film version, directed by Billy Wilder and featuring Charles Laughton and Marlene Dietrich. Although a short story, it is considered a legal thriller because of the nature of what takes place in the story and how it takes place. Leonard Vole is detained for the murder of a wealthy, older widow, Mrs. French. He has been made her main heir, although she did not know that he was already married. This does not help his defense, and his wife compounds matters by being the main prosecution witness. Yet, this is actually a convoluted plan to ensure that her husband walks free.

In the United Kingdom, Alfred Alexander Gordon Clark, a barrister and judge who wrote under the pseudonym Cyril Hare, also wrote legal thrillers. He was best known for *Tragedy at Law* (1942), which is about an inebriated judge, an exhausted barrister, and a road accident. Aside from being important in the annals of legal thrillers, *Tragedy at Law* reveals an insider's detailed knowledge of the British legal system.

Robert Travers' *Anatomy of a Murder*, which was originally published in 1958, is another legal thriller of historical significance. It is based on a true-life case, in which Travers—who was actually Michigan Supreme Court Justice John D. Voelker—acted for the defense. It is a story of treachery and murder that ends in a dramatic trial. The novel rests on the case an army lieutenant, who has allegedly killed the man who raped his wife. Both the prosecutor and the defense battle out the complex trial, each determined to win. One of the main issues covered in the novel is the defense of insanity. The surprise ending explains, at least in part, why the novel is considered to have raised the standard for legal thrillers.

One cannot write an overview of legal thrillers without mentioning Harper Lee's Pulitzer Prize–winning novel *To Kill a Mockingbird* (1960). Since this book was published, it has taken on a mystique of its own, with good reason. Set in the 1930s Depression Era and narrated by Finch's young daughter Scout, it is the story of southern lawyer, Atticus Finch, who represents an African American man accused of raping a white woman in a small southern town. His vivid cross-examination of the accuser on the witness stand destroys her story. But, despite this, his client is still found guilty and, while trying to escape, is killed. However, it is the image that he represents as a lawyer and the standard that he upholds that has made him—and the novel—so memorable and one that will always feature in the annals of legal thrillers for a long time. Southern lawyer Atticus Finch has become a role model for many a lawyer since the book was first published.

An advocate for truth, justice, and the epitome of reason, *To Kill a Mockingbird* was written in a period when lawyers were seen as principled and willing to represent an innocent man accused of a crime seen as not only horrendous, but due to the ethnicity of the accused and accuser, something of an abomination. The book is set in a time period when African Americans had few rights and what rights they did have were easily trampled on or ignored. Aside from being a legal thriller, it offers a startling look at racism. Finch portrays a humanity that is not seen as much in contemporary lawyers. This is possibly because there is now more interaction and contact on a daily basis with lawyers and the law. It is interesting to note that in 2011, the University of Alabama School of Law and the *American Bar Association Journal* instituted the Harper Lee Prize for Legal Fiction. To honor the anniversary of the publication of *To Kill a Mockingbird*, the prize is awarded annually to a published book-length work of fiction that best exemplifies the role of lawyers in society and their power to effect change. John Grisham won the inaugural prize in 2011 with his novel *The Confession* (2010).

From the late 1970s to the early 1980s, there was a dearth of legal thrillers. It was not until the late 1980s that a change took place. And it wasn't until Turow and Grisham entered the scene that the main emphasis of the legal thriller was no longer the case itself. Turow and Grisham are actually two polar opposites when it comes to legal thrillers. In his work, Turow is a lot more restrained than Grisham. His pacing is measured, meticulous, and his storylines tend to have a multifaceted psychological aspect. Grisham's, on the other hand, are faster paced and easier to read and absorb. His numerous works are considered page-turners, as readers tend to describe them as gripping, exciting, and compelling. Both authors leave us with many thought-provoking questions.

Scott Turow's 1987 seminal work *Presumed Innocent* was a commercial success that paved the way for other authors in the genre, including John Grisham. *Presumed Innocent* tells the story of a prosecutor charged with the murder of his colleague, an attractive and intelligent prosecutor, Carolyn Polhemus. The story is told in the first person by the accused, Rožat "Rusty" Sabich. In this and his subsequent novels, Turow changed the way in which the legal thriller was perceived by the public. *Presumed Innocent* required a change in public attitude toward lawyers, who were no longer idealized figures. Turow's novels are, in fact, always about the ambiguities that lie beneath the sharp edges of the law. Further, the emphasis is placed on the individual and professional life of the main protagonist (normally a lawyer) rather than on what happens in the courtroom, as was the case with thrillers written in previous decades.

Grisham's first book, *A Time to Kill*, was published in 1989, but did not initially become a bestseller. It wasn't until he published *The Firm* in 1991 that he attained the status of a best-selling author. As a result of the success of *The Firm*, *The Pelican Brief* (1992), and *The Client* (1993), *A Time to Kill* became a bestseller in its own right. *The Firm* follows the story of a young lawyer, who is one of the best students to come out of Harvard Law School. He finds himself headhunted by a small Memphis law firm that makes him an offer he can't refuse straight out of graduate school. He accepts and lives to regret it, when he realizes that the firm is not legitimate. He soon finds himself fighting to get out of the firm and stay alive.

John Grisham's popularity stems from the fact that, unlike previous authors of legal thrillers, he was not opposed to taking lawyers out of the courtroom and making them seem more human. He was also conscious of the fact that, while a lawyer would need to spend some time in the courtroom, there were also many things going on outside the courtroom that readers would be interested in. While most legal thrillers begin with the criminal and then the law, Grisham tends to write from the point of view of the law and then the criminal. His concern as an author is not for the criminal mind that forms the legal mind, but the other way round. Turow and Grisham re-energized the trend in legal thrillers and brought authority and realism to the sub-genre that, to a certain extent, had been lacking in earlier books.

In 1994, William Gaddis published *A Frolic of His Own,* which, while not strictly a legal thriller, does bear the requisite elements associated with the genre. *A Frolic of His Own* charts the legal predicament of a plagiarized dramatist, Oscar Crease, along with his idiosyncratic federal judge father and a number of other relatives, friends, and assorted people, who are solely concerned with their best interests. Written in a rather unusual manner, the novel is largely based on conversation. There are lawsuits galore and readers also find statements and legal opinions throughout. This is not a "page turner" in the same category as Grisham, but it does highlight an insight into a legal system, warts and all, and the manner in which litigation has become part of the norm. It is, in fact, an unsympathetically humorous, but extraordinarily precise story of lives caught up in the grind of the law.

In 1995, American author John Lescroart came on the scene with *A Certain Justice,* the first in the Abe Glitsky series. It was not the first book written by Lescroart, however. He had already written two books in his Auguste Lupa series and four books in the Dismas Hardy series. Alongside *A Certain Justice,* he is best known for *The 13th Juror* (1994), which is the fourth book in his Dismas Hardy series and is a suspenseful novel of moral ambiguity, good intentions, bad judgments, and the tortuous path to justice. *The 13th Juror* was nominated for the Shamus and Anthony Awards for Best Mystery Novel. Aside from the fact that they are good legal thrillers, they also show a different style in as much as Lescroart is using a series character in his legal thrillers as opposed to writing stand-alone legal thriller novels.

Toward the end of the 1990s, other authors began to emerge and publish legal thrillers. Among these, one of the most well known is Brad Meltzer. The publication of his 1997 novel, *The Tenth Justice*, marked the beginning of the rise of much younger writers working in the genre. Another author to fall into this category is David Ellis, the Chief Legal Counsel to the Speaker of the Illinois House of Representatives, who was the prosecuting attorney in the impeachment trial of former Illinois governor Rod Blagojevich. His first novel, *Line of Vision* (2001), won the 2002 Edgar Award for Best First Novel. Unlike most legal thrillers, it was told from the point of view of the accused, a non-lawyer named Marty Kalish. This is rather unconventional, as legal thrillers tend to be told from the point of view of the main protagonist, who is usually a member of the legal profession. Ellis continued to experiment with his writing style. His fourth novel, *In the Company of Liars* (2005), is told backwards. It is quite a skill to be able to maintain a sense of place and tension, while presenting the story backwards, but Ellis manages to make it possible for the reader to follow and maintain interest.

Best-selling author Michael Connelly, known for his Harry Bosch police procedural series, is also the author of a series of legal thrillers featuring Mickey Haller, who starts out as a criminal defense lawyer working out of the back of his Lincoln Town car. The title of the first book in the series is *The Lincoln Lawyer* (2005), and in keeping with stand-alone legal thrillers, *The Lincoln Lawyer* is packed full of brisk pacing, skillful twists, and clever writing. Originally a stand-alone legal thriller, it has now become a series, owing largely to the success of *The Lincoln Lawyer*. In 2012, Connelly became the second recipient of the Harper Lee Prize for Legal Fiction with his novel, *The Fifth Witness* (2011).

Mark Gimenez's *The Color of Law* (2006) tells the story of the ruthless politics of corporate law that come face to face with the ethics of public defense when a hotshot Dallas lawyer is asked to defend a black prostitute accused of murder. The lawyer is forced to question everything he previously held dear. A poignant moral tale and very reminiscent of the early works of Grisham, it also has parallels with Harper Lee's *To Kill a Mockingbird*.

Also noteworthy is William Landay's 2012 *Defending Jacob* (2012), which is about throwing the ultimate test into the hands of any parent. Respected Assistant District Attorney Andy Barber has it all: a good job and a happy home with his wife and son Jacob. Suddenly, all this disappears when his introverted, gawky, and secretive son is accused of stabbing a young boy to death. This suspenseful, character-driven legal thriller manages to combine a harrowing family drama with riveting courtroom scenes.

Ferdinand von Schirach's bestselling *The Collini Case* (2012) is another recent work that has changed the face of the legal thriller in recent years. It showcases a talented, non-American, non-British writer capable of writing a gripping legal tale. *The Collini Case,* a bestseller in Europe, has been constantly in the German charts. Fabrizio Collini has, for thirty-four years, worked diligently for Mercedes Benz. He is a quiet and respectable person until the day he visits one of Berlin's most luxurious hotels and kills an innocent man. Young attorney Caspar Leinen takes the case, as exonerating Collini would raise his profile enormously. He learns belatedly that Collini does, in fact, know the victim, who is a well-known industrialist. Leinen is now caught in a professional and personal dilemma. Collini admits the to the murder, but will not say why he did it, forcing Leinen to defend a man who will not put up a defense. To make matters worse, a close friend and relation of the victim insists that he give up the case. His reputation, his career, and this friendship are all at risk. Then he makes a discovery that goes way beyond his own petty concerns and exposes a terrible and deadly truth at the heart of the German justice system. *The Collini Case* is a legal thriller that deals with the infiltration of the post-war German political and judicial systems by former Nazis.

Von Schirach is not the only European author capable of writing exhilarating legal thrillers. Another is Italian author and former anti-Mafia prosecutor Gianfrico Carofiglio. His legal thriller *A Walk in the Dark* (2010) is a powerful example of masterful legal writing outside the United Kingdom and North America. The story deals with a man trying to fight his own demons. The laconic, crisp, and ironic narrative voice gives the reader a distinct sense of place.

While a number of authors write stand-alone legal thrillers, more authors are becoming known for legal thriller series featuring the same protagonist. In fact, some simultaneously publish more than one legal thriller series. Erle Stanley Gardner (1889–1970), for example, was author of over eighty novels featuring fictional trial lawyer Perry Mason. Gardner himself was a practicing lawyer for over twenty years and his knowledge of the law was put to good use when he began working on the Perry Mason novels. Compared to today's legal thrillers, his novels have not stood the test of time and may come across as somewhat bland and formulaic. Perhaps the one that holds the greatest historical value is the first book in the series, *The Case of the Velvet Claws*, which was first published in 1933. Other novels in the series followed a similar scenario. The case was introduced and then investigated, Mason's client was accused of the crime, more investigation took place, and then the trial began. Mason always managed to reverse the case by finding new evidence and exposing the real culprit in court at the same time. Gardner never departed from this system, and while the novels were considered entertaining, they hardly taxed the brain. One of the problems that arose in the Gardner books was, in fact, the lack of characterization. Mason and his sidekicks never really evolved.

English author Sarah Woods is the name behind the series featuring barrister Anthony Maitland. In *Bloody Instructions*, the series' first of forty-nine books, an elderly family solicitor is found dead after being served his afternoon tea. Any of the clients who consulted him that day had the opportunity to sneak back and commit the crime, including a leading actor who had a motive. It is his knife, in fact, that is found stuck in the lawyer's back. It is up to barrister Antony Maitland to find the real killer before it is too late.

Sarah Caudwell, another English author of legal thrillers, also bears mentioning. A Chancery barrister and a former Professor of Law, she only wrote four novels. Her first was *Thus Was Adonis Murdered* (1981) and introduced Oxford Professor of Law Hilary

Tamar. Her second novel, *The Shortest Way to Hades* (1986), was nominated for an Anthony Award for Best Novel in 1986. *The Sirens Sang of Murder* (1989) was nominated for an Agatha Award in 1989 and won the Anthony Award for Best Novel in 1990. Her final novel, *Sybil in her Grave* (2000), was published posthumously. Her books are erudite and very reminiscent of Golden Age authors Dorothy L. Sayers and Margery Allingham. However, it is her main protagonist and narrator that make this series so intriguing, along with the incisiveness of her legal points. One does not know the sex of Hilary Tamar and the author refused to reveal whether or not Hilary is male or female. The four books are based around a group of young London barristers in a set of chambers based in Lincoln's Inn Fields and the trouble that they manage to find themselves in. Wit, humor, and intelligence thrive in her books, and the stories are bound up in arcane areas of British law and steeped in obscure allusions to classical literature. But they are also an acquired taste, as irony abounds, and they would no doubt appeal primarily to readers who enjoy Golden Age mysteries and appreciate the classical references.

Further, her plotting is as complicated and satisfying as one could expect from an author who took pride in ensuring that the gender of her main protagonist would never be specified. While in most contemporary legal thrillers, there is an element of social commentary, this is not the case with Sarah Caudwell. Therefore, if you hanker after probing social commentary or an in-depth characterization, then these books will not meet that need. They do, nevertheless, give an insight into life in chambers and within the British legal system alongside its somewhat archaic laws.

In the late 1980s and the 1990s, writing legal thrillers was not the sole prerogative of males, though one has to appreciate the fact that a majority of legal thrillers were written by men such as William Tappley, Sheldon Siegel, Philip Margolin, William Diehl, James Grippando, Richard North Patterson, William Lashner, and Robert K. Tanenbaum, among others.

In 1987, lawyer Lia Matera wrote *Where Lawyers Feared to Tread*, the first in what became a series of books featuring lawyer

Willa Jansson. It is difficult to decide whether these can be classed as legal thrillers along the same lines as Turow and Grisham—as they are essentially a series featuring a lawyer who becomes an amateur sleuth—but they are still set within a legal milieu. Former lawyer Steve Martini also emerged around the same time with his first novel, which was not a legal thriller. However, it is his series of courtroom thrillers, featuring criminal defense lawyer Paul Madriani that put him on the map. The first book in the series is *Compelling Evidence* (1992), which sees Madriani defending his ex-lover in court when she is accused of murdering her husband. Perhaps the best book in the series is *Undue Influence* (1994), where Madriani finds himself defending his wife's sister in what was initially a contested child custody case. It ultimately becomes a murder case when she is accused of killing her former husband's new wife and their unborn child.

Lisa Scottoline published the Edgar Award-nominated *Everywhere That Mary Went* in 1993. A former lawyer herself, Scottoline favors heroines who are both smart and determined. A standout in her oeuvre is her second novel, *Final Appeal* (1994), which won her an Edgar for Best Paperback. This fast-paced thriller is designed to be read like daily newspaper headlines. Protagonist Grace Rossi finds herself investigating a murder, unearthing a secret bank account, and following a trail of bribery and judicial corruption. With end-of-chapter cliffhangers, Scottoline's stories are witty, gripping, and suspenseful, and reviewers often place them in the same category as works by such giants as Grisham and Turow.

While Nancy Taylor Rosenberg has written two different series featuring members of the legal profession, her stand-alone novels made her part of the growing trend of women writing legal thrillers. In *Interest of Justice* (1993), her first stand-alone novel, she explores the murky world of law administration, where, all too often, the lawmakers use the law instead of serving it, and the real victim of the system is justice. With an insider's knowledge of the criminal legal system, it is not so technical that it will put readers off.

Since 2000, there has been a rise in the number of female authors writing legal thrillers. They have certainly made inroads into what has normally been perceived as a male bastion. Linda Fairstein and Alafair Burke are undoubtedly two of the most prominent, and of late, Marcia Clark, who is best known as the head prosecutor in the O. J. Simpson case, has also joined them. Fairstein is a former Assistant District Attorney, who was head of the Sex Crimes Unit in the Manhattan District Attorney's Office. During her tenure, she prosecuted a number of extremely high-profile cases, including the Central Park Jogger case and the Preppie Murder Case. Her books are legal thrillers with a dose of police procedural incorporated into them as well. Her main protagonist is Alex Cooper, a sex crime prosecutor, who is helped in her investigations by her cohort's detectives, Mike Chapman and Mercer Wallace. In the first book in the series, *Final Jeopardy*, Alex Cooper finds herself investigating the murder of a glamorous film star and friend in the rarefied environment of Martha's Vineyard. The books draw heavily on her experience as a prosecutor. They are also full of tidbits about New York. One is not drowned by legalese and there is a running joke about the show *Jeopardy!* throughout the series.

Cooper is not a typical prosecutor either; she is independently wealthy, enjoys the finer things in life, and appreciates the arts. It is fair to say that Alex Cooper is Linda Fairstein's alter ego. Fairstein has gone on record to say that one of the things she thought to bring to the genre is the authenticity of her experience. The series certainly attests to that. Despite the many years that she spent dealing with high-profile crimes, Fairstein never writes about actual cases that she has dealt with. Instead, she draws from the motives and crimes that she encountered on the job, and this is what makes her writing so incisive.

Alafair Burke is, in her own right, an author well regarded by fellow crime writers. She is also Professor of Law at Hofstra University School of Law and a legal commentator. She has a distinguished pedigree when it comes to writing, as her father is the celebrated crime writer James Lee Burke. Burke's novels are known for their authenticity, and, like Linda Fairstein, she does not write about crimes that she has been involved with in real life, but she does draw upon her experience as a prosecutor. The first book in her series, *Judgment Calls* (2003), features Samantha Kincaid, an Oregon prosecutor. The storyline is based superficially on the case of Keith Hunter Jesperson, better known as the "Happy Face Killer" due to his tendency of drawing smiley faces on correspondence to the press. What comes across in Burke's novels is that she often explores one or two legal points simultaneously, like murder and corruption.

Marcia Clark's first novel, *Guilt by Association* (2011), manages not to suffer from the author's reputation. However, it is clear that Clark has used to good effect her knowledge and expertise of the nuances found in the courts of Los Angeles and the crimes that take place there. In a job that is usually occupied by men, Los Angeles D.A. Rachel Knight, her main protagonist, is a stubborn, wisecracking, and intensely gifted prosecutor. Clark's vibrant ensemble of characters, her intimate knowledge of what goes on in the Los Angeles courts, and her knack for fast-flowing action are proof already that *Guilt by Association* marks the beginning of what may turn into a prolific writing career.

Recent emergence of Scandinavian authors of legal thrillers have brought to light the works of Icelandic writers Yrsa Sigurðardóttir and Åsa Larsson. Sigurðardóttir sets her series of books, featuring lawyer Thóra Gudmundsdottir, in Reykjavik. The second book in this series, *My Soul to Take* (2009), was shortlisted for the Shamus Award for Best Novel in 2010. Larsson sets her books in Sweden and features Rebecka Martinsson, a tax lawyer. Her work has been shortlisted for a number of international awards. *Sun Storm* (2006), also published as *The Savage Altar* (2007), won Sweden's Best First Crime Novel Award and was shortlisted for the Crime Writers Association International Dagger Award in 2007.

It is clear that popular culture helps shape the views of the public in relation to how they see the law and what they expect from it. While legal thrillers have been around for some time, it did not really become an established genre until twenty years ago. The number of authors writing legal thrillers has grown significantly over the last few decades, and there are still a vast number of authors out there who are integral to the constant changing arena of the genre. Authors Greg Iles, David Ellis, Robert Rotenberg, Robert Rotstein, and Paul Goldstein are certainly among them. Although the genre will have its peaks and troughs, there is no doubt that as long as there are authors (especially members of the legal profession) willing to write legal thrillers, there will always be those willing to read them.

Works Cited

Ashley, Mike. *The Mammoth Encyclopedia of Modern Crime Fiction.* London: Robinson, 2002.

Breen, Jon L. *A Guide to Courtroom Fiction.* Metuchen, NJ & London: Scarecrow Press, 1984.

Browne, Ray B. "Why Should Lawyers Study Popular Culture." *The Lawyer and Popular Culture: Proceedings of a Conference.* Ed. David L. Gunn. Littleton: Fred B. Rothman & Co, 1993.

Burke, Alafair. *Judgment Calls.* London: Orion, 2003.

Carofiglio, Gianfrico. *A Walk in the Dark.* London: Bitter Lemon Press, 2010.

Caudwell, Sarah. *Thus Was Adonis Murdered.* London: Collins, 1981.

_____. *The Shortest Way to Hades.* London: Robinson, 2002.

_____. *The Sirens Sang of Murder.* London: Robinson, 2002.

_____. *Sybil in Her Grave.* London: Robinson, 2002.

Christie, Agatha. *Witness for the Prosecution and Selected Plays.* London: HarperCollins Publishers, 1995.

Clark, Marcia. *Guilt by Association.* London: Mulholland Books, 2011.

Connelly, Michael. *The Lincoln Lawyer.* London: Orion, 2005.

_____. *The Fifth Witness.* London: Orion, 2011.

Drell, Adrienne. "Murder, They Write" *American Bar Association Journal* (June 1994) 80: 46-52.

Ellis. David. *Line of Vision.* New York: Putnam Publishing Group, 2001.

_____. *Company of Liars.* New York: Putnam Publishing Group, 2005.

Fairstein, Linda. *Final Jeopardy.* London: Little Brown, 1996.

Friedman, Lawrence M. "Law, Lawyers and Popular Culture" *Yale Law Journal* 98 (1989): 1579 HeinOnline. The Supreme Court of the United Kingdom Library. 10 Oct. 2013.

Gaddis, William. *A Frolic of His Own*. London: Viking, 1994.

Gardner, Erle Stanley. *The Case of the Velvet Claw*. London: Pan Books Ltd, 1960.

Gimenez, Mark. *The Colour of Law*. London: Sphere, 2006.

Grisham, John. *A Time to Kill*. London: Arrow, 1992.

_____. *The Pelican Brief*. London: Century, 1992.

_____. *The Client*. London: Doubleday, 1993.

_____. *The Firm*. London: Arrow, 2010.

_____. *The Confession*. London: Arrow, 2011.

Gunn, David L. *The Lawyer and Popular Culture: Proceedings of a Conference*. Littleton: Fred B Rothman & Co, 1993.

Hare, Cyril. *Tragedy at Law*. London: Faber & Faber, 1942.

Herbert, Rosemary. *Whodunit?: A Who's Who in Crime and Mystery Writing*. New York: Oxford UP, 2003.

Landay, William. *Defending Jacob*. London: Orion, 2012.

Larsson, Åsa. *The Savage Altar*. London: Viking, 2007.

Lee, Harper. *To Kill a Mocking Bird*. London: Heinemann Mandarin, 1989.

Lescroart, John. *The 13th Juror*. London: Headline, 1994.

_____. A Certain Justice. London: Headline, 1996.

Macaulay, Stewart. "Popular Legal Culture: An Introduction." *Yale Law Journal* 98 (1989): 1545 HeinOnline. The Supreme Court of the United Kingdom Library. 10 Oct. 2013

Martini, Steve. *Compelling Evidence*. London: Headline, 1993.

_____. *Undue Influence*. London: Headline, 1995.

Matera, Lia. *Where Lawyers Fear to Tread*. New York: Ballantine Books, 1991.

Meltzer, Brad. *The Tenth Justice*. London: Hodder & Stoughton 1997.

Scottoline, Lisa. *Everywhere That Mary Went*. London: Hodder & Stoughton, 1995.

_____. *Final Appeal*. London: Hodder & Stoughton, 1995.

Shakespeare, William. *The Merchant of Venice*. London: Penguin Classics, 2007.

Sigurðardóttir, Yrsa. *My Soul to Take*. London: Hodder, 2010.

Swanson, Jean & Dean James. *Killer Books: A Readers Guide to Exploring the Popular World of Mystery and Suspense*. New York: Berkley Crime, 1998.

Travers, Robert. *Anatomy of Murder*. London: Faber & Faber, 1958.

Turow, Scott. *Presumed Innocent*. London: Bloomsbury, 1987.

_____. *Innocent*. London: Mantle, 2010.

Von Schirach, Ferdinand. *The Collini Case*. London: Michael Joseph, 2012.

White, Terry. *Justice Denoted: The Legal Thriller in American, British and Continental Courtroom Literature*. Westport, CT: Praeger, 2003.

Wishingrad, Jay. *Legal Fictions: Short Stories About Lawyers and the Law*. London: Quartet Books, 1995.

Woods, Sarah. *Bloody Instruction*. New York: Avon, 1986.

The Techno Thriller in Context _____

John A. Dowell

In the Beginning: Symbols and Supernature

In the beginning, there was the symbol, and the symbol was with story, and the story was heroic, and the heroes were divine.

Beyond the symbol is the word and its better users, who developed storytelling as a craft. In the 4,700 year-old epic Sumerian tale of thrills, prostitutes, battles, beer, and death, Gilgamesh and Enkidu were Bronze Age heroes wielding the tools of their time. Religions and philosophies developed and were cast off, gatherings became settlements then civilizations. Deities and other supernatural agents—common among these tales—were revered and abandoned. With the advent of hard metals was born the Iron Age and the powerful new transportation technologies it forged, immensely improving roads and sailing vessels, allowing greater commerce and sharing of knowledge. Following the trajectories of technologies shared, weaponry vastly improved, allowing wars to become more horrific—fresh empires formed, flourished, floundered, and fell. When bronze and iron yielded to steel and steam, heroes and their engines of creation and destruction had to "harden" as well.

Modern Ages of Technologies: The Doctors Are In

All stories use the technologies of their time, and the Industrial Age brought with it fresh magnitudes of scientific power. In 1791, Luigi Galvani published his discoveries of bioelectricity—significantly developed by nephew Giovanni Aldini—demonstrating that electricity was the medium by which nerve cells passed signals to the muscles of all creatures. Mary Wollstonecraft Shelley would certainly have been aware of Aldini's sometimes bizarre public demonstrations with freshly executed humans. While not necessarily directly linked, it is easily construed that these demonstrations were in her mind when writing *Frankenstein; or, The Modern Prometheus*. Readers only familiar with various Frankenstein films learn the book is in three sections: a narrative by the captain of the vessel who discovers the titular medical student during a voyage to the North Pole; the second by Victor Frankenstein describing his experiments with corpses and electricity in his "workshop of filthy creation" as well as the purpose of his revenge against the "creature"; the third a heartbreaking, lucid narrative from the creature himself (indeed, the most self-reflective writer of the three). Published in 1818, this parable of technology attempting to control nature—without a reliance on divinity or other supernatural agencies—was arguably the first true techno thriller.

Around the same time as Aldini's demonstrations with bioelectricity, American inventor Robert Fulton designed and had built the first practical submarine, *Nautilus*. Fulton's was a relatively crude craft, little more than a semi-buoyant, copper-clad cylinder with a leather breathing snorkel and hand-cranked propeller. However, it was eventually commissioned by the French to sink British cargo ships in stealth. Despite apparent successful testings, Napoleon lost interest in the project, and it was abandoned. Dejected, Fulton sought other investors, which he found in the British, who expressed an allure in a larger redesign of the craft, though—due to their victory against the French—it was never constructed.[1] Fulton then returned to America to design the first commercial steamboat, as well as the first steam-powered warship, intended to be used in the War of 1812 against the British. Fulton clearly cared not for politics or mode of production so much as getting his ideas weaponized.

This hardly marked an end of interest in submarines by the French. In 1870, adventure novelist Jules Verne revived daring underwater exploits with Captain Nemo's vision of the electric-powered *Nautilus* in *Twenty Thousand Leagues Under the Sea*. Best known for his pioneering work in thrilling scientific genre fiction, Verne—eldest son of a successful attorney—was recognized for his diligent attention to detail in his massive tales of dramatic fancy. Often disregarded by many literary critics of his time, he has nevertheless been recognized as a prophet of technology, influencing not only designers of many modern submarines, but bold conquests of seemingly impossible sites terrestrial,[2] aerial,[3] and extraterrestrial.[4] Along with technology detailed with enough of a sense of reality to underscore the plausibility, Verne's tales have been thrilling enough for audiences to discover and rediscover them in many languages, enjoying massive resurgences of interest after decades of near-dormancy. Though often cited as science fiction, given its level of plausibility,[5] *Twenty Thousand Leagues* may correctly be considered an early techno thriller.

Also occasionally dismissed for a time with books of children's verse and South Seas travel, Robert Louis Stevenson is nevertheless listed among the pantheon of early techno thriller writers. However, due to so many grim happenings, Stevenson's best-known novel is usually considered a horror piece, yet *Strange Case of Dr. Jekyll and Mr. Hyde* (1886) is a tale of technology run amok, a common thread among the techno thriller form. In the mid-nineteenth century, many institutions of higher learning were going well beyond armchair philosophical analysis of psychology, mental illness and criminality, personality development, and perception, and actually investigating the physiology and chemistry of various brain functions and their impact on personality and psychopathy. Stevenson's Dr. Jekyll and his brutally base counterpart Hyde have become so recognizable a trope of "the dual nature of man"—underscoring the outwardly prim and proper doctor's violent alternate self—that the technology of the tale is sometimes overlooked. Jekyll was first taking his potion to *intentionally* unleash his savage inner "id" beast (as Freud would identify the drive about a decade later) in his repressive Victorian environment when, unexpectedly, Mr. Hyde became the dominant personality. When Jekyll realized he was unable to procure the precise formula of "impure salts" for returning to his own mind—to ostensibly contain his murderous impulses, that is—he presumed his surviving dark half would either take its own life or be captured and executed. This thriller is a techno-tragedy, as the stunning conclusion reveals, when the audience at last learns the doctor and Hyde were one person, and "the life of that unhappy Henry Jekyll [comes] to an end."[6]

This late Victorian audience was stunned by the graphic gruesomeness of Stevenson's depiction of the immoral inner nature of humankind. At the same time, they were in the midst of learning a great deal of new scientific industries with advances not only in the human sciences, but also in the technologies of communication and transportation, as postal routes and vast expanses of canal ways, steamship lines, coach roads, and especially railways opened and flourished in a steam-powered world. A student of this time's, as he called it, "reaction of mechanical and scientific progress upon human life and thought" was Herbert George ("H. G.") Wells, sometimes known as a father of modern science fiction.

Schooled as a zoologist, Wells' *The Island of Doctor Moreau* (1896) and especially *The Invisible Man* (1897) investigated fictions concerning headways in modern biological sciences. *Moreau* is another speculative investigation into the inner workings of humanity attempting to circumvent nature using advanced technology. We learn from the protagonist and narrator, the shipwrecked Edward Prendick, that Dr. Moreau had been a once-respected London physiologist whose torturous experiments in animal vivisection caused him to lose favor among the scientific community.[7] On this Pacific island (actually called Noble's Isle), the doctor has been defying nature once again with vivisection, in this case, to create humans from wild animals, known as the "Beast Folk." These tormented hybrid creatures—one screaming "as if all the pain in the world had found a voice" (26)—were to never taste flesh, in defiance of their natural urgings. In time, the beast folk turn on one of their own, then on Dr. Moreau, leading to Prendick's mercy-killing of Moreau before the doctor could be torn asunder. As the beast folk are, in due course, reverting to their inborn animal behaviors, Prendick finally discovers a rowboat and makes his escape from the island. Eventually returning to London, he finds he cannot stand the company of fellow humans—seemingly on the verge of becoming their own new breed of savage city beast—and retires to a life of quiet contemplation in the country.

Wells' titular *Invisible Man*, the murderous Mr. Griffin, apparently had greater chemical resources than biomedical experimenters Moreau, Jekyll, or Frankenstein. That said, Griffin is not unlike Jekyll in several respects: he is a serious scholar who justifies his base behavior on a transformative chemical experiment gone bad—though the "reveal" is far more gradual and Griffin's rationale for his evil is slightly more sympathetic, as he is trying to survive his plights of invisibility, hunger, and poverty. Having traded his goals in chemistry for the science of optics, Griffin fused the two technologies and created a potion rendering him invisible, eventually leading to a mad new goal of creating his personal reign throughout England. To survive in the meanwhile, Griffin first seeks the assistance of vagrant Mr. Marvel, who betrays him after receiving Griffin's laboratory notes. Griffin later offers former fellow medical student Dr. Kemp a chance to be his confederate in the upcoming reign. It is to Kemp that Griffin reveals his full back-story, though Kemp also betrays him, eventually leading to Griffin's capture and violent death. The story does not quite end there, as the dénouement reveals Marvel has kept Griffin's notes, leaving the reader with a "The End?"-type conclusion, a technique such tales have often employed.

Contemporary Techno Thrillers: Just This Side

The techno thriller has an obvious reliance on science—sometimes speculative science—yet it stays "just this side of the line of reality" from science fiction, which dares to postulate alternative, fictional, science. While Shelley's reanimated "creature" of Frankenstein, Verne's reliance on electric propulsion while submerged, or Stevenson's and Wells' personality-dividing potions and surgeries may have been fictions of science, the technologies upon which these stories were predicated were nevertheless based upon genuine scientific knowledge of their time, no less than were those cutting-edge technologies of the tellers of fantastic ancient adventure tales.

As the century turned one digit closer to the millennium, so turned technologies. Louis Pasteur and Joseph Lister's advances in antiseptics and surgery were among those employed as doctors treated wounds of soldiers from the more technologically-driven wars of the time. Indeed, the very same carbolic acid used in sterilizing surgical instruments and in the creation of analgesic and life-saving pharmaceuticals was used to make the poisonous phenol gas and lethal injections administered to prisoners of Nazi death camps. While capable of peacetime advancement in agriculture, weaponized chemicals, such as phosgene, chlorine, and mustard gas were stockpiled weapons of mass destruction. The same psychotropic medications and therapeutic techniques to ease the suffering of the mentally tormented may also be turned into the compounds of hellscape nightmares. Currently, the complex powers of the computer, robotics, virus, atom, and rocket may be used for either peaceful advantage or global destruction. Former Nazi V-2 rocketeer-turned-early-NASA scientist Wernher von Braun clearly cared not if his ideas were weaponized, so long as they were realized.[8]

In any case, both the plowshare and the sword are forever double-edged. It is with this system-wide level of scientific complexity—no longer bound by the earth itself—that contemporary techno thriller writers typically draw their professional inventory. There are many forms for these breathtaking adventures—military, medical, off-worldly, cybernetic, societal, biological—but when their bark is stripped, they boil down to the employment of actual or genuinely-near-future technologies. They stay "just this side of the line of reality," which certainly does not mean these thrillers depict a "safer" world than science fiction. The inexorable tick-tock countdown of the techno thriller thus entails a more imminent threat than science fiction typically does.

The Cold Atom: *Fail-Safe*

First run as a three-part weekly serial in the *Saturday Evening Post*, "Fail-Safe" and its 1962 publication, appearing between October 13 to October 27, coincided perfectly with the Cuban Missile Crisis of October 14–28. You cannot buy advertising gold that good, and the novelization was already selling briskly by Halloween. This missile crisis has been largely accepted as the two weeks the human race came closest to being incinerated by US and USSR thermonuclear devices in what has been termed MAD—Mutual Assured Destruction. It is the very *certainty* of this mutual destruction that prevents one nation in the "nuclear club" from initiating a nuclear "exchange" of planetary annihilation—and in late 1962, this was a club with only two members. The crisis was during one of the chilliest times of the early Cold War,[9] when the nuclear clock ticked so very loudly.

Authors Eugene Burdick and Harvey Wheeler posit a framework in which the means of protection from nuclear attack itself—the "Fail-Safe"—is the very engine that guarantees nuclear devastation. In their scenario, the US Strategic Air Command detects what is believed to be an oncoming Soviet nuclear bomber, but the threat turns out to be an off-course passenger airliner. However, the recall order sent to scrambled bombers on their way to a nuclear drop over Moscow is jammed by a new Soviet technology. Having passed the Fail-Safe point, recall messages, which finally get through to the bombers, are heartbreakingly ignored—per orders and training—as they are presumed to be a Soviet trick. To keep the USSR from being bombed, initiating the MAD scenario, some of the bombers are shot down with intentional US "friendly-fire" and others are lost to Soviet defenses, but one gets through—Moscow is doomed. After admitting technological errors on both sides (the false alert, the radio-jamming), the US President and Soviet Chairman must together consider what to do next. In a shockingly desperate attempt to avert MAD, the President offers to appease the Chairman by dropping a US bomb on the Empire State Building. Knowing the President's wife is in New York City, the Communist leader responds: "Holy Mother of God." It is therefore easy to posit "Fail-Safe" as the standard-bearer for the contemporary techno thriller—you cannot buy standard-bearing gold that good.

Games of a Patriot: Tom Clancy

Among the best-known champions of the contemporary techno thriller form is Tom Clancy. So familiar is his name to readers that his characters and military groups are used in licensed video games not authored by Clancy himself. His 1984 debut bestseller, *The Hunt for Red October*, introduces audiences to his primary recurring character, CIA analyst (eventually US President) Jack Ryan. Again readers are drawn beneath the oceans to depths where only the most technologically-advanced machinery may battle, reminiscent of the troubled Captain Nemo's *Nautilus* adventures, or even those of

Clive Cussler's Dirk Pitt.[10] In a brinksmanship game of multiple tactics and counter-tactics, Ryan and defecting Soviet Captain Ramius must work together to outwit the Russian command that would prevent Ramius from delivering *Red October*—with its super-stealth propulsion system—into U.S. hands. So well-researched was the book that it was first published by the U.S. Naval Institute Press.

President Reagan's proposed Strategic Defense Initiative (SDI) to take warfare past the sky in space-platformed satellite and ICBM-killing weapons is featured in a number of Clancy's stories, most notably in his fourth bestseller, 1988's *The Cardinal of the Kremlin*, the follow-up to *Red October*. Clancy's other novels are all as renowned for their inventive logical strategies, brilliant tactical maneuverings, and detailed technologies as they are for what might be considered their chest-thumping patriotism.

Clancy's heroes sometimes rival the exploits of Gilgamesh himself and would make Robert Fulton proud. This is true whether battling the USSR and KGB of the Cold War;[11] or *alongside* the post-USSR Russians against the Chinese;[12] against China alone;[13] a thinly-disguised Irish Republican Army;[14] drug lords;[15] Pakistani and other "Arab terrorists;"[16] or even a recently-denuclearized Japan, after the US and Russia have themselves denuclearized.[17] Clearly, an American life in one of Tom Clancy's universes is apparently one very much in need of the "off-the-books black-ops" teams he offers.[18]

Angles and Demands: Dan Brown

Leaning a bit closer to the cryptographic than the catastrophic, Dan Brown has enjoyed an unusual career as a techno thriller writer in that he has outsold nearly all his leading peers, while, among them, writing the fewest books in the genre. His main recurring protagonist is Harvard cryptologist[19] Robert Langdon, a sort of gun-for-hire, mytho-religious scholar. Langdon has appeared in four novels to date: *Angels & Demons* (2000), *The Da Vinci Code* (2003), *The Lost Symbol* (2009), and 2013's *Inferno*.

Brown expects a reasonably sophisticated audience willing to play along with the demands of various angles in his puzzle-piece stories. Two years prior to *The Da Vinci Code*, the last page of

Brown's *Deception Point* had the character sequence of: "1-V-116-44-11-89-44-46-L-51-130-19-118-L-32-118-116-130-28-116-32-44-133-U-130," which could easily have been dismissed as mere press error. However, some fans applied the characters as a code within *Deception Point*'s various chapters and found this 25-letter sequence: "TVCIR HIOLF ENDLA DCESC AIWUE." Twenty-five letters is five squared, so if every fifth letter is read in sequence, it spells out "THE DA VINCI CODE WILL SURFACE." Brown maintains he has perhaps another dozen Langdon novels in mind—a claim not hard to believe, given the incredible success of the franchise.

The Doctor Is Back: Robin Cook

In a nearly H.G. Wellian style, physician Robin Cook has an uncanny knack of anticipating actual scientific events and medical controversies. His first such novel, 1977's *Coma*, was notable not only for its timely investigation into the patriarchy of the medical profession, but malpractice, patients' rights, and the black market of organ donation and transplantation. Harkening back to the roots of the genre, his Dr. Victor Frank (yes) explores the familiar realm of creating a superior "son"—albeit on a molecular-genetic level rather than gross anatomy—in 1989's *Mutation*; again, the remarkable son and disappointed father meet their watery dooms.

Cook's work consistently explores medical ethics, whether dealing with organ transplantation, gender discrimination, or viral mutation. *Outbreak* (1987) and *Contagion* (1996) anticipated variant strains of the flu and ebola, potentially earth-killing "bugs," and the inevitability of disaster when conflicting agencies put their institutional egos ahead of medical efficacy. Cook's heroic duo, medical examiners Laurie Montgomery and Jack Stapleton, appear in ten stories,[20] contending with institutional resistance, genetic manipulation, governmental malfeasance, and scientific criminal masterminds, as well as their own evolving relationship. As is typical of the genre, Cook demonstrates that the more sophisticated a technological system is, the more things there are to fail catastrophically—*and* the more likely it *will* happen.

This One is REAL: *The Hot Zone*

A panic-inducing clockwork frightscape is lifeblood for any technology thriller, and one book delivers a unique variant: reality. Among the laudatory blurbs on the jacket of journalist Richard Preston's *The Hot Zone* (1994) is this: "The first chapter of *The Hot Zone* is one of the most horrifying things I've read in my whole life—and then it gets worse. That's what I keep marveling over: it keeps getting worse." This from no less a reader of horrifying things than Stephen King, correct in his assessment of the eighteen days the "Level Four" biohazard of Ebola Reston gripped the Hazelton Laboratories of Virginia.[21] Those days also held the entire medical community in terror, to say nothing of rendering the Centers for Disease Control and the Army's USAMRIID[22] at loggerheads. The simple truth is, had "RESTV" ultimately been pathogenic in humans—given the outbreak's proximity to the nation's capital—a viral apocalypse may have actually occurred. As with techno-master Michael Crichton, Preston persuasively underscores the theme that technological terrors are exponentially amplified when institutional egos are placed ahead of medical efficacy. So devoted is he to this theme, Preston's *Micro* (2011) was co-authored with Crichton.

What Could Go "Wrong"?[23] Michael Crichton

Michael Crichton's nuts-and-bolts-level of scientifically-detailed offerings may be among the most wide-ranging of the lot. A Cold War graduate from Harvard Medical School (a distinction which likely lends itself to an attention to detail), Crichton maintained a focused vision of asking "what-if?" and "now-what?" throughout his *oeuvre*. The inevitable response to that question is a recognition that all technological things—especially those dealing with complex technologies—are not only fallible, but most certainly *will* fail at some point, and that point may well be catastrophic. The thrill, of course, is in that very point.

The Andromeda Strain (1969) put Crichton on the bestseller list.[24] A medical mystery within a fail-safe countdown begins when a military satellite unexpectedly crashes to earth near a secluded Arizona town, and soldiers sent for retrieval instantly die. When it appears the town has died as well, alarms signal and the "Wildfire" protocol is initiated, indicating the presence of an extraterrestrial organism with the potential to infest earth. The satellite and the only two town survivors, an inconsolable baby and a sterno-swilling drunk, are contained and brought to the wildfire facility deep underground. The "Andromeda strain," as the microbic contagion is code named, mutates with every growth cycle, yet is eventually discovered to have a narrow pH range—within that of human blood—explaining the sudden deaths of unprotected retrieval soldiers and townspeople. The screaming baby and besotted drunk's blood had pH levels not promoting growth, and Andromeda eventually mutates into a nonlethal form. But the seals of Wildfire's lower levels were compromised and the self-destruct mechanism meant to obliterate organisms that might escape the facility is initiated—a nuclear fail-safe. Should it detonate, Andromeda will transform the energy into matter and be unleashed, un-mutated, into Earthling bloodstreams. Luckily, the only person in the facility with the key disarms the nuke in the nick of time. Again, this is a format typical of Crichton and many such genre writers: establish a terrifying *what-if?* and keep asking the frustrating *now-what?* questions that keep the clockwork mechanisms ticking—though sometimes the hands tick very far backward.

Jurassic Park (1990) marked another peak in Crichton's career, combining the cutting-edge technology of DNA research with a childlike interest in dinosaurs—not static, fiberglass-skinned museum pieces, but fast-moving, flesh-rending monsters on a secluded island "theme park" set to bubble in a pressure cooker countdown. *What-if*: reptiles extinct for 70 million years were cloned from DNA found in amber-trapped mosquitoes of the period? They cannot reproduce, however, as only females were cloned, keeping the population easy to maintain and control. *Now-what*: as there were missing sequences in the DNA that were filled in the laboratory with amphibian DNA—amphibians such as frogs, capable of "protogynous hermaphroditism"—thus able to switch their gender from female to male. That, naturally (as it were), led to reproduction and inexorably to the catastrophic ending, with most characters on the island torn asunder, not unlike Moreau on Noble's Isle or Frankenstein and his creature in the Arctic wastes in their own "science versus nature" tales. The island is finally blasted with air strikes by the nearby Costa Ricans, killing the land-bound dinosaurs. *Now-what*: some of these creatures were swimmers; there are reports of odd reptilian footprints in Costa Rica where there should have been chicken tracks. *Now-what?* Indeed. *The End?* Certainly not, given the franchise.

A Techie for the Rest of Us: Daniel Suarez

A former information technologist to massive, complex agencies,[25] relative newcomer to the techno thriller field, Daniel Suarez burst into the genre with his one-two slam of *Daemon* (2006) and *Freedom™* (2010). Using a groundbreaking self-publication strategy, Suarez effectively explains an Internet doomsday non-techies can understand, in which detective Peter Sebeck susses the brilliant killing AI (artificial intelligence) that was posthumously unleashed by mad programmer Matthew A. Sobol into the "darknet." In due course, the AI controls world economies and political forces, as well as manufacturing facilities, creating self-aware—and self-driving—weaponized automobiles and motorcycles. (Driverless cars? *Check.* The technology of "Google Chauffeur," for example, is well in development.)

What-if: there existed fully autonomous missiles, flying killer robots? (*Check*: the US regularly uses "drones" in warfare.) *Now-what?*: these faceless death machines have been hijacked and given insectile intelligence by an unknown military force. *Kill Decision* (2012) not only posits these aerial terrors, but also forces the reader to consider what would happen if human intervention were entirely removed from decisions regarding the "termination" of "targets"—particularly when they target US citizens. (And armed robots have gained the ability to acquire targets autonomously? Yes, they have.)[26]

Beyond Time and Gods

Around 40,000 years ago, early humans—perhaps proto-human Neanderthals—made symbolic images on cave walls, producing the earliest surviving art-stories. Mastodons and other terrifying beasts populate these, along with people who saw heroic deeds—even divinity itself—in the symbols. The tools of those Paleolithic storytellers were, by definition, limited to stone—but while prehistoric, they were certainly not pre-story, and most certainly not pre-technology.

Ancient and contemporary heroic sagas are dependent upon the crafts, interpersonal organization, and tools—the technologies—of their age. Sometimes the stories are driven by the teller, and sometimes by the technology: the flame, the wheel, the arrow; the armor, the blade, the catapult; the canon, the firearm, the steam engine; the computer, the hydrogen bomb, the weaponized virus. These tales are the techno thrillers, regardless of the technology employed. Then as now, such stories may ask questions of their heroes to which one may not always want answers, their divinity be damned.

Notes

1. Ironically, the blueprints were long abandoned at the American consul in London.

2. For example, *Journey to the Center of the Earth* (1864), *Around the World in Eighty Days* (1873), and *The Adventures of Captain Hatteras* (1874).

3. Compound helicopters detailed in *Robur the Conqueror* (1886).

4. Rocketry of *From the Earth to the Moon* (1865).

5. *Nautilus* was also the name of the world's first nuclear-powered electric submarine, which the US Navy took under the North Pole's ice cap in 1958.

6. For the complete text, visit: http://www.bartleby.com/1015/10.html

7. Vivisection was no small matter among the English; the Royal Society for the Prevention of Cruelty to Animals was established in 1824.

8. When hearing of the 1960 American film lauding von Braun, satirist Mort Sahl observed that while the biopic is titled *I Aim at the Stars*, it should be subtitled "But Sometimes I Hit England." (Hendra, 14 n.)

---

9. The Cold War lasted from 1945's Yalta Conference to 1991's dissolution of the Soviet Union in a post-Berlin Wall, post-*perestroika* (economic restructuring) world, after Soviet forces withdrew from Afghanistan.

10. Perhaps only Clive Cussler's green-eyed Dirk Pitt, Sr. is as recognized in the techno thriller depths as Ryan and his cadre. While every bit the all-American as Ryan, Pitt's adventures are generally more personal than patriotic, as he outwits criminal masterminds with cunning, and is more reliant upon regular sidekick Al Giordino, a friend since childhood and Vietnam service.

11. *The Cardinal of the Kremlin* (1988) and *Red Storm Rising* (1986).

12. 2000's *The Bear and the Dragon.*

13. *SSN: Strategies for Submarine Warfare* (1996) and *Threat Vector* (2012).

14. The "Ulster Liberation Army" in *Patriot Games* (1987).

15. *Clear and Present Danger* (1989) and *Without Remorse* (1993).

16. *The Sum of All Fears, Locked On,* and *Against All Enemies* (all 1991), *Executive Orders* (1996), and *Dead or Alive* (2010).

17. *Debt of Honor* (1994). A central plot-point in this thriller is a hijacked airliner used as a missile exploding into the US Capitol during a joint session of Congress—instantly vaporizing nearly all; a matter reflected upon after the September 11, 2001 terrorist attacks on New York and Washington, DC.

18. Such as "*Rainbow Six*" (1996) and "The Campus," found in *The Teeth of the Tiger* (2003), *Dead or Alive* (2010), and *Locked On* (2011).

19. A self-identified "symbologist" (an invented term), Langdon is largely modeled on Columbia University mythologist Joseph Campbell.

20. *Blindsight* (1992), *Contagion* (1996), *Chromosome 6* (1998), *Vector* (1999), *Marker* (2005), *Crisis* (2006), *Critical* (2007), *Foreign Body* (2008), *Intervention* (2009), and *Cure* (2010).

21. There is no Level Five.

22. United States Army Medical Research Institute of Infectious Diseases.

23. From an advertisement for Crichton's original screenplay *Westworld*.

24. Several previous pot-boiling paperback "science caper" novels were published as "John Lange," including 1972's *Binary*, published under

that pseudonym, as well as 1968's medical mystery *A Case of Need*, published as "Jeffery Hudson."

25. Including defense, Fortune 1000, and entertainment companies.

26. Gaudin, Sharon. "Machine gun-toting robots may soon back up US soldiers." *Computerworld*. 11 Oct. 2013. Web. 7 Feb. 2014. <http://bit.ly/HoGt7l>.

Works Cited

Brown, Dan. *Deception Point*. New York: Simon & Schuster, 2002.

Crichton, Michael. *The Andromeda Strain*. New York: Alfred A Knopf, 1969.

_____. *Jurassic Park*. New York: Alfred A. Knopf, 1990.

Fischer, Adam. "Inside Google's Quest To Popularize Self-Driving Cars." *Popular Science*. 18 Sept. 2013. Web. 1 Oct. 2013. <http://bit.ly/1aKMipl>.

Gaudin, Sharon. "Machine gun-toting robots may soon back up U.S. soldiers." *Computerworld*. 11 Oct. 2013. Web. 7 Feb. 2014. <http://bit.ly/HoGt7l>.

Harvey, Eugene & Burdick Wheeler. *Fail-Safe*. New York: HarperCollins, 1962.

Hendra, Tony. *Going Too Far*. New York: Doubleday, 1987.

McHugh, Josh. "How the Self-Published Debut *Daemon* Earned Serious Geek Cred." *Wired*. 21 Apr. 2008. Web. 2 Oct. 2013. <http://wrd.cm/13TtV>.

Preston, Richard. *The Hot Zone: A Terrifying True Story*. New York: Random House, 1994.

Stevenson, Robert Louis. *Strange Case of Dr. Jekyll and Mr. Hyde*. New York: Scribner, 1886; Bartleby.com. 2000. Web. 22 Dec. 2013. <www.bartleby.com/1015/>.

Verne, Jules. *Twenty Thousand Leagues Under the Sea*. Trans. m. Chicago: Rand McNally & Company, 1922.

Wells, H. G. *The Island of Dr. Moreau*. New York: Penguin, 1988.

_____. *The Invisible Man*. Cutchogue, NY: Buccaneer Books, Inc., 1985.

Wolf, Leonard. *The Annotated Frankenstein*. New York: Clarkson N. Potter, Inc., 1977.

The Psychological Thriller in Context _____

Kristopher Mecholsky

Oh, I wasn't touched. I was fascinated. It was as though a veil had been rent.
—Joseph Conrad, *Heart of Darkness*

The psychological thriller is a contradiction, a self-conflicted genre with a central dialectic: we can understand the mind/we can't understand the mind. In both cases, the mind reveals itself to be almost unspeakable, defined simply and inscrutably in Conrad's *Heart of Darkness* by Colonel Kurtz in his dying breath: "The horror! The horror!" And like Marlow, quoted in the epigraph, readers often respond less with sympathy than with *schadenfreude*. Looking at the kinds of fiction most contemporary American readers seem to consider "psychological thrillers," a number of motifs dominate:

- serial killers
- psychotic protagonists
- children in danger
- apparent paranormal danger and/or paranormal gifts
- revenge plots
- psychotic antagonists who stalk the protagonist and who often are (or seem) beyond the reach of the law
- crucial scenes that depict psychological torture
- misleading narratives and unreliable narrators (often resulting from some kind of psychosis)
- psychotic parents/spouses/significant others/apparent-innocents who seemed good
- obsessive investigations (often of unsolved cases)
- severe psychological illness, trauma, or memory loss in a main character;
- and past traumas that revisit in a new danger

Many of these recent psychological thrillers illustrate more than one of these traits. For instance, S. J. Watson's *Before I Go to Sleep* (2011) involves psychotic parents/spouses who seemed good, in addition to a main character with severe psychological illness or trauma. Stephen King's *Doctor Sleep* (2013) concerns apparent paranormal danger and/or paranormal gifts, as well as children in danger. And A. S. A. Harrison's *The Silent Wife* (2013) employs misleading narratives and revenge plots. In some cases, the accumulation of conventions approaches, reaches, and passes absurdity. In James Patterson's *Alex Cross, Run* (2013), the twentieth novel in his popular Alex Cross series, the plot involves obsessive investigations of unsolved cases, psychotic antagonists who seem beyond the law, serial killers, children in danger, revenge plots, psychotic spouses who seemed good, crucial scenes that depict psychological torture, severe psychological illness, and past traumas revisited. Why did these specific themes and patterns arise in this genre in America? What gave it its form?

In many essential ways, the psychological thriller is simultaneously the most modern *and* the most postmodern of literary forms, in the sense that its basic characteristics and development and its role in American culture mark it as demonstrative of how the modern period distinguished itself from the past—and how the postmodern period has moved to question it. Although writers, like Edgar Allan Poe and Henry James, importantly prefigure today's psychological thriller, the fiction that resembles it prior to 1940 is associated primarily with genres other than the psychological thriller (e.g., Gothic fiction, the sensation novel, and the detective story). At what point, then, did the psychological thriller become recognizably its own genre and why? Ultimately, three recent historical trends prompted the rise of the psychological thriller: Gothic fiction, Freudian psychoanalysis, psychological realism in fiction, and mass-market publishing.

No one seems to agree on one definite method for determining which works belong in which genres, or when the traits of one genre have become a new one. So how should the psychological thriller be classified? As an evolutionary biologist might do, the literary critic can test theories of phylogeny (a history of a species) for genre, moving backward through history via groups called *clades*—members of which all descend from a common ancestor—to find unique ancestors to the genre in question, as well as common ancestors that genre shares with those similar to it. Evaluating the motifs that I listed earlier, which indicate the "speciation events" that prompted the many overlapping strains among psychological thrillers, I suggest the following as the strongest currents that have come to define the genre:

- psychotic killers as antagonist or protagonist, often beyond the reach of the law and often prompting obsessive investigation; in many cases, the antagonist is a family member
- children in danger
- revenge for psychological trauma, often perpetrated by a family member
- unreliable narrators whose unreliability usually comes from some kind of psychosis, sometimes in the form of found documents
- prominent citizens, close family relations, or presumed innocents who turn out to be psychotic
- severe psychological illness, trauma, or memory loss in a main character that often haunts and threatens long past the traumatic event, often caused by a family member

Looking at the list, social and personal fear surface as the main instigators of the psychological thriller; specifically, these patterns reveal a profound dread that, underneath appearances—either one's own, one's family's, or others'—lurk insidious secrets that threaten social and personal identity.

The dread that dangerous secrets lie beneath once-safe sectors of life resonates strongly across the nineteenth century, echoing particularly in Gothic fiction. That dread and the patterns listed above come from anxiety about the modern age and its implications—especially with regard to the limits of science; the simultaneous reliance on and unknowability of the individual, particularly concerning the distribution of land and wealth into private property to individuals; the overwhelming importance of family lineage to wealth and property; and the limits of the law. The psychological thriller comes, then, from peculiarly modern dynamics: it confronts the modern anxiety about the nature of the mind and self through the Enlightenment struggle to subjugate myth and superstition by way of science and rationality. But it simultaneously seeks to reveal the limits of knowledge of the individual self: humanity might be ultimately unknowable and uncontrollable. The mind may even be unknown to itself.

The growing nineteenth-century understanding of the world primarily through empiricism and objectivity ultimately compelled a radical equivalence of objects and people in reasoning. "The real *telos* of reason," Carl Freedman writes in *The Incomplete Projects*, "is not just philosophical but social: modernity's goal is to allow us to live rationally" (19), a goal it draws from the Enlightenment. Indeed, rationality and objective equivalence was borne out in capitalism, industrialization, and scientific progress, even as contemporary thinkers like Marx challenged its cultural implications. Such critics were an effect of the Enlightenment worldview. While rationality, reason, and mastery over nature were lauded in their replacement of the mystery of superstition, unquestioning trust in authority, and fate, the limits and extremes such a worldview presented were immediately feared. This dialectic found cultural expression in Gothic art.

Jerrold E. Hogle remarks, in his introduction to *The Cambridge Companion to Gothic Fiction*, "the longevity and power of Gothic fiction unquestionably stem from the way it helps us address and disguise some of the most important desires, quandaries, and sources of anxiety, from the most internal and mental to the widely social and cultural, throughout the history of western culture since the eighteenth century" (4). Gothic fiction is an uncanny extension of the neoclassical, realistic phase that emerged in the early novel. Fiedler argues that "its fables represent the hopes and fears of a group of intellectuals turned toward the future at a moment of revolutionary readjustment" (136). The American and French Revolutions were the logical cultural goals of Enlightenment thought, and when the latter resulted in horrific terror and wanton murder, it cast a pall over former successes of rationalism. How could reason be so wrong about humankind? Fiedler suggests that "the guilt which underlies the gothic...is the guilt of the revolutionary haunted by the (paternal) past which he has been striving to destroy; and the fear that possesses the gothic and motivates its tone is the fear that in destroying the old ego-ideals of Church and State, the West has opened a way for the inruption of darkness..." (129). The positivity of knowledge in the Enlightenment was replaced by a new knowledge: there is something unknown *we did not know was unknown*.

Since the modern period is defined largely through the rise of capitalism and an educated and politically liberated middle class—cultural products of Enlightenment rationalism—the secrets of the individual in relation to society are the limits with which Gothic fiction is fundamentally concerned. Gothic obsession with the individual's place in a property-mutable world arguably resonated more strongly than most other themes of the genre. The hierarchy of society was no longer understood in terms of an unyielding and religious cosmos that dictated how land was distributed, but rather in terms of how individuals related to each other through the possession and retention of property. Subsequently, the control of accumulating and shifting property was fundamentally mysterious, since the individual remained mysterious. For all of the realistic psychological probing that prompted the rise of the novel, Gothic fiction revealed how unknown the individual could be.

While several Gothic writers from all over Europe and America are worthy of record in helping shape the contemporary psychological thriller, none has had more lasting influence than Edgar Allan Poe (1809–49). He is the most important forebear of the psychological thriller. In addition to the techniques and themes of his stories—which include unreliable narrators, revenge plots, close relations who turn out to be psychotic, descriptions of the psychology of criminals and victims as well as psychological torture—Poe's prescient work within what would become many of the various genres that proceeded from Gothic fiction also helps demonstrate how the psychological

Critical Insights

thriller developed particularly from Gothic fiction. Poe's attention to psychological terror had its greatest impact in horror, a genre intimately related to the psychological thriller, but the motifs of the mystery of private individuals and property were explored with greater zest and to greater effect in an off-shoot genre of Gothic fiction: sensation fiction. Along with the Newgate novel of the early nineteenth century, the sensation novel was an important genre in the development of crime fiction, and it was an important conduit to the psychological thriller for the Gothic obsession with mysterious and perverted families. Unlike Gothic fiction, sensation fiction was placed firmly in contemporary times and focused more often than not on middle-class, country living. In novels like Wilkie Collins' *The Woman in White* or Mary Elizabeth Braddon's *Lady Audley's Secret*, mysteries of inheritance and family lineage are uncovered in the light of fantastic and horrifying incidents that appear supernatural (ghosts and curses) but are revealed to have rational explanations, often based in new science (such as psychoactive drugs). Moreover, sensation fiction's attention to *thrilling* the reader and its great commercial success in doing so illustrate the importance of genre fiction in the age of mass publishing.

Gothic art declined sharply after the beginning of the twentieth century. As Richard Davenport-Hines notes in *Gothic: Four Hundred Years of Excess, Horror, Evil and Ruin*, the decline coincided with the rise of Freudianism (325). Whereas Gothic and sensation fiction capitalized on the boundaries of scientific discovery and hinted at the unknown in seemingly undiscoverable human mind, the Vienna School of psychoanalysis began to give explanations for that unknown. Mark Edmundson suggests that Sigmund Freud did nothing less than take "the props and passions of terror Gothic... and...relocate them inside the self" (32). By describing childhood in terms of psychosexual development and modeling the Self on an engagement between an instinctual drive (the Id), a realistic mediator (the Ego), and cultural internalization controls (the Super-Ego), Freud provided a working model that depicted the Self as fundamentally split, confirming the anxieties many were feeling after the upheavals of the nineteenth- and early twentieth centuries.

In some ways, this made the terror of the unknown even worse. If everything is simply wrapped up in some mental tissue, all of humanity should be knowable. But Freud was also exposing the irrationality at the center of rational humanity. The fact that the essence of humanity remained so elusive despite its apparently physical basis was more terrifying than supernatural phenomena.

Simultaneously motivated and scarred by humanity's achievements following the Enlightenment, late-nineteenth-century and early-twentieth-century writers sought to break free from old modes of representation and more accurately describe the fractured sense of self and community that many people felt in the post-industrial age. A major Anglo-American precursor to the modernists of the twentieth century, Henry James (1843–1916) developed and popularized an approach to fiction firmly rooted in an unflinchingly realistic look at the psychological mechanics of living without reference to mythology, melodrama, or religion. And in *The Turn of the Screw*, before Freud had even published his culture-shattering theories, James demonstrated how Freudian psychological realism could reinvigorate Gothic fiction by grounding it in the mind. Perhaps more important, James also greatly altered the literary depiction of the child. Whereas nineteenth-century writers "paid tribute to the idyll of childhood innocence," as Ellen Pifer comments in her comprehensive book on children in contemporary literature (21), James explored what Freud was developing at the same time in Austria: a "conscious intellectual exploration of states of childhood" through his own "unconscious experience" (Edel 480). As Pifer argues, "it is clear that James participated in the same intellectual ferment that led Freud, along with Charles Darwin, Karl Marx, and others, to dismantle the edifice of nineteenth-century thought" (25). As argued here, that edifice of thought already housed its own contradictions, which the psychological thriller unveils.

But these literary–historical movements had not coalesced in any consistent or recognizable format. As these anxieties over modernism fermented in various theories of life, society, and the mind, industrialization moved inexorably forward, finding more efficient ways to produce mass quantities of commodities to sell at higher profit margins. Although mass publications had been targeting segments of the reading public with genre fiction throughout the nineteenth century, those forms were mainly in serial magazines of varying quality (including the penny dreadfuls of the nineteenth century and the pulps of the early twentieth century, as well as the "slicks," like *The Saturday Evening Post* from every decade in both centuries). But these formats were short and shoddy. They could not keep pace with the sale of novels, which had the advantage of longevity and cultural legitimacy. In the late 1930s and early 1940s, Penguin Books and Pocket Books began selling pocket-sized, paper-covered books with durable, relatively high-quality paper. They sold a combination of content, from reprinted classics to contemporary "fluff" entertainment. And they sold quite well, especially after a heavy push to soldiers stationed overseas with stretches of time to read. Soon after, more companies joined the innovative market. The paperback boom of the 1940s was a quantum leap for publishing and fiction, opening up the length and respectability of the novel form to new, more specific markets.

I mark the beginning of the early psychological thriller, then, with the intersection of mass-marketing, psychological realism, and Gothic-inspired fiction. In this context, a useful starting point for the first early psychological thriller would be the Daphne du Maurier (1907–1989) novel *Rebecca* (1938), which represents a transition from the Gothic (epitomized by her grandfather's Gothic fiction) and the contemporaneous popularity of historical romances. But the popularity of the psychological thriller could not have reached the heights it has in fiction without the formal constraints the contemporary thriller imposes, which earlier books, like *Rebecca*, exhibit to only a small degree. As a thriller, the psychological thriller should include significant danger threatening the protagonist or someone/something the protagonist values to keep the reader reading. That kind of tension sells well. But thrillers are also defined by their ability to maintain suspense—tension about whether the protagonist will lose what he/she values. While terror and suspense are relatively easy to create for a moment, they are difficult to sustain reasonably over longer plots. The psychological thriller appears earlier in film, since suspense is easier to create and maintain through visual and sound cues. Thus, readers of genre fiction in the 1940s were used to reading shorter, serialized thrills in cheap magazines, including *Black Mask*, rather than in novels. The hard-boiled fiction, as it was called, that appeared in these magazines was violent and filled with the uncertainty of the modern world. The heroes are deeply flawed and the criminals are often regular people pushed into unforgiving circumstances. While Dashiell Hammett, Horace McCoy, and Paul Cain, and others honed their craft on the pages of *Black Mask*, they found promising new income in the form of the explosion of new paperback presses. And the paperbacks that sold best were those that could grab readers' attention and keep it throughout. No doubt, the gripping allure of film also inspired the publishing industry to find new ways to keep its readers.

Two writers deserve special credit for popularizing the darker, more psychologically-oriented thriller writing that would come to prominence in the 1950s: William Faulkner (1897–1962) and James M. Cain (1892–1977). In 1930, Faulkner published *Sanctuary*, in between *As I Lay Dying* and *Light in August*. He claimed it was originally written solely for money. As he wrote in his preface to the 1932 Modern Library edition of the book, "I took a little time out, and speculated what a person in Mississippi would believe to be current trends, chose what I thought would be the right answer and invented the most horrific tale I could imagine..." (Faulkner 323). Faulkner reports that his publisher replied, "Good God, I can't publish this. We'd both be in jail" (323). Whatever rewritings he did in the meantime (and he claims they were extensive), the book was published, and it did make a lot of money. Tawdry potboilers were proven hits, as Erskine Caldwell, John O'Hara, and writers following proved. While the style of most thrillers in the 1950s and later do not approximate Faulkner's entirely well, no standard had yet been established. Thus, while it might seem indecorous to include a Faulkner novel as a psychological thriller, it *was* just that—more so than du Maurier's *Rebecca*, in fact. Kevin Railey points out that the novel "has frequently been discussed as an exploration of evil and more recently as a text delineating the

---

cultural significance of the Oedipal conflict," and Railey further argues that the "psychoanalytical readings have in fact been the best readings of the novel..." (69). Arguably, one could synthesize these statements to say that *Sanctuary* is an exploration of evil *because of* its exploration of Freudian psychosexual behavior and attitudes, particularly in its depiction of the extreme violence that stems from repression and systemic psychosexual paternalism. Throughout *Sanctuary*, Railey observes, a pervasive and oppressive social paternalism unremittingly punishes Temple Drake for her "loose" ways (83).

If Faulkner's writing has been too aligned with the twentieth-century canon to be considered much of a psychological thriller, James M. Cain's astonishing commercial success with his first novel, *The Postman Always Rings Twice*, marks a clear point after which the psychological thriller is a recognizable, if somewhat ambiguous, genre. In addition to his taut writing, Cain also probed what was relatively deviant psychosexuality in its time, roping in mythological and psychoanalytical themes into his nightmare visions of the American dream. His work demonstrates a consistent interest in the psychological inner-workings behind the façade of modernity. For instance, his widely-praised *Double Indemnity* opens by promising to tell about "this House of Death, that you've been reading about in the papers," swearing that "it didn't look like a House of Death....just a Spanish house, like all the rest of them in California..." (217). Furthermore, Cain's second full-length novel, *Serenade*, depicts an opera singer's psychological struggle to repress his homoerotic feelings for an old conductor through his relationship with a Mexican prostitute. For all of the book's explicit references to mythology, Cain claims the book was prompted into publication by a prominent physician (Dr. Samuel Hirschfeld), praised by a psychiatrist (Dr. James M. Neilson), and prescribed as reading in psychiatry courses all over the country (Madden and Mecholsky 20–21). Of course, the book's views on race and homosexuality are caustically heteronormative and would never be read now for educational purposes. Nevertheless, Cain's work also announces a new period in fiction via dual publishing, with respectable hardcover editions (from Alfred A. Knopf) and paperback editions (from a publisher like Avon). His cultural hybridity illustrates how increasingly meaningless the divisions between high, middle, and low fiction would become by the twenty-first century.

After Faulkner and Cain's work in the 1930s (and 1940s for Cain), as the paperback industry developed, the psychological thriller took on more contemporary characteristics as various writers explored the combined themes and techniques of Gothic fiction, psychological realism, and hard-boiled writing. In the late 1940s and throughout the 1950s, Freud's theories became much more mainstream, echoing to the depths of popular fiction. From the late 1940s through the 1960s, armed with the tenets of pop psychology, crime writers forayed into the thoughts and actions of the psychologically disturbed. Two of the most important early paperback writers involved in popularizing and capitalizing on Freudian themes were Cornell Woolrich (1903–1968) and Horace McCoy (1897–1955), both of whom wrote throughout the 1940s and '50s. Both writers owe a major thematic debt to Cain, but each explored noir themes in stylistically individual ways. In fact, Woolrich is hardly hard-boiled in that sense. His work is much more atmospheric and operatic, and he delights in ruminating explicitly and unremittingly on universalities and eternal symbols—a far cry from Hammett. Woolrich's plots center on strikingly psychological terror, usually from the reader and/or character's foreknowledge of a fatal situation. In fact, Woolrich's ability to conceive of such plots led to the adaptation of a number of his stories, including "It Had to Be Murder" into Hitchcock's *Rear Window*. Raymond Chandler gave him a back-handed compliment, calling him "the best idea man" (O'Brien 91). McCoy is also interested in depicting people on the precipice of sanity, although much of his writing is stylistically hard-boiled. McCoy is well known for *They Shoot Horses, Don't They?* (1935), but it is with *Kiss Tomorrow Goodbye* (1948) that he points toward the greater possibilities of the psychological thriller, since it is the first major book of the period to really explore the psychology behind a psychopathic killer. In fact, the intelligent, sadistic, violent, and psychologically traumatized Ralph Cotter narrates the whole book, which follows his escape from prison and criminal dealings with a gang and a corrupt police force. However, the real story and mystery is what haunts Cotter. Whereas Cain presupposes flaws and trauma, McCoy seeks to explore in greater depth what kind of past could have made such a man. Leonard Cassuto points out how McCoy's novel prefigures the serial killer novel, but instead of a catalog of the horrors a psychotic can commit, *Kiss Tomorrow Goodbye* explores how a trauma (in this case his confused murder of his own grandmother) can damage someone for life.

Along with Woolrich and McCoy, the first writers who might be considered consistent writers of the psychological thriller are Patricia Highsmith (1921–1995) and Jim Thompson (1906–1977). And with them, the genre arguably reaches its zenith, particularly since both of their writings epitomize the most postmodern aspects of the psychological thriller, in the sense that Jean-François Lyotard meant it in *The Postmodern Condition*: as an "incredulity toward metanarratives" (xxiv). Leonard Cassuto calls Highsmith the "quintessential fifties crime writer" for her exploration of the psychological effects of guilt in an era "in the shadow of a mushroom cloud…where the long arm of the House Un-American Activies Committee (HUAC) reached into people's most private spaces" (135). Highsmith's 1950 debut was *Strangers on a Train*, which was adapted to the screen by Alfred Hitchcock, and its themes are indicative of much of the rest of her fiction. Cassuto argues in *Hard-Boiled Sentimentality* that:

> rootless, pervasive anxiety nourishes Highsmith's paranoid creative vision. Pursuit is a persistent theme…but her characters don't know where to run because they don't know where the threat is coming from. For Highsmith's characters, the danger usually originates within—and it's inexorable (135).

In addition to depicting psychopaths, as she does so memorably in her Ripley novels, Highsmith also casts light on how psychologically destructive—but bearable—guilt can be for an average person. Like Woolrich, Highsmith is an inheritor of Poe who importantly transforms Poe's themes to a modern world. In Highsmith's universe, as Cassuto remarks, "her characters never get comfortable with themselves or each other in an ominous-feeling world... They're always looking around as though something terrible is going to happen to them—and something frequently does" (135). Unlike Poe's more Gothic universe, though, the full weight of literary modernism and realism have crushed the sentimentality out of Highsmith's fiction. In *The Talented Mr. Ripley* (1955), for instance, Ripley is on the run from the very beginning from his wrong-doing in the world, and while he is threatened at every turn, no external force ever actually stops him. Nor does he stop himself. While Raskolnikov in *Crime and Punishment* escapes justice only to find guilt too unbearable to live with, eventually turning himself in to the police for proper punishment (and ultimately religious forgiveness), Ripley escapes justice, but is too self-preserving to end the guilt that yet seems to dog him. Ripley's sad fate is his inability to escape himself. Freud offered explanations for how the subconscious might make the mysteries of the mind surface, but Highsmith showed how they might just release themselves without being identified or stopped by a panoptic society.

With Highsmith, the psychological thriller finds greater sophistication than it had before. Nevertheless, Jim Thompson just might be the psychological thriller author *par excellence*. Whatever niceties in description Thompson lacks compared to Highsmith, he is her equal (and occasional better) in terms of psychological depiction. As Geoffrey O'Brien contends, Thompson's ability to narrate so convincingly from within the mind of a psychopath leaves the reader with "the uncanny feeling that *this is too real* to be fiction, that only a true psychopath could so expertly have charted thought and abrupt, equally fragmented action..." (121). David Glover argues that the characters in Thompson's fiction "have become thoroughly demented and the descent into the nether world of Norman Bates in Robert Bloch's *Psycho* (1959) and thence of Dolarhyde, Francis ('the Tooth Fairy') and Hannibal Lecter in *Red Dragon* is about to begin" (146). Indeed, Thompson's works are the beginning of the clearest examples of psychological thrillers, and they are, in many respects, the epitome of the genre because "in each case what starts out as a disarmingly upfront first person narration is revealed as something far more impenetrable and unsafe, enmeshed in its own craziness to the point where it is no longer really clear what kind of entity is doing the speaking" (147). In Thompson's fiction, more so than that by any writer before, the genre finally adopts an unusual characteristic that is unlike many others. Genres usually tell what will take place in the narrative events (as in the espionage thriller, the legal thriller, the medical thriller, and so on), but psychological thrillers also describe the *effect* they have on the reader: this book is not only be about psychological thrills, it will thrill *you* psychologically. Thus, from Thompson on, psychological thrillers in fiction and film often experiment with ways to perturb the audience to greater degrees, frequently through terrifying and horrifying plot points (which often appear at the end).

Thompson is one of the last of the hard-boiled writers in the psychological thriller genre. In the 1950s, two writers began publishing works that mark the transition in the genre from its hard-boiled era to the present one of mass-marketed, professional, commercial fiction: Robert Bloch (1917–1994) and John D. MacDonald (1916–1986). Bloch, a protégé of H. P. Lovecraft, originally wrote for pulps like *Weird Tales*, but he soon moved away from more supernatural horror and began writing more realistically-based crime and horror. He published his first novel, *The Scarf*, in 1947, an early psychological thriller that follows a writer who compulsively kills the women he patterns his characters from. It's somewhat unaccountable that this novel did not catapult him to fame. But it was in fact his 1959 novel, *Psycho* (and its massively successful Hitchcock film adaptation), that really transformed the genre. Inspired by real-life serial killer Ed Gein, Bloch drew effectively and scientifically on modern psychology to push the limits of horror away from the supernatural. The horror Bloch evoked was disgust in personality, which he achieved by narrating within the psychotic mind and by portraying the actions of that mind. *Psycho* begins with Norman Bates reading about Incas flaying people alive, making drums of their skin, before following an age-inappropriate conversation he has with his mother. The reader follows along as a creepy voyeur, interested in Bates' unusual life, inducing a sensation similar to that of reading Woolrich's fiction, but with far more eager revulsion. The cultural effect of Bloch's approach was the popularization of the serial killer novel, the most important subgenre of the psychological thriller.

As important as Bloch's contributions have been—particularly for his example to later films and to Thomas Harris—John D. MacDonald's writing signifies a broader, but noticeable, shift. Although he is well known for his Travis McGee detective novels, MacDonald was a prolific writer in other areas, publishing paperback novels and short stories in a wide variety of pulp and slick magazines before finally publishing hardcover books. In some of MacDonald's 1950s writing, the style and thematic attention approaches Thompson's writing. Leonard Cassuto describes many of MacDonald's '50s paperbacks as depicting "morally detached murderers who maim and kill for the pleasure of it" (241). Furthermore, MacDonald's relation to Thompson and Highsmith extends to their mutual affinity for questioning the metanarrative of modern progress. MacDonald said when he wrote of evil, it was "a kind of evil which defies the Freudian explanations of the psychologists, and the environmental explanations of the sociologists" (69). In his *PopMatters* review of MacDonald's paperback novels, Jeff Tompkins suggests that MacDonald's portrayal of a criminal personality in *Soft Touch* (1957) is "as chilling as any of the psychopaths who stalk through Thompson's fiction, and all the more effective for being so understated…" But MacDonald did not always eschew psychology and sociology's explanations. In his early novels like *The Executioners* (1957), *The Price of Murder* (1957), *The End of the Night* (1960), and many more, MacDonald vigorously explored the psychology of criminals, particularly of self-centered sociopaths in violent confrontation with society. In fact, his literary output from the 1950s into the 1960s reflects the central conflict at the heart of the psychological thriller's development. Steve Scott argues on his blog, *The Trap of Solid Gold*, that MacDonald's fiction moved steadily from a "fascination with the environmental forces that shape criminal action…seen in his early pulp stories but [which] really began to blossom in his mid-period novels" to a conviction that he could not "offer any answers or opinions as to why people turn out the way they do." Current trends in psychological thrillers still usually vacillate between the poles of understanding (even commanding) aberrant behavior and staring into the ultimately unknowable void of the human psyche.

By the end of the 1950s, all of the cultural elements of the contemporary psychological thriller had been introduced. The 1970s produced a blitz of writers who stressed the particular patterns of those elements: Sidney Sheldon, Lawrence Sanders, Mary Higgins Clark, Stephen King, V. C. Andrews, Thomas Harris, and more. In fact, thriller writers of all kinds were coming into their own. Lawrence Sanders (1920–1998) popularized the motif of the obsessive detective figure who is often personally involved or implicated in the crime being investigated. His first novel, *The Anderson Tapes* (1970), is a political thriller of the kind so popular in the 1960s, but it was in his second novel, *The First Deadly Sin* (1973), that Sanders first used "the sure-fire formula of crime, sex, violence, and moral highhandedness that would sustain his career," as his *New York Times* obituary put it. As Patrick Anderson affirms, although Sanders gambled with detective Edward X. Delaney and *The First Deadly Sin*, given its length and complexity, he "achieved a psychological depth rarely seen in crime fiction" (75). Many writers (like James Patterson and Patricia Cornwell) have followed Sanders' pattern into the present, with greatly varying levels of capability and success.

In the 1970s and 1980s, then, the psychological thriller bloomed. Writers of all kinds popularized and capitalized on the inchoate strains of the genre embedded by Gothic fiction, psychological realism and Freudian psychoanalysis, mass marketing, and hard-boiled fiction. Mary Higgins Clark harnessed the Gothic and Freudian interest in lost innocence, threatened and murdered children, and the psychopaths who endanger families in novels like *Where Are the Children?* (1975) and *A Stranger is Watching* (1977). Stephen King, an iconoclast whose work transcends genre, has made important contributions to psychological thrillers with a great number of his novels, such as *The Shining* (1977), *The Dead Zone* (1979), *Thinner* (1984), *Misery* (1987), *The Girl Who Loved Tom Gordon* (1999), and *Doctor Sleep* (2013). King certainly participates in and influences an aspect of the psychological thriller more closely aligned with the Gothic interest in the supernatural and with pulp fiction horror, as preceded by Lovecraft and Bloch. V. C. Andrews (1923–1986) yoked Bloch's psychological horror approach, Gothic family mystery, and Freudian fears and fascinations with familial sexuality and murder in novels like *Flowers in the Attic* (1979).

The most important among these writers of the psychological thriller is Thomas Harris, who, now flourishing, emerged on the publishing scene in the 1970s and altered the landscape of psychological thrillers with his series involving Hannibal Lecter: *Red Dragon* (1981), *The Silence of the Lambs* (1988), *Hannibal* (1999), and *Hannibal Rising* (2006). While Stephen King has had an incalculable effect on publishing since his arrival, his oeuvre has been so idiosyncratic that it has inspired few real imitators. But Harris' Lecter marked what Patrick Anderson calls "a turning point in the amount of sadistic stomach-turning violence that was acceptable in mainstream fiction" (153). Anderson grants that "Harris' intelligence and wit made the depredations of Dr. Lecter and his other killers more or less acceptable to readers" (153), but later imitations often simply capitalized on gore. Nevertheless, Harris' second Lecter novel, *The Silence of the Lambs*, advanced the serial killer subgenre even further by pitting Dr. Hannibal Lecter against a woman, Clarice Starling. This pairing injects into the serial killer genre the hunter/hunted dialectic between the detective and the serial killer with even greater force than *Red Dragon*'s FBI agent Will Graham provided. Harris was so successful with his overall formula that all of his Lecter novels have been made into highly successful film adaptations, and in 2013, NBC launched a television series based on Hannibal Lecter and Will Graham's burgeoning relationship.

Although the serial killer novel (and film) has dominated the psychological thriller genre, a number of recent writers have still been evolving the genre. Dennis Lehane seems to be the most conspicuous writer to follow Harris' dominance of the genre. In fact, in many ways, Lehane is the consummate descendent of almost all of his predecessors in the genre. As he demonstrates in *Darkness, Take My Hand* (1996), his second of the Kenzie–Gennaro novels (which focus on Boston private detectives), Lehane's writing can fall in the tradition of detective novels (especially following Ross Macdonald and Lawrence Sanders' psychological depth), but it also operates within the horrific violence and psycho exploitation initiated by Bloch and Harris. Furthermore, in novels like the Kenzie–Gennaro *Gone, Baby, Gone* (1998) and the stand-alone *Mystic River* (2001), Lehane positions himself as a more competent writer than most when depicting child abuse and its consequences. Long after Henry James, Mary Higgins Clark, V. C. Andrews, and many other followers, the use of children in psychological thrillers can be trite and mawkish. Particularly with *Mystic River*, though, Lehane manages to confront childhood innocence and violence in immediate, realistic, and thus psychologically terrifying ways. Lehane's dedication to psychological realism in *Mystic River* necessitated a slower pace than in most thrillers, indicating that perhaps the newer generation of genre writers, like Lehane, Karin Slaughter, and Gillian Flynn, may break free somewhat from the hold thrillers have on commercial fiction.

Aside from the high points of books like Lehane's *Mystic River*, Slaughter's *Kisscut* (2002), and Flynn's *Gone Girl*, most psychological thrillers have continued to push, with mixed results, the limits of taste and psychological horror to convey what David Glover calls the potential monstrosity at the core of humanity that "resists or challenges scientific expertise, a kernel of pure unmotivated evil that will always lie just outside official knowledge" (148), yet which is still controllable and knowable. If the psychological thriller tries occasionally and valiantly to invalidate psychiatric progress through its depictions of psychopathy (as Harris did in *The Silence of the Lambs*) then it is also often yanking readers back to the cocoon of Enlightenment thought to reassure them that the most sadistically evil thing imaginable can still be explained by a bad childhood (as Harris did in *Hannibal Rising*). Within that dialectic, new breadths of psychological realism are broached in the best fiction, but the psychological thriller remains a conflicted genre with a dissociative identity disorder, wanting to explain horror when horror proclaims itself to be unexplainable. As Marlow says in *Heart of Darkness*,

> The mind of man is capable of anything—because everything is in it, all the past as well as all the future. What was there after all? Joy, fear, sorrow, devotion, valour, rage—who can tell?—but truth—truth stripped of its cloak of time. Let the fool gape and shudder—the man knows, and can look on without a wink (32).

Or can he?

Works Cited

Cain, James M. "Double Indemnity." *Three of a Kind*. New York: Alfred A. Knopf, 1944.

Cassuto, Leonard. *Hard-Boiled Sentimentality: The Secret History of American Crime Stories*. New York: Columbia UP, 2009.

Conrad, Joseph. *Heart of Darkness*. 1902. Dover Thrift Edition. Ed. Stanley Appelbaum. New York: Dover, 1990.

Davenport-Hines, Richard. *Gothic: Four Hundred Years of Excess, Horror, Evil and Ruin*. New York: North Point Press, 1998.

Darwin, Charles. *The Origin of Species By Means of Natural Selection, or the Preservation of Favoured Races in the Struggle for Life*. 6th ed. London: John Murray, 1876. *Darwin Online*. Web. 5 Oct. 2013.

Edel, Leon. *The Life of Henry James*. New York: Harper & Row, 1985.

Edmundson, Mark. *Nightmare on Main Street: Angels, Sadomasochism and the Culture of Gothic*. Cambridge, MA: Harvard UP, 1997.

Erkkila, Betsy. "Perverting the American Renaissance: Poe, Democracy, Critical Theory." *Poe and the Remapping of Antebellum Print Culture*. Eds. J. Gerald Kennedy & Jerome McGann. Baton Rouge: Louisiana State UP, 2012. 65–100.

Faulkner, William. Preface to the Modern Library edition. *Sanctuary*. New York: Vintage International, 2011. 321–24.

Fiedler, Leslie. *Love and Death in the American Novel*. Champaign, IL: Dalkey Archive Press, 1960.

Fox, Margalit. "Sidney Sheldon, Author of Steamy Novels, Dies at 89." *The New York Times* 1 Feb. 2007. Web. 5 Oct. 2013.

Freedman, Carl. *The Incomplete Projects: Marxism, Modernity, and the Politics of Culture*. Middletown, CT: Wesleyan UP, 2002.

Glover, David. "The Thriller." *The Cambridge Companion to Crime Fiction*. Ed. Martin Priestman. Cambridge, UK: Cambridge UP, 2003. 135–53.

Hogle, Jerrold E. "Introduction: The Gothic in Western Culture." *The Cambridge Companion to Gothic Fiction*. Ed. Jerrold E. Hogle. Cambridge, UK: Cambridge UP, 2002. 1–20.

Horkheimer, Max & Theodor W. Adorno. *Dialectic of Enlightenment*. Ed. Gunzelin Schmid Noerr. Trans. Edmund Jephcott. Stanford, CA: Stanford UP, 2002.

Houghton, Walter E. *Vienna School of psychoanalysis*. New Haven: Yale UP, 1957.

James, Henry. "The Art of Fiction." *Longman's Magazine* 4 (September 1884): 502–21. Google Books, 7 Oct. 2009. Web. 2 Oct. 2013.

Lyotard, Jean-François. *The Postmodern Condition: A Report on Knowledge*. 1979. Trans. Geoff Bennington & Brian Massumi. Minneapolis: U of Minnesota P, 1984.

MacDonald, John D. "Introduction and Comment." *Clues: A Journal of Detection* 1.1 (1980): 63–74.

Madden, David & Kristopher Mecholsky. *James M. Cain: Hard-boiled Mythmaker*. Lanham, MD: Scarecrow, 2011.

Marx, Karl. *Capital: A Critique of Political Economy*. Ed. Frederick Engels. Trans. Samuel Moore & Edward Aveling. Vol. 1. Moscow: Progress Publishers, 1887. Marxists Internet Archive. Web. 1 Oct. 2013.

O'Brien, Geoffrey. *Hardboiled America: The Lurid Years of Paperbacks*. New York: Van Nostrand Reinhold, 1981.

Pifer, Ellen. *Demon or Doll: Images of the Child in Contemporary Writing and Culture*. Charlottesville: UP of Virginia, 2000.

Pykett, Lyn. "The Newgate Novel and Sensation Fiction, 1830–1868." *The Cambridge Companion to Crime Fiction*. Ed. Martin Priestman. Cambridge, UK: Cambridge UP, 2003.

Railey, Kevin. *Natural Aristocracy: History, Ideology, and the Production of Faulkner*. Birmingham: U of Alabama P, 2012.

Scott, Steve. "The Price of Murder." *The Trap of Solid Gold: Celebrating the Works of John D. MacDonald*. Steve Scott. 20 Aug. 2011. Web. 20 Oct. 2013.

Stasio, Marilyn. "Lawrence Sanders, 78, Author of Crime and Suspense Novels." *The New York Times* 12 Feb. 1998. Web. 4 Oct. 2013.

Tompkins, Jeff. "The Connoisseur of Crime, John D. MacDonald, Is Shadowing the E-Book World." *PopMatters*. PopMatters.com. 25 Sept. 2013. Web. 20 Oct. 2013.

CRITICAL
READINGS

Death's Head: Thomas Harris _____

Abby Bentham

When one realizes that an entire generation is unable to think of
fava beans without immediately thinking of Dr. Hannibal Lecter,
Thomas Harris' most famous creation, then one must acknowledge
that the author has been impactful. Indeed, 'impactful' could be
selling him short. In much the same way that Lecter transforms his
victims into works of visual or culinary art, he has helped Harris
to metamorphose from the author of a fairly orthodox political
thriller to a multi-millionaire literary phenomenon. Harris has been
described as "perhaps the most influential American crime writer
since Dashiell Hammett" (Cassuto 242); globally famous, his works
have been translated into more than a dozen languages (O'Brien 9),
and he is broadly credited with having established the serial killer
subgenre of the crime thriller. Impressive as Harris' achievements
are, they seem all the more incredible when one considers that, in
a career spanning thirty-one years, he has written just five novels.

Born in April 1940 in Jackson, Tennessee, Harris was an insular,
bookish child. His interest in crime seems to have developed during
his time at Baylor University in Waco, Texas when, alongside his
studies, he worked as a police beat reporter on the Waco Tribune-
Herald. A move to New York for a job at Associated Press in 1968
saw him hone his reporting skills and develop what his agent, Mort
Janklow, has described as "an intimate knowledge of police procedure
and of homicide investigations and, indeed, of the psychology of
murder" (Cowley)—skills which were to prove instrumental in his
literary career. Harris remained at Associated Press as a reporter
and editor until the sale of the film rights to his first novel, *Black
Sunday* (1975), allowed him to concentrate on fiction writing full-
time (Cowley).

Black Sunday enjoyed limited success on its release, although it
gained in popularity following the release of John Frankenheimer's
film adaptation in 1977 and went on to become a bestseller. It began

as a collaborative endeavor with Dick Riley and Sam Maull, two of Harris' colleagues at Associated Press, and, initially, the three men researched and wrote together before Harris assumed full responsibility for the project. The novel follows the political thriller conventions established by writers such as Frederick Forsyth who, like Harris, had a journalistic background and applied journalistic techniques to the writing of his novels. Forsyth's novels blend fact and fiction to create believable narratives (his most famous novel *The Day of the Jackal*, 1971, depicts an assassination plot against French President Charles de Gaulle, masterminded by the OAS, or Organisation de l'armée secrète, a group of French paramilitary dissidents, operational in the mid-twentieth century), and Harris similarly weaves his tale to incorporate real-life terror organizations and political figures. *Black Sunday* tells of a deranged American pilot who, with the help of a ruthless PLO terrorist cell, plots to detonate an airship on Super Bowl Sunday, potentially killing eighty-one thousand spectators and the President of the United States as the whole world watches on TV. Although the plot was dismissed by some contemporary reviewers as implausible, it has proved to be remarkably prescient, with its central themes of international terrorism, Middle East tensions, and American homeland threats retaining resonance some thirty-eight years after publication. The cover of the 1977 Bantam movie tie-in edition heralds the novel as the #1 SUPERTHRILLER OF THE YEAR and warns: "Do not read it unless you are prepared to finish it in one sitting!" Popular fiction, mass-produced for quick turnover, often relies on the consumer being able to make quick purchasing decisions based on assumptions relating to the specific genre the narrative belongs to. As Scott McCracken observes, characteristics including "[t]he cover and the marketing of the book set up certain expectations in its readers, even before they buy the novel, alerting them to anticipate a certain kind of narrative" (13). By heralding *Black Sunday* as a high-octane, bestselling 'superthriller' that readers won't be able to put down, Bantam promises that the reader's expectations of high narrative tension and a fast-paced plot will be exceeded. Yet this vow to smash the genre is in itself conformist, as David Glover explains: "the thriller was and still is to a large extent marked by the way in which it persistently seeks to raise the stakes of the narrative, heightening or exaggerating the experience of events by transforming them into a rising curve of danger, violence or shock" (137). The experienced thriller reader is able to purchase a novel with very little background information on the plot or author, but still feel assured that they know what they are getting, even when the cover matter promises an experience unlike anything they have previously encountered.

As a genre, the thriller depends on pace and intensity to deliver its thrills, and *Black Sunday* is short of neither. Harris also does an excellent job of creating the verisimilitude upon which the plausibility of the storyline rests. The thriller genre typically demands a sense of realism from its narrative, and Harris develops this by skillfully weaving references to real politicians, such as Yasser Arafat, Muammar Gaddafi (spelled Khadafy by Harris) and even JFK; genuine organizations, like Black September, the PLO, and Mossad; and terrorist events, such as the massacre of eleven Israeli athletes at the Munich Olympics and the Lod airport massacre (both of which occurred in 1972) into his fiction. The result is a tale so realistic that, at times, one finds oneself wondering whether it is actually based on real events.

However, the intermingling of fact and fiction not only augments the authenticity of the tale, it also adds resonance. This kind of intertextuality invokes the Bakhtinian notion of dialogism, whereby the references to characters, like Arafat or Kennedy, carry with them any number of associations based on the reader's understanding of these figures in the world beyond the text. Within the dialogic, these external denotations interact with those created within the text itself to create new shades of meaning. References to Arafat and Al Fatah, for instance, bring with them implicit allusions to revolutionary and guerrilla ideals and to Al Fatah's commitment to international terrorism in the early-mid 1970s, which in turn invoke certain value judgments in the reader. Similarly, evoking the failure of the Secret Service to identify Lee Harvey Oswald as a risk to JFK (218) adds emotional resonance and increases narrative tension, while also making the threat posed by Lander appear weightier and more realistic. The reader maps their understanding of Harris' text onto graphic and emotive memory images of the President's assassination, to create a blood-soaked vision of human tragedy, which is threatened in the novel on a massive scale.

Harris' intertextuality also works on a more subtle level, when he adds inferences to the narrative, which again bring with them dialogic shades of meaning that color our reception of the text. Although the novel presents as a conventional political thriller, it also carries overtones of noir. The novel's femme fatale is Dahlia Iyad, and her name evokes the 1946 film noir *The Blue Dahlia*, in which Johnny Morrison, a discharged Navy bomber pilot, returns home from the war and is suspected of murdering his unfaithful wife. Significantly, the killer in writer Raymond Chandler's original script was Morrison's mentally discharged fellow airman, Buzz Wanchek, but objections from the US military forced a rewrite. The dialogic association invoked by Harris' choice of name for his femme fatale and the comparisons that can be drawn between Lander and Morrison/Wanchek suggests that Harris is offering a veiled challenge to American idealism of the kind that Chandler was denied. While the Cold War had provided material for countless other political thrillers of the period, Harris' choice of the more complex political question of the Israeli/Palestinian struggle offers a direct challenge to America's self-assurance.

Although many Americans in the 1970s were aware of the terrorist events in Munich, Tel Aviv, and so on, a far greater majority of the American public was not. Domestic issues, including the oil price crisis, racial unrest, the rise of the Christian right, and political assassinations dominated popular consciousness, and Harris' novel offers a stark warning about the consequences of America's foreign policy and of its complacency. By supporting Israel financially and supplying it with arms, America was breeding resentment in the Arab world; failure to recognize the threat this posed could ultimately have disastrous consequences. Lander is humiliated at home and at school then betrayed by the military, his anger building to a crescendo that jeopardizes the safety of the American public.

When viewed in the context of East/West relations and international politics, the scale of the danger that Lander presents is suddenly revealed to be vast.

Like her first name, Dahlia's surname also has dark undertones, in that she shares it with Abu Iyad, the Deputy Chief and Head of Intelligence of the PLO. Iyad was a founder of the Black September group, which was behind a number of international terror plots, including the Munich massacre and a failed attempt to detonate three car bombs in New York in 1973. Like Dahlia, Iyad was an advocate of PLO terror campaigns. As well as providing creative inspiration, the use of Iyad's name adds weight to Dahlia's characterization, and fact and fiction are mingled further when we learn that "Dahlia had helped train the three Japanese terrorists who struck at Lod Airport in Tel Aviv, slaying at random" (3). The novel's noirist tones can be felt in the novel's bleak view of human nature; its focus on the darkness at the core of the human psyche and the impossibility of redemption in a world fractured by twisted ideology. Even the end of the novel—when the hero Kabakov has thwarted Lander's plan and saved thousands of lives—is bleak. The President has been saved and the threat posed by Lander and Dahlia has been eliminated; Fasil will be extradited to Israel to stand trial for his role in the Munich massacre. Yet the suggestion that order will be restored is not enough to lift the mood. Kabakov is dead, and his body is never recovered. There is no rejoicing; no suggestion that evil has been vanquished. Rather, the novel's final image is of Kabakov's bereaved girlfriend, Rachel, and his enormous henchman, Moshevsky, dwarfed by their pain; the human capacity for evil is revealed as vast, unconquerable, and enduring. The enormity of the threat this poses and the intensity of the storytelling are key aspects of the thriller genre, and part of the appeal for the reader lies in the challenge they present to his or her sense of self, a challenge which is complicated by the novel's noir ending. Harris' use of multiple genres in a single narrative is a common technique of popular fiction which, as McCracken notes,

> can allow a more complex exploration of self-identity while still giving the reader familiar boundaries within which to project his

or her fantasies…however, the fragility of the self means that there can be no simple reflection of a pre-existing identity. The different genres…must supply a setting in which the permeable boundaries of the self can be transgressed even if they are then re-fixed (13).

This idea of the multiple self runs throughout *Black Sunday* and, indeed, on through Harris' later novels. When the novel opens, it is initially difficult to distinguish between the heroes and the villains, with both al Fatah and Mossad portrayed in a light that is simultaneously flattering and bloodthirsty. Even as the narrative progresses and the characters become more polarized (due largely, in Kabakov's case at least, to the civilizing influence of the principled doctor, Rachel), there is a recognition that there is a duality to man's nature. When Kabakov watches an eagle circling a flock of sheep his instinctive identificatory pull towards the predatory animal forces him to acknowledge his own destructive drives: "he realized that he loved the eagle better than the sheep and that he always would and that, because he did, he could never be perfect in the sight of God" (200). The monster within is explored in the novel on both a literal and a figurative level. Both Lander, the American hero turned murderous fanatic, and Fasil, the hubristic psychopath, are described as monsters in the text, yet there is an implicit distinction made between the two. Fasil's is "conditioned hatred," whereas Lander's is the result of "injury and madness" (125), we are told, "and though Lander could not have defined the difference, was not consciously aware of the difference, it made him uneasy" (125). This sense of unease is shared by the reader and it is based in the fact that we empathize with Lander due to the biographical detail we receive about the life events, which have turned him from a tormented child into a crazed and murderous war veteran. Lander is a cruel and impetuous man, who thinks nothing of shoving a live kitten into a waste disposal unit or giving a pregnant woman a ticket to the Super Bowl, knowing that she and her baby will most likely be killed there. He is also a genius, and his meticulously engineered bomb, packed with steel flechette darts, holds deadly fascination for the reader. Harris' great skill is in making the reader oscillate between opposing positions of identification—having endured the exquisite agonies of the highly wrought narrative, we will Lander towards the fulfillment of his plan, even as we hope that Kabakov will be able to stop him in time. Recognition of this tension is a sobering experience for the reader, who is forced to confront his or her own preference for the eagle over the lamb. Ultimately though, Harris' poetics lead the reader towards identification with Kabakov's mission, and, as the narrative reaches its crescendo, our resistance to Lander also peaks.

Although the tropes and techniques used in *Black Sunday* are not especially innovative, they are expertly handled, and Harris delivers a breathless superthriller, which suspends the reader in a state of exquisite agony as s/he navigates the twists and turns of the highly wrought plot. We see, too, those elements that would become Harris' trademarks: the extraordinary level of detail and painstaking research; the close weft of fact and fiction; the inside glimpse into the workings of shadowy organizations; the flawed maverick hero who succeeds where the police or state fall short; the unflinching psychological focus; and, of course, the irresistible pull of the enigmatic psychopath. One of Harris' key strengths is the insidious way that he controls the reader's empathetic identification with the novel's characters, often in ways that override conventional morality and subvert traditional response. Indeed, Harris' manipulation of the reader was to become something of a trademark in his later novels, and his trope of the charming psychopath versus the flawed investigator was cemented in the developing serial killer subgenre, which proliferated in the 1980s and 1990s. Although Harris did not invent serial killer fiction, the genre-bending techniques he developed during the writing of *Black Sunday* did lead him to create a template for it, which Philip L. Simpson has defined as a "controlling Gothic tone, two killers, [and] a dark and troubled law enforcement outsider in uneasy alliance with a murderer" (70). The verisimilitude, mounting tension and fascination with the darker side of human nature that characterize *Black Sunday* remain as primary components, joined by the investigative focus of the police procedural and the psychological emphasis of the Gothic. Harris' formula has spawned countless imitators and "ensured his status as the foremost writer of serial killer fiction" (Simpson 70).

The police procedural, as the name suggests, details the investigative process of the detective (however loosely that term is applied) and the structures that contain him or her. Significantly, the form often also offers a bifurcated narrative, which provides psychological access to both the investigator and the killer. Combining the rough edges of the hard-boiled detective with a Holmesian, uncanny intuition, the investigator is typically a troubled outsider operating on the limits of the law, bending or breaking the rules in order to achieve results. The liminality of the investigator mirrors that of his or her quarry, drawing an uncomfortable parallel between the two. Harris' Gothicism destabilizes the certainties of the police procedural and its move towards narrative closure, instead focusing ever-greater attention on the grey areas of human psychology. As McCracken observes, "Gothic horror is more inward than outward looking. It explores the limits of identity rather than its metamorphoses: the point at which coherence cracks and crumbles and the reader is left struggling for rational explanations" (184). The disruptive influence of the Gothic brings with it a sense of quiet panic, as surfaces are revealed to be misleading and the depths they expose unsettling in the extreme. In the serial killer subgenre, the ratiocination and clear binaries of the detective genre (and its police procedural offshoot) give way to a troubled doubling of detective and killer as "[t]he killer's text is one that works to implicate the detective who decodes it (and thereby the reader and the literary critic) in his own crimes and cultural attitudes" (Horsley 141). It is significant, therefore, that the Harris character, who most grips the public, is not a righteous law enforcer, but a cannibalistic serial killer, who has now transcended his literary base to become a part of the cultural imaginary. More than thirty years after his first appearance in the 1981 novel *Red Dragon*, Lecter continues to hold a vital and evolving place in popular culture, having appeared in four Harris novels, five Hollywood adaptations of those novels, countless sketch shows, spoofs, documentaries, comic books, and, most recently, an NBC television series. Although the media may change, what remains consistent is the public's fascination with the inscrutable killer.

It is interesting to note that, although in the first two novels of the Lecter series, the Doctor is merely a supporting character (appearing in less than three percent of *Red Dragon*'s 420 pages), he occupies a key narrative space. Held in a secure psychiatric facility, Lecter is a source of fascination for the staff, who hope to study him, and for the FBI, which wishes to harness his unique skill-set (he is both a brilliant psychiatrist and a serial killer) and use his insight to catch other offenders. When the FBI's Behavioral Science Unit struggles to catch a serial killer who is preying on entire families, its head, Jack Crawford, turns to two liminal figures for help: Special Investigator Will Graham and Dr. Hannibal Lecter. Graham is possessed of "pure empathy and projection" (179) a 'gift,' which allows him to psychologically connect with the monstrous psychopaths he is hunting. Lecter, by contrast, "has no remorse or guilt at all" (64). Both men exist on the margins and both have killed, Lecter recreationally and Graham in the course of duty. The novel suggests that, in projecting himself into the minds of the killers he pursues, Graham psychologically enacts their crimes and, in so doing, brings himself dangerously close to his own instinctive aggressive drives. His conflict in empathizing with killers mirrors that of the reader who, while enjoying close proximity to the monstrous Lecter, is challenged by Harris to acknowledge his or her own appetite for violent excess. *Red Dragon* ends with Will Graham's "memory-dream" (418) about his visit to Shiloh, the site of the 1862 Battle of Shiloh in the American Civil War, the bloodiest battle in American history up to the date. Graham visited Shiloh after he shot serial killer Garrett Jacob Hobbs. Although the act was necessary to prevent further loss of life, Graham was unable to reconcile it, and the aftermath of the shooting saw him confined to a mental institution after suffering a breakdown. The scene at Shiloh, which has an other-worldly Gothic essence, functions as both a meditation on man's true nature and as a warning to the reader about his or her relationship to violence and its exploration in literature. In Graham's 'memory-dream,' a broken-backed snake, run over by a car, loops endlessly around in the road, making figures of eight; Graham picks it up by its tail and cracks it like a whip: "Its brains zinged into the pond. A bream rose to them" (419). In its agony, the injured snake enacts the symbol of infinity; although brutal, Graham's violent action is really an act of mercy, as he puts the snake out of its ceaseless misery. The bream rising to consume its brains, or essence, represents the circle of life and, as he considers "the indifference of nature" (419), Graham realizes that human nature is instinctively brutal. Nature is life and death, going on and on, forever and ever, and concepts, such as murder (wrongful killing) and mercy are merely human constructs. Graham knows that he is capable of murder, but his capacity for mercy remains only a possibility. As he muses on "the vicious urges we control in ourselves" (419), we are reminded of Freud's assertion that the "residues and traces" of the "animistic stage in primitive man" are still "capable of manifesting themselves" (Freud), a sobering thought for the consumer of serial killer fiction. Yet ultimately, the novel ends on a positive note: as Graham wonders "if old, awful urges are the virus the makes the vaccine" (420), the reader is reassured that men's knowledge of their base and vicious nature is what helps them to protect themselves from becoming brutes who act on these instincts.

The Silence of the Lambs (1989) builds on many of the themes explored in *Red Dragon*; indeed, it has been argued that it is essentially the same story but with different protagonists. As in *Red Dragon*, the detective is a liminal character (this time not a Special Investigator, but a trainee FBI agent who also happens to be a woman and is, therefore, doubly marginalized) who must draw on the expertise of Hannibal Lecter in order to catch a serial killer. And, as in the previous novel, the serial killer is a terrifying figure of extreme Gothic proportions, who stands in stark contrast to the cultured, lucid Lecter. Lecter himself enjoys greater prominence in this novel, fulfilling the promise he showed in *Red Dragon* as a beguiling and enigmatic antagonist. Although arguably not the most monstrous figure in the book (that honor must surely go to Jame Gumb), Lecter is positively satanic in his depiction, from his maroon eyes, which 'reflect the light in pinpoints of red' that sometimes "fly like sparks to his center" (15), to his partiality for human flesh. A great deal of his appeal lies in his combination of knowingness and inscrutability; his preternatural ability to penetrate a person's psychic defenses and discern their core secrets is at odds with his own air of mystery. Lecter defies quantification, insisting "You can't reduce me to a set of influences" (20). When invited by Starling to participate in a psychological study, he warns, chillingly "A census taker tried to quantify me once. I ate his liver with some fava beans and a big Amarone" (22–23). That this line (slightly amended in Demme's film to include a glass of Chianti) is one of the most quotable and recognizable in popular culture speaks volumes about the novel's reach. Indeed, since it was published twenty-five years ago, *The Silence of the Lambs* has sold over eleven million copies worldwide and is now recognized as "the most influential crime novel of this generation" (Cassuto 185). Jonathan Demme's film adaptation in 1991 launched it into the cultural stratosphere; Anthony Hopkins' definitive performance secured Lecter's position as one the most memorable movie villains of all time, and the film itself made movie history, becoming one of only three films to ever win the 'Big Five' Academy Award categories for Best Picture, Best Director, Best Actor, Best Actress, and Best Screenplay. No other film has since won in all five categories.

The Silence of the Lambs' status as the premier example of the serial killer thriller is well-deserved. In it, Harris has honed his genre formula to perfection and, via painstaking research, has created an unsurpassed level of verisimilitude. Harris' commitment to creating a convincing portrayal of the internal workings of the FBI has been so successful that "at the FBI training academy in Quantico—which Harris, researching his novel, briefly attended—the case of Ed Gein, on whom Buffalo Bill is based, is taught alongside Harris' book" (Haut 215). Of course, such a merging of fact and fiction is characteristic of the Gothic, where boundaries become blurred and thresholds, particularly into darkness, are rendered more inviting. The success of *The Silence of the Lambs* is due in large part to the way that Harris manipulates the reader's empathy towards identification with Lecter. Lecter's extraordinary intelligence and sensory perception are impressive, and there is a degree of whimsy to the staging of his murders and his matching of fate to victim that is highly seductive (these are elements, which are particularly highlighted in Bryan Fuller's NBC series *Hannibal*). As Lee Horsley explains: "An increasingly mythic figure, he is an artist whose Grand Guignol crimes combine with an aesthetics of murder so darkly humorous that we find it hard to resist the force of the images produced by Hannibal's satiric art" (140), and this combination of Gothicism, mythic status, and seduction is suitably vampiric for a liminal character, descended from a count, and with genetic links to "the Mediterranean and the Baltic, with just a hint of the Carpathians in between" (Horsley 143). While the reader does empathize with Starling and support her mission to free Catherine Martin and catch Buffalo Bill, when Lecter escapes at the end of the novel, the reader is in the curious position of willing a killer to get away scot free. Harris' power, then, lies not just in his ability to bend genre conventions, but also in his ability to twist the reader into a position of acceptance and identification, banishing moral surety along the way.

If a large part of Lecter's allure lies in his mysteriousness, it is surprising to find his aberrance explained away in the final two books of the series. In *Hannibal* (1999), the hotly anticipated follow-up to *The Silence of the Lambs*, we begin to receive biographical details of the formerly closed Lecter's life, which reveal the psychological bases for his monstrosity. Cassuto explains:

> Lecter changes from a killer without a past ('Nothing happened to me, Officer Starling. *I* happened.') to a sensitive, haunted man in terrible pain from the destruction of his own family, especially his sister. The Lecter of *Hannibal* and *Hannibal Rising* is a tragic hero to whom something terrible *did* happen (254).

As Hannibal becomes the central focus of the narrative, the police procedural element of Harris' format gives way to Gothic romance and a probing metaphysical exploration of relativity, love, and loss, in which, as Horsley has observed, "the standard moral polarities of a conventional detective story are displaced" (143). As we have come to expect from Harris, Lecter is juxtaposed with another, more monstrous villain—this time in the shape of Mason Verger, the only one of Lecter's early victims to have survived. During a therapy session, Lecter fed Verger psychotropic drugs, then encouraged him to cut off his own face with a shard of broken mirror and feed it to the dogs. Although he survived, Verger remains trapped in a half-life; with very little capacity for movement and unable to breathe unaided, he is lidless, lipless, and entirely dependent on others. His vast, inherited fortune ensures that he is able to purchase the services of people who will facilitate his evil whims, be they the abuse of disadvantaged children or the capture and torture of Hannibal Lecter. Although in the mold of Francis Dolarhyde and Jame Gumb, Verger is psychopathic rather than psychotic and, as such, more closely aligned with Lecter than with his monstrous predecessors. In a way similar to how Lecter 'took a single sip of [Senator Martin's] pain and found it exquisite' (Harris, *Silence* 191), Verger drinks martinis infused with the tears of orphans. Yet, whereas Lecter's act is evidence of his connoisseurship and restraint, Verger has no finesse. Our dark fascination with Lecter thrills at such details, but with Verger, they seem crass and farcical, galvanizing the reader's resistance rather than empathy. But of course, the most startling manipulation of empathy in the novel relates to Harris' treatment of Clarice Starling. Her grudging identification with Lecter blossoms in the novel, by way of hypnotic drugs, into a warped Gothic love, which sees her joining Lecter as his cannibalistic bride. This element of the narrative was met with scathing disapprobation by critics and readers alike, but within the context of Harris' hyperbolized Gothic romance, it offers a logical conclusion to the merging of investigator and psychopath, which has typified the Lecter series.

Hannibal Rising (2006), the final installment of the Lecter series, charts Lecter's early life, and in so doing, completes the humanization of the diabolical villain. Indeed, our identification with the killer is such that he becomes Hannibal, rather than Lecter, an act that strips him of the ghastly connotations wrought from the earlier novels. Like the other books in the series, *Hannibal Rising* was a bestseller, yet it came in for almost universal criticism. Although Cassuto suggests that the novel's shortcomings are evidence that Harris' tautly constructed formula for the serial killer thriller "has boxed everyone into a narrow space (including himself...)" (242), I find that this novel does depart slightly from the narrative structure of the earlier works. Rather than overlaying the police procedural and Gothic genres, these elements recede as *Hannibal Rising* combines a Grimm fairy tale first half (Karim 152) with more conventionalized thriller elements in the second section. Harrowing exposition of Hannibal's boyhood war traumas, when his family is slaughtered and his sister cannibalized, secures the reader's empathy. As the novel progresses, Hannibal defends the honor of his lady and redresses heinous crimes with intelligence, humor, and panache, and here, Harris borrows from the trope of the righteous avenger so common to heroic quest narratives and the Hollywood box office. The novel's thrilling dénouement is formulaic, but perfectly executed; the kidnapped Lady Murasaki becomes the imperiled loved, one that is a staple of the thriller and Hannibal's rescue of her is riven with danger. As he sets out to rescue her, Hannibal takes a samurai tantō dagger from the shrine to Lord Dante Masamune in Lady Murasaki's home. This situates him within the samurai trope, and the positive, heroic associations this intertextuality creates in the dialogic further endears him to the reader. Hannibal is an honorable lover on a sacred quest, not a crazed killer like his enemy, Grutas. As Karim has noted, the final battle is reminiscent of a Bond movie (158), but unlike Bond, Hannibal does not "get the girl." During his frenzied attack on Grutas, Hannibal reveals to Lady Murasaki the extent of his debasement, and when he turns to her and declares his love, she spurns his advances before making an ostentatious exit: "'What is left of you to love?' she said and ran from the cabin, up the companionway and over the rail in a clean dive into the canal" (360). Harris' self-conscious use of generic convention here suggests a tongue-in-cheek nod to the limitations of his well-worn formula, but it is effective nonetheless.

Murasaki's recognition of Hannibal's darkness reconciles the hints that have peppered the novel with the knowledge we have of Lecter from the rest of Harris' corpus. Relatively early on in the narrative, Inspector Popil, who "had considerable experience and knowledge of the awful" (144), hears in Hannibal's voice a "specific wavelength he had not heard before, but he recognized it as Other" (144) and, as Hannibal's resolve hardens during his search for Mischa's killers, we learn that he is "growing and changing, or perhaps emerging as what he has ever been" (191). Thus the "ideological tension" (86–87) that Simpson detects between the mystification and humanization of the many killers in the Lecter series is resolved; Harris' novels, *Black Sunday* included, are about becoming, about the search for self, the impossibility of ever truly knowing or defining the inscrutable mystery of the human psyche, and of the dialectical pull between self and Other, which is both the fascination and the reward of reader engagement with dark psychological fiction.

If, as McCracken asserts, popular fiction exists in the interface between the world, reader and text (2), then Harris' extraordinary, best-selling success can perhaps be attributed to his understanding of the complex relationship between these three elements. In addition to his considerable skills as a writer, researcher, and creator of worlds, Harris appears to have an uncanny knack for capturing the concerns of the zeitgeist. His understanding of the human condition has allowed him to create one of popular culture's most enduring mythic figures, one with the resonance to transcend his historical moment and captivate generations of audiences. His trope of the charming psychopathic killer, with whom audiences can empathize created the conditions for such cultural icons as Bret Easton Ellis' Patrick Bateman and Jeff Lindsay/Showtime's *Dexter*, securing his position as Death's Head, the most successful and influential writer of modern times.

Works Cited

Black Sunday. Dir. John Frankenheimer. Paramount, 1977.

The Blue Dahlia. Dir. George Marshall. Paramount, 1946.

Cassuto, Leonard. *Hard-Boiled Sentimentality: The Secret History of American*

Crime Stories. New York: Columbia UP, 2009.

Cowley, Jason. "Creator of a monstrous hit." *The Observer*. 19 Nov. 2006. Web. 17 Oct. 2013. <http://www.theguardian.com/books/2006/nov/19/fiction.thomasharris>.

Dexter. Showtime, 2006–Present. Television.

Ellis, Bret. *American Psycho*. London: Picador, 1991.

Forsyth, Frederick. *The Day of the Jackal*. 1971. London: Arrow Books, 2011.

Freud, Sigmund. *The Uncanny*. Trans. David McLintock. London: Penguin, 2003.

Glover, David. 'The Thriller.' Priestman, 135-154.

Hannibal. Dir. Ridley Scott. MGM, 2001.

Hannibal. Creator Bryan Fuller. NBC, 2013. Television.

Hannibal Rising. Dir. Peter Webber. MGM, 2007.

Harris, Thomas. *Black Sunday*. 1975. New York: Bantam, 1977.

_____. *Red Dragon*. 1981. London: Arrow Books, 2009.

_____. *The Silence of the Lambs*. 1989. London: Mandarin, 1991.

_____. *Hannibal*. London: Heinemann, 1999.

_____. *Hannibal Rising*. 2006. London: Arrow Books, 2007.

Haut, Woody. *Neon Noir*. London: Serpent's Tail, 1999.

Horsley, Lee. *Twentieth-Century Crime Fiction*. 2005. Oxford, UK: Oxford UP, 2007.

Karim, Ali S. 'Hannibal Rising: Look Back in Anger.' Szumskyj, 147–159.

Lindsay, Jeff. *Darkly Dreaming Dexter*. London: Orion, 2004.

McCracken, Scott. *Pulp: Reading Popular Fiction*. Manchester & New York: Manchester UP, 1998.

Manhunter. Dir. Michael Mann. De Laurentiis Entertainment Group, 1986.

Morris, Benny. *Righteous Victims: A History of the Zionist-Arab Conflict, 1881–2001*. New York: Vintage, 2001.

O'Brien, Daniel. Foreword. *Dissecting Hannibal Lecter: Essays on the Novels of Thomas Harris*. Ed. Benjamin Szumskyj. Jefferson, NC and London: McFarland & Co., 2008. 1–5.

Priestman, Martin, ed. *The Cambridge Companion to Crime Fiction*. Cambridge, UK: Cambridge UP, 2003.

The Silence of the Lambs. Dir. Jonathan Demme. Orion, 1991.

Simpson, Philip L. *Psycho Paths: Tracking the Serial Killer Through Contemporary American Film and Fiction.* Carbondale & Edwardsville: Southern Illinois UP, 2000.

Szumskyj, Benjamin, ed. *Dissecting Hannibal Lecter: Essays on the Novels of Thomas Harris.* Jefferson, NC, and London: McFarland & Co., 2008.

Lee Child's Pure, Uncomplicated Hero _____

Elizabeth Blakesley

Lee Child was born as Jim Grant in Coventry, England, in 1954 and was raised in Birmingham. After attending law school and working in the theatre, he joined Granada Television, where he worked as a presentation director. After being downsized at age forty, he decided to try his hand at writing fiction. He bought six dollars' worth of paper and pencils, did some market research, and started to create the character of Jack Reacher, a "pure, uncomplicated hero" in the "tradition of the American Wild West" (Ayers 19).

The initial product of that experiment was *Killing Floor*, the first novel in the Reacher series. It received a great deal of critical acclaim and commercial success. He has received a number of awards and nominations throughout his career, and Child was the 2013 recipient of the Crime Writers Association's prestigious Diamond Dagger Award. According to his website, Child's novels have been published in ninety-six countries and in forty-one languages, with over eighty million copies sold worldwide. E-book sales have also been phenomenal. He was one of the first authors to sell over a million Kindle editions on Amazon (Campbell). Given all that success, his six-dollar investment has certainly paid off well.

All of Child's novels have been optioned for cinema, and as of this writing, one feature film has been made. Titled simply "Jack Reacher," it was released in December 2012 and received a mixed reception from fans and critics. As is often the case, some people who have read the book have issues with the film, particularly regarding the casting of the main characters, while others enjoy it as a stand-alone movie, and others, who were unfamiliar with the series, become interested in reading the books. This film adaptation was based on *One Shot*, the ninth novel in the series. Child was not involved in the writing or production, although he made supportive comments about the film, particularly in response to criticism about the casting of Reacher (Bethune 68; Cannon 17).

In the series, Jack Reacher is a larger than life character, described as 6'5" tall, 220–250 pounds with a 50" chest, although other physical attributes are left unclear. Child believes that leaving such things to the reader's imagination is part of the collaborative relationship between a writer and a reader (Ayers 20). A West Point graduate, Reacher served in the Army for thirteen years, working as a military policeman. A demotion from Major to Captain derailed his career in some regards, although he had earned the rank of Major again before his discharge. Reacher's parents and brother are deceased, and he has no fixed address, few possessions, and his own code of honor.

The series begins with *Killing Floor*, which won both the Anthony and Barry Awards for best first novel and was a finalist for two others, the Macavity and the Dilys. It opens at a breakneck pace and doesn't slow down. Reacher is traveling on a Greyhound bus and, on a whim, decides to disembark at a stop in Georgia to hunt down a memorial to a blues musician. He stumbles into a situation and finds himself arrested for murder. Given this welcome, Reacher plans to leave as soon as his alibi checks out, but when he learns the murder victim is his brother, a US Treasury agent, he stays to uncover the truth and solve the case.

Most reviews were generally positive, with some critique typical of that leveled at first-time novels, such as overly coincidental plot points. *Publishers Weekly* chose to put that in a positive light, noting that the coincidence was "as big as the author's talent" (Zaleski 393). The *Library Journal* review was harsher, with Elsa Pendleton describing Reacher as "creepily amoral, violent, and generally unpleasant" (161). While Pendleton obviously did not care for Reacher, most reviewers found him to be an intriguing hero from the start. Child has noted that he writes Reacher "warts and all because it hurts a series when the author falls in love with his or her character" (Ayers 20). Child also initially anticipated that Reacher was "too much of a barbarian to appeal to women," but was happy to be proven wrong (Donahue, "*PW* Talks " 48). The series remains a strong favorite of female readers. In later interviews, Child has been asked about why women love Reacher so much. His theory is that Reacher is attractive due to the "absolute impossibility of him sticking around" (McGrath E6).

In the follow-up novel, *Die Trying*, Reacher is again in the wrong place at the wrong time. Walking in Chicago, he finds himself caught in the middle of an abduction and is taken prisoner along with a female, who turns out to be an FBI agent. Dick Adler, who was the crime fiction reviewer for the *Chicago Tribune*, notes that Child addresses those critiques of unlikely coincidences directly in the novel. After the kidnapping, Reacher reflects on the event, noting that "he understood freak chances. Life was built out of freak chances, however much people would like to pretend otherwise" (Adler).

Tripwire finds Reacher living incognito in Key West and working as a day laborer. His quiet life is interrupted when a private investigator comes looking for him and is disrupted further still when the detective is found murdered. Michele Leber praised Child's "crisp prose, intriguing protagonist and storytelling skills," also noting that this plot was built less on coincidences, as if Child had "actually [taken] note" of the earlier critiques (Leber, "Tripwire" 134). Sybil Steinberg notes that while Reacher's physical strength is portrayed as hulking and massive, he is "actually a dynamo of a character, wily in a sort of innocent way, and the anchor to one of the best new series in thriller fiction" (Steinberg, "Tripwire" 63), further lauding Child for writing Reacher as "spellbinding whether he's kicking in doors or just kicking around a thought in his brain" (Steinberg, "Tripwire" 64).

In *Running Blind*, Reacher is the link between the victims of a serial killer. He knew all the women when they served in the Army, and he was aware of the fact that they all filed sexual harassment claims against superior officers. Although the conclusion wraps up with some "disappointing convenience," Sybil Steinberg nonetheless praises the book for two elements that "separate it from the pack: a brain-teasing puzzle" and a protagonist with a "Robin Hood-like integrity and an engaging eccentric approach to life" ("Running Blind" 47). Marilyn Stasio found Reacher's "romantic persona of the rootless hero" to be wearing thin, but praises the clever plotting and the fact that Reacher uses "honest ingenuity" to solve the case (BR20).

Hitchhiking lands Reacher into trouble in the fifth novel, *Echo Burning*. Accepting a ride places Reacher in the debt of Carmen Greer, a woman whose abusive husband is due to be released from prison soon. Although Reacher declines her request to kill her husband, he does agree to work on the Greer ranch and keep an eye on things. When Carmen's husband returns home and is murdered with her gun, Reacher applies himself to solving the case, although as *Publishers Weekly*'s Jeff Zaleski notes, "most wandering heroes would move on at this point" ("Echo Burning" 45). Wes Lukowsky's review in *Booklist* calls Reacher "a one-man wrecking crew nourished only by the hunt," and recommends the book "for anyone who thinks the hard-boiled genre is growing soft around the edges" (1624).

Without Fail finds Reacher in Atlantic City, doing some small-scale security work. He is contacted by Secret Service agent M.E. Froelich, who once was his brother Joe's girlfriend. In addition to the personal connection, Froelich offers a tantalizing assignment and Reacher agrees to pose as an assassin in order to uncover who is making death threats against the Vice President-elect. The book was another winner with the critics. Michele Leber noted in her review that the "political scene adds interest to Child's trademark intricate plotting" and that, in this outing, Reacher becomes "an even more rounded character, revealing some of his background as his intelligence, intuition, and physical prowess all shine" ("Without Fail" 131).

Persuader features a complicated plot with plenty of twists and turns. The novel opens with an explosive rescue scene, in which Reacher thwarts an attempted kidnapping. Child "pulls the rug out from under the reader" with the chapter's conclusion, which reveals the truth behind the incident and Reacher's real agenda, and then keeps the pace brisk, while "tension runs high, then extremely high" (Zaleski, "Persuader" 50). Bill Ott notes that the tropes of violence in the novel are never portrayed "generically, and the mayhem, both physical and emotional, never feels gratuitous" ("Persuader" 82).

In *The Enemy*, Child takes readers back to Reacher's Army days in his role as military police. Set in January 1990, against the backdrop of the fall of the Berlin Wall, Reacher is called in to investigate the murder of a general, whose body in found in a disreputable motel. The case becomes more complex when the general's widow is also murdered. Turning the clock back also allows Child to provide character development for Reacher's mother, as well as for his brother Joe, whose post-mortem influence has been a key element in many of the novels of the series. Jeff Zaleski praised Reacher for "dig[ging] deep, in his usual brilliant and vilent way" to solve the crime ("The Enemy" 59). Zaleski further opined that this novel would "convince those who still need convincing that Child has few peers" ("The Enemy" 59).

One Shot opens with a sniper preparing for work, killing five people and upon his capture, asking for Reacher. Reacher is already on his way to Indiana, having seen the news coverage. He knows the shooter and knows his past, but the present case is not as it seems. *Publishers Weekly* referred to the novel as being "written lean enough to make Hemingway seem chatty" ("One Shot" 55). Child builds suspense to the point that "readers will be torn between reading slowly to prolong their pleasure or skimming quickly to see how Reacher makes it out alive" (Leber, "One Shot" 68).

In *The Hard Way*, Reacher agrees to take a case from a shady client for a hefty fee. A mercenary whose first wife was kidnapped and murdered recruits Reacher to help recover his second wife and daughter from kidnappers. Reacher makes assumptions that prove costly in this one, doing things, as the title suggests, the hard way. As Michele Leber puts it, Reacher knows "the time to the minute without a watch," but has to "sweat the details and work the clues" in this case, because even though he has "acute observation and intuition" in his arsenal, this case is more complex than he expects ("Hard Way" 77).

Bad Luck and Trouble finds Reacher in Portland, Oregon, living off the grid as usual. A series of events leads Frances Neagley to track him down, and when Reacher learns that members of his team of Army investigators are being killed, he is compelled to join Neagley and the other remaining members of the team to solve the case. Bill Ott notes that this plot line is often used to bring back old characters, but that in this case, "there's more going on here than a class reunion. Readers know Reacher only as a loner, a tough guy with his own agenda who falls into stranger's problems, solves them, and moves on, Shane-like. But here we see him functioning as part of a team, almost an organization man, and it reveals new and fascinating aspects to his character" (2007:4). *Kirkus Reviews* concluded that there might be other writers better known than Child, but that no one could offer a "tighter-plotted, richer-peopled, faster-paced" novel (241).

Nothing to Lose finds Reacher stopping for coffee in Colorado, near the neighboring towns of Hope and Despair. Although he is minding his own business, he is pulled into a case involving corruption and a religious fanatic. At that point, Reacher "happily takes things into his own hands" (Conroy 72). *Kirkus Reviews* notes that, as always, Child "constructs sentences like a flurry of jabs, before delivering a knockout punch of a climax" ("Nothing to Lose" 4). In an interview, Child noted that he "instinctively chose a writing style that does in fact contribute to the description of Reacher's character just as much as physically descriptive passages do. It's terse, spare and no-nonsense, like the man himself. In other words, yes, the style maketh the man. I hear from readers that they feel like they are thinking along with Reacher" (*Kirkus Reviews*, "Nothing to Lose" 4).

Gone Tomorrow opens with Reacher on a New York subway at two a.m., observing a fellow passenger who is exhibiting the textbook signs of a suicide bomber. Reacher opens the novel, indicating that "suicide bombers are easy to spot. They give out all kinds of tell-tale signs. Mostly because they're nervous. By definition they're all first-timers" (Child, *Gone Tomorrow* 1). As it turns out, Reacher is right and wrong, and as usual, nothing is ever simple and straightforward in a Child novel.

Lee Child has noted that he wanted to try something different with *61 Hours*, and this novel is set in South Dakota during a blizzard. Reacher is catching a ride on a tour bus filled with senior citizens, and they are marooned in a small town when the bus skids off the road during the storm. The pacing seems slower, with a marked decrease in physical violence. Chapter headings count down the sixty-one hours during which the book is set. This structure leads Janet Maslin to state that "such a hackneyed device ... has no business working so well" (21). The fact that readers do not know what awaits them at the conclusion of the countdown keeps suspense taut. Another change is that Child wrote a cliffhanger ending for the first time. Even with these alterations, reviewers had positive reactions.

Worth Dying For opens a few days later, with Reacher recuperating from the events in South Dakota while hiding out in a small town in Nebraska. Reacher has bad luck selecting places to settle and finds himself caught up in corruption and crime from the present and the past. An unsolved case from decades earlier, involving a missing child, pulls Reacher in as much as his accidental involvement in helping an abused woman. Reviews remain uniformly positive, with praise for Child's writing and Reacher's portrayal.

Child has noted that the two most frequently asked questions from readers are about Reacher's work in the Army—which, as mentioned above, was covered in *The Enemy*—and how he left the Army, which is covered in *The Affair*. This novel recounts Reacher's last case, an undercover operation, during which he uncovers the truth about allegations leveled at a solider whose family has powerful connections in Washington, D.C. Set in March 1997, this novel takes Reacher to Mississippi and sets the stage for the Reacher that readers have come to know throughout the series. Child has also written short stories that take place when Reacher was younger; these have been sold as e-book singles and also printed in paperback editions as a bonus item. In "Second Son," a thirteen-year old Reacher is settling into the fortieth place his family has lived, while in "High Heat," Reacher is seventeen and stops in New York on his way to visit his brother. It happens to be 1977, and Reacher is there for the famous blackout during the hunt for the Son of Sam killer.

In *A Wanted Man*, Reacher is done with his business in the Midwest and is heading toward Virginia. He hitches a ride with a suspicious group of travelers, one of whom may be a hostage, and begins to unravel the mystery before being shot and left for dead. Reacher is not seriously injured and then joins forces with the FBI to bring the crew to justice. As Bill Ott notes, "if a Lee Child novel begins with Jack Reacher standing by the side of a highway with his thumb out, you can be sure the wrong guy is going to pick him up" ("Wanted Man" 32). As in the other books in the series, Reacher rights the wrongs and makes it to the next stop. Tom Nolan praises it as "a page-turning caper filled with well-timed surprises" and Reacher's trademark grace under pressure, "whether in math-induced meditation or in chilling battle mode" (C 8). Nolan also highlights the wry humor that Reacher can exhibit, recounting a scene where Reacher is using a key to saw on the rope binding a captive, who asks him if he has a knife and is unimpressed when Reacher responds that he only has a toothbrush (C 8).

Never Go Back, the eighteenth novel in the series, finds Reacher finally arriving in Virginia to meet Major Susan Turner, who was first introduced via a phone conversation in *61 Hours* and is now commanding Reacher's former unit. Instead of Turner awaiting their planned dinner date, however, she is facing trial for conspiracy, and Reacher finds himself summarily re-drafted into the Army so that he can face charges of his own, including a paternity suit. Although this plot may sound extremely contrived even for a thriller, reviews were uniformly positive, even glowing. Janet Maslin went on record to say that this "may be the best desert island reading in the series. It's exceptionally well plotted. And full of wild surprises. And wise about Reacher's peculiar nature. And positively Bunyanesque in its admiring contributions to Reacher lore" ("His Workout" C15). Reviewers reacted positively to the possibility of Reacher having a daughter, with Maslin calling their meeting "superbly staged and completely unexpected, featur[ing] some of the best, wiliest writing Mr. Child has ever done" ("His Workout" C15).

Many series in the mystery and thriller genres lose steam along the way, or at least have some weaker entries in the series. The reviews of the Reacher novels indicate that, along with their commercial success, this is one series that gets better with each episode. Although the Reacher series has not yet received scholarly scrutiny, the novels are more than just best-selling beach reads.

A good deal of criticism regarding mystery fiction focuses on one or more of these three areas: the role of the detective's family and friends, the setting of the series, and the detective's profession. Perusing the Modern Language Association International Bibliography (MLAIB) database shows published research for the role of family in the detective novel, from Willkie Collins to James Ellroy to Reginald Hill, and from Agatha Christie to Margaret Maron to P.D. James. Cities such as Chicago, London, and Los Angeles have been studied in terms of their function as a main character in a series or in a subgenre. Given Reacher's personality and travel habits, Child's work defies such study.

Child has noted that he did not want to do a "standard recurring-cast soap-opera type of series," and he believes the lack of recurring characters helps him keep the series fresh (Igler 32). As Child further explained, the "no job, no-location structure" provides him with "infinite flexibility," since Reacher can "get involved anywhere with anything" (Igler 32).

Another area of criticism of hard-boiled mystery fiction revolves around the treatment of or attitude toward women, and how the writers, particularly male ones, create their female characters. Although aspects of Child's female characters are stereotypical in some ways, these women are much more than pretty faces or potential love interests for Reacher, although many of them do play those roles. These women can hold their own and back up Reacher in what needs to be done, including scenes of physical violence and the strenuous activity required to bring the criminals to justice.

A third area of potential critical assessment involves the novels' points-of-view. Some are written in first person—that is, from Reacher's perspective—and others are written in third person. When asked about this choice, Child noted that writing in first-person feels more natural, but that writing in third-person gives him "more freedom when building suspense," allowing for the reader "to see around corners and anticipate events about which Reacher has no knowledge" (Ayers 20).

Topics such as these, along with the portrayal of Reacher as the archetypal lone hero—arguably the true heir to Dashiell Hammett and the Continental Op—make Lee Child's novels worthy of further study.

Works Cited

Adler, Dick. "Die Trying." *Amazon.com.* n.d. Web. 20 Oct. 2013. <http://www.amazon.com/Die-Trying-Jack-Reacher-No/dp/0515142247>.

Ayers, Jeff. "Lee Child Crafts a Rootless Hero Who Resonates." *Writer* 123.1 (January 2010): 18–21.

"Bad Luck and Trouble." *Kirkus Reviews*, 15 Mar. 2007: 241.

Bethune, Brian. "How Dare Tom Cruise." *Maclean's*, 17 October 2011: 68–70.

Campbell, Lisa. "Stockett and Evanovich Hit Kindle Milestone." *Bookseller. com.* 16 Aug. 2011. Web. 20 Oct. 2013. <http://www.thebookseller.com/news/stockett-and-evanovich-hit-kindle-milestone.html>.

Cannon, Peter. "Lee Child Reaches the Heights with Latest." *Publishers Weekly*, 24 Sept. 2012: 17.

Child, Lee. *Bad Luck and Trouble*. New York: Delacorte, 2007.

_____. *Die Trying*. New York: Putnam, 1998.

_____. *Echo Burning*. New York: Putnam, 2001.

_____. *The Enemy*. New York: Delacorte, 2004.

_____. *Gone Tomorrow*. New York: Delacorte, 2009.

_____. *The Hard Way*. New York: Delacorte, 2006.

_____. *High Heat*. New York: Delacorte, 2013.

_____. *Killing Floor*. New York: Putnam, 1997.

_____. *Never Go Back*. New York: Delacorte, 2013.

_____. *Nothing To Lose*. New York: Delacorte, 2008.

_____. *One Shot*. New York: Delacorte, 2005.

_____. *Persuader*. New York: Delacorte, 2003.

_____. *Running Blind* (UK title: *The Visitor*) New York: Putnam, 2000.

_____. *Second Son*. New York: Delacorte, 2012.

_____. *61 Hours*. New York: Delacorte, 2010.

_____. *Tripwire*. New York: Putnam, 1999.

_____. *A Wanted Man*. New York: Delacorte, 2012.

_____. *Without Fail*. New York: Putnam, 2002.

_____. _Worth Dying For_. New York: Delacorte, 2011.

Conroy, Robert. "Nothing to Lose." _Library Journal_, 1 Apr. 2008: 72.

Donahue, Dick. "Lee Child: Late to the Crime Scene." _Publishers Weekly_, 31 May 2004: 44–45.

_____. "_PW_ Talks with Lee Child." _Publishers Weekly_, 22 Apr. 2002: 48.

Igler, Marc. "Reacher on the Move." _Publishers Weekly_, 5 Sept. 2011: 32.

Leber, Michele. "The Hard Way." _Library Journal_, 1 Mar. 2006: 77.

_____. "One Shot." _Library Journal_, 15 Mar. 2005: 68.

_____. "Tripwire." _Library Journal_, 15 Aug. 1999: 134–5.

_____. "Without Fail." _Library Journal_, 1 May 2002: 131.

Lukowsky, Wes. "Echo Burning." _Booklist_, 1 May 2001: 1624.

Maslin, Janet. "He Needs Only His Wits And the Shirt on His Back." _New York Times_, 13 May 2010: 21.

_____. "His Workout: Beating People Up." _New York Times_, 30 Aug. 2013: C15.

McGrath, Charles. "Creating a Don Quixote of the Cheap Motel Circuit." _New York Times_, 3 Jun. 2008: E1, E6.

Nolan, Tom. "A Wanted Man." _Wall Street Journal_, 7 Sept. 2012: C8.

"Nothing to Lose." _Kirkus Reviews_, 15 Feb. 2008: 4.

"One Shot." _Publishers Weekly_, 3 Oct. 2005: 55.

Ott, Bill. "Bad Luck and Trouble." _Booklist_, 15 Feb. 2007: 4.

_____. "Persuader." _American Libraries_, Mar. 2006: 82.

_____. "A Wanted Man." _Booklist_, 11 Sept. 2012: 32.

Pendleton, Elsa. "Killing Floor." _Library Journal_, 15 Feb. 1997: 161.

Stasio, Marilyn. "Crime." _New York Times Book Review_, 23 Jul. 2000: BR20.

Steinberg, Sybil. "Running Blind." _Publishers Weekly_, 26 Jun. 2000: 47.

_____. "Tripwire." _Publishers Weekly_, 31 May 1999: 63-4.

Zaleski, Jeff. "Echo Burning." _Publishers Weekly_, 22 Apr. 2001: 45.

_____. "The Enemy." _Publishers Weekly_, 22 March 2004: 58-9.

_____. "Killing Floor." _Publishers Weekly_, 20 Jan. 1997: 393.

_____. "Persuader." _Publishers Weekly_, 10 Mar. 2003: 50.

Robert Bloch's Archetypal Thriller: *Psycho*, The Novel

Garyn G. Roberts

> *Psycho* all came from Robert Bloch's book.
> —Alfred Hitchcock

Folklore, anecdotes, and trivia regarding Alfred Hitchcock's 1960 movie adaptation of Robert Bloch's 1959 novel, *Psycho*, are prolific and legendary. Even mediocre fans of Hollywood and Hitchcock's film know that Hitch used chocolate syrup to simulate blood in the famed shower scene with Janet Leigh. More experienced fans know that Hitchcock made his famous cameo early in the film, outside of Lowery's real estate office, where Marion Crane works, and they know that Hitch's daughter, Patricia, acts as Marion's associate in that office. Entire books have been written from various perspectives about *Psycho*, the movie. The two best are probably by movie star Janet Leigh and Hollywood scholar Stephen Rebello.

However, the focus of this essay is the often underappreciated Robert Bloch novel that was the basis for the movie. The novel had gone through more than forty printings at the time of Bloch's death in 1994—there have been other printings since—and it has been translated into a range of languages. Bloch's novel is an archetypal thriller.

While there is little need to provide a plot synopsis for Robert Bloch's novel and Hitchcock's adaptation here, there are some important considerations. One very viable way to appreciate Robert Bloch's novel is to consider it a murder mystery. A seasoned scribe of crime and mystery fiction, Bloch plots *Psycho* as a puzzle complete with a private investigator named Arbogast. While Bloch masterfully intertwines the mysterious lives of Mary (Mary is renamed "Marion" in the movie) and Norman and while he develops storylines of other characters past and present, he lays out clues throughout the story that something else is going on. Throughout the novel, there is an unrelenting and ever-building suspense that makes his tale an absolute thriller.

While the sexually charged, voyeuristic, and then brutally violent sequence with Mary Crane in the shower stall is the pinnacle of thrill in the novel, it is not the only thrill. The legendary scene in the Bates Motel shower stall sets up the thrill that accelerates throughout the remainder of the novel. With the dramatic and very final demise of Mary, all bets are off. In a strange way, Mary Crane has become our heroine. In this movie, Bloch develops her as our sympathetic character starting right away in chapter two, and he is very effective in doing so. (In chapter one, we meet Norman and Mother.)

Mary is on the path to correcting her horrible mistake of stealing the $40,000 from the real estate office when she disrobes and steps into the shower. She is on the path to doing the right thing, and while we the readers reluctantly support Mary in her crime, we are even more supportive of her plan to make amends. However, a turn off the highway down a wrong road seals her destiny. And she knows this—the novel and, even more, the later movie makes this very clear. In a very inventive way, Bloch kills off our heroine early in the novel, and we are left to wonder what is next. And a great deal is next.

In fact, the mystery is about to become very complex. We, the readers, know that all bets are off. Lila Crane (Mary's sister), Sam Loomis, and Arbogast are now all potential victims, and we learn a great deal more about each of these characters. To make matters worse, we develop and continue to develop a genuine, if not misplaced, empathy for Norman. We agonize with him because of his long-term abuse at the hands of Mother, and we agonize with him as he tries to cover up the sins of Mother. Bloch is breaking all the rules of his previously conventional genre—much as Agatha Christie had in *The Murder of Roger Ackroyd*. Unbeknownst to Bloch, he was creating what would become a unique, inventive archetypal thriller.

And there is more to the success of Robert Bloch's *Psycho*. The author's dark fantasy (oh, let's be honest—his intense and thrilling horror, terror fiction) deals with some of the grimmest realities of the human condition. In the second decade of the twenty-first century, that type of story is commonplace. However, in the 1950s and the decades before and immediately after the novel's publication, the culture did not accept this kind of tale. In addition, Robert Bloch had higher standards for storytelling himself. The result was that Bloch incorporated levity, and some of the best dark comedy ever found in the dark fantasy and thriller genres. This lightened the mood of what would otherwise have been some pretty rough material. This conscious incorporation of comedy is a significant component to the success and the art of Bloch's *Psycho*. Much of this comedy is the product of coincidence, and fate is the product of the characters' bad behavior. Much of this comedy is based on word play.

And word play figures prominently into the single biggest hallmark of most Robert Bloch thrillers. This is the twist ending. Often, when asked how he constructed his short stories, Ray Bradbury would say that he used "free word association." Bradbury would say that he would start out with an object or a concept—like a blue bottle. Then he would ask himself, "where is the blue bottle located?" and "where did it come from?" Robert Bloch's short stories were constructed by placing the beginning at the end, where there would be a pun or twist. He would then work backwards to tell the story that led to the surprise ending. There are so many wonderful examples of this in Bloch's short stories. Though not a short story, Robert Bloch's *Psycho* features this very same construction.

Robert Bloch

A straight, comprehensive bio-bibliography of Robert Bloch (1917–94) is fascinating, but much too detailed to record here. The single-most important biography of the author is his *Once Around the Bloch: An Authorized Autobiography*. Beyond in-depth personal, cultural, and literary history, *Once Around the Bloch* is one of the funniest biographies of the twentieth century. This volume is not only a must-read for Robert Bloch fans (beginning and advanced alike), it provides unique insights into the history of twentieth century thrillers. Randall Larson has provided the most complete Robert Bloch bibliography to date.

Robert Bloch was very talented. He was a "writer's writer," and one helluva a good friend to those who knew him. Bob was a kind man.

Since 1935, magazines, books, radio, motion pictures, television, and other media have showcased the psychological horror and suspense—the thrillers of Robert Bloch. (He also wrote in other genres besides thriller, suspense, horror, crime, and mystery fiction. These include science fiction and Damon Runyonesque comedies.) These thrillers have spawned many imitators, but in his unique style of prose, Bloch was and is unequalled. The O. Henry of the twentieth century, this wordsmith enthralled readers and viewers for sixty years of his lifetime and will undoubtedly thrill audiences for generations to come.

A variety of scholarly and semi-scholarly inquiries into Robert Bloch's life and work have appeared sporadically in recent decades, but, interestingly enough, as was initially the case with Poe, it may be the German and French cultures that have been Bloch's lead celebrants. For decades, the works of Robert Bloch have been some of the most collected and some of the most difficult to find in collectable bookshops.

Why is most of Robert Bloch's work out of print and so difficult to procure, and why has it not been the subject of detailed intellectual analysis? The finest scholarship on this wordsmith has come from the ranks of fandom—not necessarily an uninformed group—but not academe.) Much of the body of Bloch's work (pun intended) is difficult to obtain for the same reason it has not yet received the degree of scholarly attention it deserves—it's popular and hits a responsive chord in its audience. Readers hang on to their Robert Bloch books. And there's the anomaly. Bloch is habit-forming, like the best of formula television programming; yet at the same time, he has not yet received the critical attention he deserves.

Though Bloch immodestly and sincerely doubted that his *Psycho* influenced any author that followed him, there is little doubt that he did indeed influence many of his contemporaries and will influence storytellers to come. Some, like H.F. Heard and Stephen King, closely imitated, if not outright stole from Bloch.

Cultural Context

Social commentary and psychological intrigue pervade the thrillers of Robert Bloch, and this commentary and intrigue enhance, rather than detract from, his writing. So, Bloch's *Psycho*, like Charlie Chaplin's motion picture classic, *Modern Times* (1936) and Ray Bradbury's *Fahrenheit 451* (1953), have one important similarity: they are transformed from good stories into great stories because of, not despite, their astute commentary on both the social and human condition. Norman Bates falls victim to the world that created him, just as "the Little Tramp" is overrun by the inevitable evils of the corrupt, bourgeois, capitalist society in *Modern Times*, and Montag is burned by the anti-book, anti-intelligence society in which he lives.

Howard Phillips Lovecraft (1890–1937), the famed master of dark fantasy, mentored Bloch, then in his late teens, through extensive correspondence in the early- and mid-1930s. Bloch has the distinction of being the only other author that Lovecraft incorporated into his stories in *Weird Tales* and other dark fantasy publications. Bloch appeared in several Lovecraft stories as the character "Robert Blake." In his rich, varied and complex career, Bloch was clearly influenced by Lovecraft. And Bloch would often note that Lovecraft had a direct influence on *Psycho*. Specifically, Bloch pointed to Lovecraft's short story, "The Picture in the House" (1920), as a significant contributor to the atmosphere that pervades the world of Mary Crane and Norman Bates. "The Picture in the House" was not only important to Bloch, but to the continued Americanization of the "Gothic" story. In this tale, the master expanded the extensive traditions and trappings of European Gothic fiction and early American writers, like Charles Brockden Brown and Edgar Allan Poe to include rural, small-town New England and, by extension, Middle America. The horrors found in Lovecraft's house and picture are atmospheric and are based in a sleepy, naïve community, where everyone thinks they know everyone else's business. But they don't. And this is where a new, even more thrilling terror is born. The romantic farmhouse becomes intensely monstrous, almost supernatural, in its reality. And the picture in this house reveals taboo that would later be associated (if not entirely accurately) with Ed Gein and Norman Bates.

Other origins of Robert Bloch's *Psycho* long predated the real-life depredations of Ed Gein, the person often cited as the model for Norman Bates. And these are found in at least two 1950s Robert Bloch short stories. "Lucy Comes to Stay" and "The Real Bad Friend" foreshadow themes and storylines found in *Psycho*. Psychological terror pervades all three stories. Subsequently, all three 1950s tales are thrillers, which define and reflect the fears and tensions of the Cold War years. And they mirror the state of psychiatric/psychological sciences at the time. "Lucy Comes to Stay" is a short and very effective story of schizophrenia. The conclusion of the story is a twist-ending that very much predicts, seven years earlier, the conclusion of *Psycho.* In "Lucy Comes to Stay," we ultimately learn that Lucy and Vi, who has escaped from the sanitarium, are one in the same—just as Norman and Mother are one in the same.

"The Real Bad Friend" appeared in print two years before *Psycho*. Here, George Foster Pendleton is a prototype for Bloch's Norman Bates, though George is a vacuum cleaner salesman instead of a motel proprietor. If Lucy is Vi's alter ego, and Mother is Norman's, Roderick is George's id. As in "Lucy Comes to Stay," themes of schizophrenia and split personalities, insanity and murder are central to "The Real Bad Friend." As in Bloch's later novel *Psycho*, George, like Norman, is stricken with an Oedipal complex, where first his mother and then his wife, Ella, are his obsessions. There is a detective in both "The Real Bad Friend" and *Psycho*. Robert Bloch had successfully begun the *Psycho* storyline years in advance of his novel and years before the Ed Gein case broke.

A few weeks after the publication of "The Real Bad Friend," a real-life inspiration for Robert Bloch's *Psycho* appeared. In the December 2, 1957 issue, *Life Magazine* broke the story of Ed Gein to the nation: "Most of the time, Plainfield, Wisconsin, is a quiet town, a shopping center for the surrounding farmers….But one shocking day last week, peaceful Plainfield found that it had been harboring a monstrous criminal, and that his ramshackle house was the scene of murder and depravity" (*Life* 24).

When Bloch's novel, *Psycho*, debuted in 1959, many then and since thought that Bloch was creatively, if not somewhat fictionally, chronicling the Ed Gein story. The actual genesis of *Psycho* was even more amazing. On several occasions, in later years, Bloch recounted the same explanation: "It [*Psycho*] was inspired by the murders, *not* by Ed Gein. I was sitting in Weyauwega, Wisconsin, a town so small.... [that e]veryone knew everybody else's business" (Steranko 6–7). Bloch continued, "Some 40-odd miles away in an even smaller town, Plainfield, on a Saturday morning, somebody walked into Gein's shed....The police arrested Gein, and suspected he may have murdered others, too" (Steranko 6–7).

Interestingly and ironically, most of the uncanny parallels between the real-life horrors of Ed Gein and the thrilling escapades of Norman Bates were the products of Bloch's imagination. Robert Bloch's story of Norman Bates is only initially and partially influenced by the story of Ed Gein. Bloch stressed that he "knew very little about the Gein case *per se*, and nothing whatsoever about him, except he was a 42 [*sic,* 51]-year-old man, a respected man, a respected citizen his entire life" (Steranko 7). Themes of an Oedipal complex, schizophrenia, and more were developed by Bloch independently from, and without knowledge of, the specifics of the Gein case in Plainfield. Bloch had extrapolated cultural fears and concerns of the times and had then incorporated these matters into Norman Bates and the novel. It was only later that Bloch discovered that his storyline in *Psycho* closely paralleled the fact and mythology of Plainfield, Wisconsin. The Gein case served to galvanize work Bloch already had underway. In interviews years later, Bloch recalled, "I was amazed that Gein could conduct himself without *anyone* suspecting the truth. I said, 'There's a book here'" (Steranko 7).

And what happened to Ed Gein? He spent the rest of his life confined to Wisconsin state mental health facilities for the criminally insane. For quite some time before his death in 1984, Gein—mercifully (for him)—remembered nothing of his crimes of decades ago. Near the end, he had little idea who he was, and he knew nothing of his age, infamy, or crimes. In his last days, he was described as a gentle old man.

More Analysis of the Story

To the human, the most important intellectual pursuits are those that deal directly with the human experience and the parameters of that experience. Social scientists tell us that the single most important parameter of life as we know it is death. Each of us has a vested interest in this topic, and each of us will inevitably do firsthand research on the subject. Popular fiction, in whatever medium it is disseminated, is rich with tales of morality and proposals regarding the nature of a possible, but not guaranteed, afterlife. Life—or, more specifically the termination of life—pervades our thought processes more than anything else. The only possible exception occurs during adolescence, when sex largely drives thought and action. And yet, sex is directly tied to death. Without sex there is no life and subsequent death. Without sex, Jack the Ripper's atrocities in White Chapel may never have happened and most assuredly would have been infinitely less heinous and, perversely, less thrilling. Ed Gein in Plainfield, Wisconsin, in 1957 would never have had his horrible secret to hide—which he harbored for years in the sleepy little Midwestern farming community. Norman Bates would not have killed Mary Crane in as sensational a fashion as he did in Robert Bloch's *Psycho*. In short, our constructed realities and fantasies thrive on the thrill of death, and death defines life. About this, Bloch writes:

> After the kids have grown up and moved away, a new child comes into your house. His name is Death. He comes quietly without the wail of an infant, and he won't keep you up all night or make daily demands on your attentions. But, somehow you'll know he is there to stay. As he keeps growing, getting bigger and stronger with each passing day, you become smaller and weaker. Sooner or later there'll be the inevitable confrontation—and when it comes, you're the one who'll have to go (Bloch, "Reaper").

There is nothing like social taboo to spawn an enthralling thriller. Modern television programming and modern movies prove this. And, there are no bigger taboos than murder, cannibalism, necrophilia, and incest. Three of these involve death. In the 1950s, transvestitism was categorically condemned as well. By exploiting the social concerns of the day in *Psycho*, Bloch consciously and unconsciously, intentionally and unintentionally, created a thriller that would later be recognized for its archetypal proportions. Remember that the real-life tragedies of Ed Gein were only the impetus for the novel that Bloch later developed. It was Robert Bloch who told the story.

The horror and thrill of *Psycho* is born in the quiet little hamlet where everyone leaves their doors open and in that confined shower stall where, alone and naked, no one can escape. No person on Earth is more trustworthy and safer than Mother, are they? Bloch writes, "What interested me was the notion that a ghoulish killer with perverted appetites could flourish almost openly in a small rural community where everyone prides himself on knowing everyone else's business" (Bloch, "Shambles" 19). The author continued:

> The concept proved so intriguing that I immediately set about planning a novel dealing with such a character. In order to supply him with a supply of potential victims, I decided to make him a motel operator. Then came the ticklish question of what made him tick— the matter of motivation. The Oedipus motif seemed to offer a valid answer, and the transvestite theme appeared to be a logical extension. The novel which evolved was called *Psycho* (Bloch, "Shambles" 19).

Consider how like Poe Bloch is when he writes, "Basically my novel isn't about murder; it's about the person who commits them. It's about the vulnerability of our society, naked and exposed once its flimsy curtain of concealment is ripped aside" (Bloch, *Psycho 35th* 18). The House of Usher falls; the facade is destroyed. "If *Psycho* has any distinction it lies in the fact that unlike most writers in this *genre* I took criminals out of a bad neighborhood and put them in a home right next door to the reader" (Bloch, *Psycho 35th* 18).

Alfred Hitchcock's Movie Adaptation

From all accounts, Joseph Stefano was an arrogant scoundrel. Even Alfred Hitchcock, on several occasions, expressed concern that Stefano took way too much credit for the storyline in the movie, *Psycho*. Stefano did nothing to dissuade fans who congratulated him on *his* story in the movie. He often promoted himself as the author of *Psycho*, a conscious deception. Apparently, Stefano had a history of doing this and shamelessly took sole credit for other motion picture storylines and adaptations.

There is also the legendary story of the blind purchase of the movie rights to the novel by Hitchcock. The anonymous purchase of film rights to Robert Bloch's novel is discussed several places. The rights sold for a paltry (even by late 1950s standards) $9500. Bloch received less than $6000 of this amount.

In an interview with Charles Higham and Joe Greenberg, which appears in *The Celluloid Muse: Hollywood Directors Speak*, Hitch says, "*Psycho* all came from Robert Bloch's book. The scriptwriter, Joseph Stefano, a radio writer—he'd been recommended to me by my agents, MCA—contributed dialogue mostly, no *ideas*" (Steranko 6). Still, there were distinctions between book and movie. The movie changes Mary Crane's name to "Marion." In the novel, Norman doesn't just slash Mary to death, he decapitates her. And while the relatively young, slender Anthony Perkins plays Norman in Hitchcock's film adaptation, Bloch's Norman is shorter, heavier, wears glasses, and is ten years older than Perkins' portrayal. Bloch's novel does not begin with a voyeuristic view through a window into a motel room, nor does it consciously use a "Nazi motif" as does Hitchcock's movie. Dark comedy and puns appear in both the novel and the movie, but are even more pronounced in Bloch's novel. Both novel and movie employ a "bird motif," and the ultimate bird in *Psycho* is named "Crane."

A Kind Man Writes a Monstrous Thriller

For better or worse, Robert Bloch knew that he would always be best remembered as the man who wrote the novel that Alfred Hitchcock made into the movie *Psycho*. He had mixed feelings about this, since he had many hundreds of successful short stories, radio dramas, television plays, and movie scripts of which he was justifiably proud. Robert Bloch was as nice a man as he was a terrific writer. He was a writer's writer, and he was quiet and humble. Robert Bloch was unassuming and literally had a wicked sense of humor. He was the master of the twist-ending, and this led readers to compare his work to that of O. Henry. In his vast correspondence to the author of this essay, Bloch included the following:

> All I ever acquired were the simple tricks of my trade—the ability to play games with words. This is only enough to provide me with a half-life, hidden away in the pages of books which are in turn hidden away on bookshelves here and there, now and for a little while in the immediate future. After that there'll be nothing; the memories of those who knew me will fade, and my name will be referred to in passing only by those researching the "pop culture" of this soon-to-vanish century. (Personal interview)

Time will tell, but it is likely that the life and works of Robert Bloch and the origins of his thrilling novel, *Psycho*, will continue to be the source of popular and academic inquiry for years to come.

Works Cited

Bloch, Robert. "Lucy Comes to Stay." 1952. *The Living Demons*. New York: Belmont, 1967.

_____. *Once Around the Bloch: An Unauthorized Autobiography*. New York: TOR, 1993.

_____. Personal interview. 26 Jul. 1994.

_____. *Psycho*. New York: Simon & Schuster, 1959.

_____. *Psycho: The 35th Anniversary Edition*. Springfield, PA: Gauntlet, 1994.

_____. "(The) Really Bad Friend." *The Mike Shayne Mystery Magazine*. 1957. *The King of Terrors*. New York: The Mysterious Press, 1977.

_____. "Reaper." *Cutting Edge*. Ed. Dennis Etchison. Garden City, NY: Doubleday, 1986.

_____. "The Shambles of Ed Gein." 1962. *Murder Plus: True Crime Stories from the Masters of Detective Fiction*. Ed. Marc Gerald. New York: Pharos, 1992.

_____. "Society as Insane Asylum." *Rod Serling's The Twilight Zone Magazine* 1.3 (Jun. 1981): 13–17.

Gollmar, Judge Robert H. *Edward Gein: America's Most Bizarre Murderer*. Delevan, WI: Halberg, 1981.

"House of Horror Stuns the Nation." *Life* 43.23 (2 Dec. 1957): 24–31.

Larson, Randall D. *Robert Bloch: Starmont Reader's Guide #37*. Mercer Island, WA: Starmont, 1986.

Leigh, Janet, with Christopher Nickens. *Psycho: Behind the Scenes of the Classic Thriller*. New York: Harmony, 1995.

Rebello, Stephen. *Alfred Hitchcock and the Making of Psycho*. New York: HarperCollins, 1990.

Steranko, Jim. "A Nice Quiet Evening with Robert Bloch." *Halls of Horror*. London: Quality Communications, 1982.

The Elusive Genius of Michael Crichton _____

Chris Richardson

We may never really know Michael Crichton (1942–2008). Professionally, he was a doctor who didn't practice medicine, a science fiction writer who hated science fiction, and a Hollywood director who refused to become "a Hollywood type." Privately, he was closely aligned with the conservative right, dismissing "political correctness" and testifying against global warming activists, but also voicing his approval of abortion, marijuana, and euthanasia, among other controversial topics.

In the late 1960s, Crichton had two desks in Cambridge, where he would write books, like *The Andromeda Strain* (1969), under the name "Michael Crichton" (his full name is John Michael Crichton) and pulp fictions, like *Easy Go* (1968) and *Zero Cool* (1969), as "John Lange" (the combination of his real first name and the last name of a Scottish folklorist). He told *American Film* magazine that it was "like being Zorro…The whole thing just entertained me to no end" (McGilligan 16).

From the 1960s to the 2000s, Crichton would pop up each year like a masked avenger to leave his mark on subjects as diverse as illegal medical practices in *A Case of Need* (1968), computer-human interfaces in *The Terminal Man* (1971), nineteenth-century gold heists in *The Great Train Robbery* (1975), contemporary art in *Jasper Johns* (1977), underwater explorations in *Sphere* (1987), international trade relations in *Rising Sun* (1992), dinosaur cloning in *Jurassic Park* (1993) and *The Lost World* (1995), time travel in *Timeline* (1999), nano-engineering in *Prey* (2002), and seventeenth-century seafaring in *Pirate Latitudes* (2009). On most occasions, Crichton's best-selling thrillers became top-grossing films, directed by such Hollywood heavyweights as Steven Spielberg with the theatrical release of *Jurassic Park* in 1993 and *The Lost World* in 1997, and Barry Levinson with *Disclosure* in 1994 and *Sphere* in 1998. Crichton himself directed an adaptation of *The Great Train*

Robbery in 1979, where he began a long-time friendship with Sean Connery, and Crichton wrote such original screenplays as *Westworld* (1973), *Coma* (1978), *Looker* (1981), and *Runaway* (1984), which he also went on to direct. At one point, Crichton was responsible for the top television program, the top fiction publication, and the top box office film in America *simultaneously*. Despite his idiosyncrasies— or perhaps because of them—Michael Crichton became one of the most important authors of twentieth-century American thrillers.

Crichton was born in Chicago, Illinois to John Henderson Crichton and Zula Miller Crichton on October 23, 1942. He grew up in a Long Island suburb of New York, the eldest of four children. His brother Douglas recalled Crichton "always out in the backyard with a telescope he had built, looking at the sky" (Chambers 96). Writing of his early connection to literature, Crichton recalls in his autobiographical *Travels* (1988):

> When I was nine, my third-grade class was told to write a puppet show. Most of the students wrote brief skits; I wrote a nine-page epic involving so many characters that I had to get my father to retype it for me with multiple carbon copies before it could be performed. My father said he'd never read anything so cliché-ridden in his life (which probably was true); this hurt me and confirmed a pattern of conflict between us that persisted for many years (77).

His father was a journalist, an editor of *Advertising Age,* who went on to become the president of the American Association of Advertising Agencies. Like many things in Crichton's life, his relationship with his father remained complicated. Crichton thanked his parents frequently for encouraging his interests in science and technology. He also relates the story of his father's death in *Travels*, "I had to go back to attend the son of a bitch's funeral and mess up my much-needed vacation. And all his goddamned friends were going to be there, telling me what a great guy he was…" (193).

As an adolescent quickly approaching his adult height of 6'9, Crichton was an awkward student, smart but aloof. At fourteen, he sold his first article to *The New York Times'* travel section for sixty dollars. Despite being exposed to teasing and bullying in his youth, he achieved long-lasting records on the high school basketball team and considered his experiences in New York so formative that he moved back decades later when his daughter was ready to attend school. In 1960, Crichton enrolled in Harvard University. He received Cs in English classes, making him rethink his calling. "At eighteen, I was vain about my writing and felt it was Harvard, and not I, that was in error" (Crichton, *Travels* 4). At one point, he submitted a paper by George Orwell. "I hesitated because if I were caught for plagiarism I would be expelled; but I was pretty sure that my instructor was not only wrong about writing styles, but poorly read as well. In any case, George Orwell got a B- at Harvard, which convinced me that the English department was too difficult for me" (Crichton, *Travels* 4). In 1964, he earned a degree in Anthropology, graduating *summa cum laude*. After some travels, he enrolled in Harvard Medical School, writing paperback potboilers on weekends and holidays to earn money for school.

Crichton worked toward a medical degree while writing, first as John Lange for his pulp fictions, then as Jeffery Hudson (the name of a dwarf employed by Charles I) for *A Case of Need* (1968), his first medical thriller. He also wrote a book with his brother under the name "Michael Douglas." *Dealing: or The Berkeley-to-Boston Forty-Brick Lost-Bag Blues* (1970) was an anti-drug story of an undergraduate, which became a pro-drug film two years later. In 1968, Crichton won an Edgar Award from the Mystery Writers of America for *A Case of Need*, a novel about secretive abortion practices in a Boston hospital (he would win the prize a second time for *The Great Train Robbery* in 1979). It wasn't until 1969, when he was about to graduate, that Crichton published a book under his own name.

The Andromeda Strain (1969), the first "Michael Crichton" book, follows a week-long ordeal in which scientists try to make sense of a deadly new virus that has killed almost the entire population of a small town in Arizona. It quickly rose on the bestseller list and established Crichton as a force in what would later be deemed the "knowledge fiction" or "techno thriller" genre. Soon, the movie rights to *The Andromeda Strain* had been purchased by Universal

Studios for $250,000 and Crichton took a post-doctoral fellowship at the Salk Institute for Biological Studies in California. Crichton was named Writer of the Year by the Association of American Medical Writers for *Five Patients: A Hospital Explained* (1970), which detailed his real-life Emergency Room dramas and would later become the impetus for his hugely successful television series *ER* (1994–2009). A later printing of *Five Patients* captures the successes Crichton would soon experience (and even spurred a neologism to describe his work); in the words of the publicity blurb appearing on the back cover of *Five Patients*, the book is: "Written with the same honesty, suspense, technological detail and excitement that have made *Jurassic Park* and *Airframe* No. 1 bestsellers worldwide, *Five Patients* is an unputdownable account of life as it really is in a hospital."

Crichton moved into a house in a remote area outside Los Angeles designed by the famous modern architect Richard Neutra. He took an office in Santa Monica, which he filled with paintings by Frank Stella, Jasper Johns, and Claes Oldenburg and began to write full time. He would later claim the pseudonymous paperbacks were "wonderful training" and that "most of the problems beginning writers have dealing with their egos, deciding if what they're writing is good enough for them, didn't affect me at all" (Rezek and Sheff 154). He became meticulous, writing in the mornings and working more and more as he got into a project. He has said many times that he is neither the most creative nor gifted writer. But he's likely the hardest working. At his most productive, he wrote 10,000 words per day over a period of fifteen hours. He has claimed to read three hundred books and watch sixty films per year. When engaged in the writing of a novel, he begins to spend more and more time in his office, getting up "at five, then it's four, then it's three…eventually, I'm going to bed at ten and getting up at two" (Heller 63). This manic process of research followed by intensive writing has allowed Crichton to produce seventeen novels under his own name, four non-fiction books, and dozens of screenplays, films, and television shows. He's sold more than two-hundred million copies of his publications worldwide, and titles continue to be released after his death in 2008.

Crichton loved Alfred Hitchcock and suggests that they shared a sadistic pleasure in manipulating their audiences:

> What you're really doing in a narrative is paying out information bit by bit, which also means you're holding back—trying to make people worried about something. You know how it's going to turn out but you want the reader to have this feeling intermediately, and in that kind of manipulation—which is very pleasurable to experience if it's done well—there's something like sadism (C. Rose 166).

Many of Crichton's books take place in less than a week. He often divides the narrative by day, whereby Monday all is well, Wednesday the world is about to end, and Friday everything returns to normal—sort of. When writing *The Andromeda Strain*, he said that "I found you could make something more believable if you pretended not that it might happen or was happening, but that it had happened. You are not there, and it's over" (B. Rose 6). This formula continued to be a fixture of his writing style. While chapters are generally written in third person and present tense, the reader frequently gets the sense of reading a recent journal entry rather than a futuristic science fiction.

It's not hard to see why *The Andromeda Strain* was deemed "knowledge fiction" by *The New York Times Book Review* (Schott 4). Full of schematics, computer analyses and scientific procedural explanations, the novel begins "THIS FILE IS CLASSIFIED TOP SECRET." Unlike many other pseudo-confidential fictions, however, the ruse continues throughout the novel. While we know that this event has not in fact occurred, the sustained verisimilitude and the integration of very believable scientific and military practices, including redacted page transcripts, security codes, chain-of-command procedures, etc., make the tale utterly believable.
Perhaps the most impressive iteration of Crichton's knack for technically convincing fiction is his account of dinosaur cloning in *Jurassic Park* (1990):

"Here you see the actual structure of a small fragment of dinosaur DNA," Wu said. "Notice the sequence is made up of four basic compounds—adenine, thymine, guanine, and cytosine. This amount of DNA probably contains instructions to make a single protein— say, a hormone or an enzyme. The full DNA molecule contains three billion of these bases. If we looked at a screen like this once a second, for eight hours a day, it'd still take more than two years to look at the entire DNA strand. It's that big."

He pointed to the image. "This is a typical example, because you see the DNA has an error, down here in line 1201. Much of the DNA we extract is fragmented or incomplete. So the first thing we have to do is repair it—or rather, the computer has to. I'll cut the DNA, using what are called restriction enzymes. The computer will select a variety of enzymes that might do the job" (101).

Following this passage are multiple graphics that imitate DNA codes and computer models of the dinosaurs, along with more richly detailed explanations. While knowing the impossibilities of these technologies—the human genome project hadn't even been completed yet—Crichton paints a picture that reads more like a science report than a fantasy novel.

Crichton claims to be most influenced not by other fiction writers but by academics. He often publishes a bibliography at the end of his works, listing hundreds of scholarly articles and monographs about the subjects he covers. But despite his unconventional taste for dry, academic texts, Crichton's prose reads more like his idols Edgar Allan Poe, Charles Dickens, Louis Stevenson, and Sir Arthur Conan Doyle (also a doctor). Crichton's 1995 follow-up to *Jurassic Park* was even a wink to Conan Doyle, named after his 1912 novel *The Lost World*, which featured an expedition to South America, where the protagonists encounter surviving pre-historic animals and ape-men.

Crichton's style can, at times, be a pastiche, or a kind of literary play with traditional genre conventions. He admits to being drawn to genre fiction because "there's a set of preconceived notions that you can play with, a set of expectations that you can meet or fail to meet. And I like to work inside an established form" (McGilligan 19). *The Great Train Robbery* (1975) can be read as a combination of the Western and the Victorian novel of manners, in addition to the crime thriller. *Eaters of the Dead* (1976), which features Vikings pitted against cannibalistic smoke monsters, retains many traditional elements of gothic fiction. *Congo* (1980) plays on the historical convention of the fantastic voyage, in which travelers set out on an adventure to a strange and foreign land. He said that "the original impulse for *Congo* was from the nineteenth-century romantic adventures in faraway places. The difference was to do it in a contemporary way" (Warga 24). *Timeline* (1988), set simultaneously in the present and the Hundred Years' War, plays with notions of the historical romance, combining chivalry tales with historical fiction and the more contemporary genre of quantum fiction. *Rising Sun* (1992) fits well within the detective, murder mystery genre. *Jurassic Park* (1990) and *The Lost World* (1995) share links to the "lost world" adventure subgenre. And, of course, many of his novels are more straightforward legal-, medical-, and, above all, techno thrillers.

From early on, many critics complained that Crichton's characters remain shells with little or no explanation of their desires, motivations, and choices. In response, Crichton has insisted "I don't really believe most psychological explanations for why people are the way they are or why things turn out as they do" (C. Rose 162). He adds that:

> when I was younger, I was interested in situations in which individual personality didn't matter. Once an oil spill starts, I don't think it matters who the president of Exxon is, whether he's a good or bad guy...Once [disaster] happens, almost everything you do is going to make it worse. In such stories, the personalities of the people don't matter (C. Rose 162).

Toward the end of his career, Crichton even suggested that he would write a book explaining why it's impossible to truly know one's desires and why he thus strips his characters of any such explanations.

Crichton insists that this unknowable aspect of human choice and motivation applies also to himself. He said in a *Vogue* interview that "I make up little stories about how I get ideas, but I really don't know most of the time" (B. Rose 10). He begins *The Terminal Man* with a quotation from J.B.S. Haldane, the British scientist: "I have come to the conclusion that my subjective account of my own motivation is largely mythical on almost all occasions. I don't know why I do things." When it comes to understanding his unconscious motivations, he minces no words. Crichton calls Sigmund Freud "the greatest novelist of the twentieth century" (C. Rose 182). "If you define the impact of a novelist as the ability to impose a fictional view of the world—their personal and fictional view of the world—and to make it real and persuasive to other people, which I suppose is a good description of Tolstoy or Dostoyevsky, Freud beats everybody hands down" (C. Rose 182). He claims to have read Freud's books avidly, but disagrees with virtually everything they contain. Elsewhere, he has said "Bring me someone's superego— cut a brain open and hand it to me. It's not there! It's all baloney, all late-nineteenth-century Viennese wank" (Heller 69).

Critics have also suggested that Crichton writes, not as an inspired artist, but as someone looking to sell his paperbacks to Hollywood. He has replied, "I see pictures in my head and I describe them; my way of writing is cinematic. It's just the way I work. Robert Louis Stevenson is phenomenally cinematic, and there weren't any movies at the time he was writing. If he wrote *Treasure Island*, today, people would say, 'He's writing with a movie in mind'" (Rezek and Sheff 150). Crichton's popularity soon became a source of joy as well as frustration for him. "At a certain point what you do won't get reviewed anymore—you get reviewed" (C. Rose 133). Quickly, critical circles pegged him as a popular writer and, despite his academic credentials, he was denied a place among the great literary artists to which he aspired. In an interview with Charlie Rose in 1996, Crichton discusses his admiration for Clint Eastwood, who, unlike Crichton, was able to step out of such typecasting and reach a higher level of respect within his field. "There's something else that I, at least, think about when I think about Clint Eastwood—which is all those years when people said, 'Oh, yeah. Clint Eastwood—spaghetti westerns.' And he was continuing to work...He was going forward and going forward. Now, he has this other kind of respect...I think of that whenever I'm feeling that I'm not getting enough respect" (C. Rose 132–133). Ironically, Crichton expressed these ideas long before Eastwood's most significant acclaim for films like *Million Dollar Baby* (2004), which earned him Academy Awards for Best Motion Picture, Best Director, and many other accolades. Eastwood was pigeonholed in American popular culture and successfully transcended that narrow categorization. Perhaps Crichton might have overcome his status as a generic bestseller if he had lived as long as Eastwood.

Regardless of what could have been, Crichton remains "father of the 'techno thriller'" (Blair 92). Writing one of the first popular explanations of computers in the late-twentieth century, Crichton begins his non-fiction *Electronic Life: How to Think About Computers* (1983):

> This is a book about people and computers. It proceeds from several fundamental assumptions:
>
> 1. People are more important than computers.
> 2. Much of what we believe about computers is wrong.
> 3. It is easy to use a computer.
> 4. This is fortunate, because everybody's going to have to learn.
> 5. It is not so easy to use a computer wisely.
> 6. This is unfortunate, because everybody's going to have to learn.
> 7. Computers can actually be a lot of fun.
> 8. There are people who want to put a stop to that (3).

If we treat "computers" as advanced technologies more generally, we have the general principles of virtually all of Crichton's thrillers. Whether it's the *Frankenstein*-like transformation of a human through computer-assisted enhancements that go horribly awry, as in *The Terminal Man* (1972), computer-assisted DNA sequencing that allows humans to play with evolutionary patterns by creating dinosaurs in the contemporary world, as in *Jurassic Park* (1990), nano-computers that begin to adapt to their environments and murder everything in their paths, as in *Prey* (2002), or skewed computer-generated projections of Earth's temperatures over time, as in *State of Fear* (2004), the basic tenants he lays out at the beginning of *Electronic Life* apply equally well. In virtually all Crichton plotlines, human lives are put in jeopardy by those seeking to control and harness new technologies for the financial benefits, with little consideration for the ethical, political, and social consequences.

More than anything, Crichton is known for his nuanced scientific explanations. His first best-seller, *The Andromedia Strain* (1969), takes place in a secret complex buried deep under the Nevada desert to quarantine the most deadly viruses on the planet. His descriptions are sharp and meticulous:

> Except for the clotted blood, there was nothing unusual about them at all. He knew that these same pieces of tissue would now be sent to the microscopy lab, where another technician would prepare stained sections, using hematoxylin-eosin, periodic acid-Schiff, and Zenker-formalin stains. Sections of nerve would be stained with Nissl and Cajal gold preparations (*Andromedia Strain* 132–133).

This kind of detail, which makes it virtually impossible to separate the science from the fiction, especially for readers without specialized knowledge, would become Crichton's calling card.

While technology, even in his historical texts, remains an important element of each plotline, it is never celebrated blindly. More often than not, Crichton's interest is in the darker side of technology's utopian promises. Such skeptical attitudes have led some scientists to claim his books are bad for science. *Jurassic Park*, in particular, came under attack by members of the scientific community who found his tale of cloning run amok to be counterproductive to medicine. The *Journal of the American Medical Association* published a piece that stated, "Crichton's monster tale should appeal to these enemies of science better than any Frankenstein incarnation ever did" (Skolnick 1253). Ironically, Crichton pointed out that more people were interested in dinosaurs and science than ever. "If it were true that *Jurassic Park* is anti-science and impeding progress and people's interest in science, why are so many natural history museums in the U.S. now running shows called "Jurassic Park" or "The Real Jurassic Park?" They perceive that the effect of these stories is to arouse tremendous interest and enthusiasm—more than scientists are generally able to" (Rezek and Sheff 151–152). Seeming to support his argument, a genus of dinosaur found in China was even named Crichtonsaurus in honor of the author (Minzesheimer). In relation to the backlash, however, Crichton likens the issue of cloning to medical practices at the time he attended Harvard Medical School when artificial respiration systems were being introduced and keeping alive many aged patients who would not have been able to survive otherwise. "We had the machines well before we started the debate…We were being forced by technology to make decisions about the right to die—whether it's a legal or a religious issue—and many related matters" (Rezek and Sheff 152). His goal throughout his life was to ask questions about technological progress before they became uncritically accepted.

One of the difficulties in assessing Crichton's cautionary tales rests in his impartial narrative style. While he often pits free-thinking professionals against corporate megalomaniacs who meet their demise at the hands of the former, it's not always clear where Crichton falls within such debates. One of the most striking aspects of this controversial style can be seen in *Rising Sun*, which many critics saw as a racist and xenophobic tale of unfair competition by a ruthless, secretive, and homogenous Japanese society. In scenes where protagonists refer to "fucking japs," it's easy to see why critics might argue "Crichton has turned alarmism into one of the most profitable shticks in the history of publishing" (Denby 50). Despite these criticisms, Crichton remained adamant that he loved Japan and its customs and merely wanted to see America remain economically competitive. He also, however, told interviewers that political correctness "gives me the creeps" (Rezek and Sheff 146).

Following this controversial novel came *Disclosure* came an even more controversial narrative about a happily married executive in Seattle who is the victim of sexual harassment by an attractive, sexually-aggressive female boss—who also happens to be incompetent at her job. While Crichton claims to have chosen this atypical case to ask questions about the power of "victims" in new and provocative ways, many readers were not pleased with his seeming trivialization of a hot-button issue. As Terry and Schiappa contend, "despite being framed as an egalitarian feminist exploration of the power dynamics of sexual harassment, *Disclosure* can be read ideologically as anti-feminist backlash characteristic of some mainstream popular culture of the late 1980s and 1990s" (69). Crichton's relationship with women, both romantically and professionally, represented a source of tension in his life. He once joked in a speech that his hobbies were "scuba diving, tennis, and getting divorced" (Warga 24). He was married five times. His first few wives made him see a psychotherapist, an experience for which he would later tell interviewers he was very thankful.

His final major controversy occurred when, despite many of his liberal views—pro-gun control, pro-choice, pro-health care—Crichton became a poster boy for the American right with *State of Fear* (2004). The novel challenged the importance of carbon emissions and other manmade pollutants that those aligned with the political center and left—Al Gore being one of the most well-known—were arguing caused irreparable damage to our ecosystem and needed drastic intervention to prevent floods, famines, and other global disasters. Ironically, Crichton told a group of high school students in 2005 that, after publishing *The Andromeda Strain*, "people said, 'Aren't you afraid you're going to be enhancing biological warfare and giving the government ideas?' I thought, 'If the government has to get ideas from novels, we're in terrible trouble'" (Students & Leaders Program 216). That same year, Crichton spoke at the Senate Committee on Environment and Public Works on the issue of global warming, arguing that much of the scientific foundations for global warming fears were unfounded. Jeanne Hamming later argued in her essay, under the subheading "Michael Crichton's *State of Fear;* Or, How to Stop Whining about Climate Change and Be a Real Man," that "while much attention has been paid to Crichton's dubious, pseudo-scientific arguments regarding climate change, less attention has been given to the political framework in which these arguments are embedded" (27). Tellingly, Republican President George W. Bush met with Crichton privately to discuss the issue in which they reportedly "were in near-total agreement" (Barnes 23). Ultimately, as Crichton became a household name and earned millions for each new book and movie deal, he seemed to embrace the controversial nature of his interests. "I've always been called anti-whatever; anti-feminist, anti-Japan, anti-science. There's a long list" (Rezek and Sheff 151). Reportedly, when someone once suggested Crichton was a contrarian, he shouted back, "I'm not contrary!" (Heller 70). This refusal to agree, even with those who suggest he's contrarian, speaks volumes of his *oeuvre* more generally.

Crichton's final book, published posthumously as *Micro* in 2011, was incomplete at the time of his death in 2008. Crichton passed away from throat cancer in Los Angeles, leaving behind his daughter Taylor Anne and his six-months-pregnant wife Sherri Alexander, who gave birth to John Michael Todd Crichton in February 2009. He also left behind a completed manuscript for *Pirate Latitudes*, which was published in 2009 and a "Cryptic road map for an unfinished techno thriller...scrawled in two notebooks and on scraps of hotel stationary [*sic*]" (Alter D4). HarperCollins brought in non-fiction author Richard Preston, best known for his book about the Ebola virus *The Hot Zone: A Terrifying True Story* (1994), to complete the novel. Like many Crichton plots, *Micro* (2011) involves a maniacal executive in a life sciences research corporation who, using state-of-the-art technologies, shrinks a group of graduate researchers to half an inch. To survive, the students must use their scientific knowledge of the tropical forest to fend off deadly insects and sneak into the facilities to return to normal size and expose the criminal dealings of the antagonist. Again, like many Crichton plots, this genre-bending techno thriller is filled with scientific minutia to demonstrate how such incredible feats could potentially become possible. And, as he frequently does, Crichton (and Preston) provide an extensive bibliography. While *Micro* has been his last novel to date, there may be more posthumous works in the pipeline. "He always worked on a lot of projects," Crichton's widow Sherri told reporters, while alluding to a "treasure trove" that remained of her husband's notes and sketches of stories (Alter D4).

In the fall of 2013, Hard Case Crime re-released all of the pulps Crichton wrote as "John Lange" in the 1960s. The covers of each of his Lange novels feature provocatively dressed women and dangerous situations, much like Ian Flemings' James Bond novels of the same period. In a 1969 *New York Times* interview, Crichton says, "it appeared to me that almost any idiot could write a spy story, and I discovered that almost any idiot can" (Shenker 5). The back covers read like B-movie tag lines: "Can an Egyptologist and his band of thieves find a lost tomb buried for centuries in the desert—and get away with its treasure?" (*Easy Go*); "An expert on venomous snakes and smuggler of rare artifacts accepts an assignment working as a bodyguard to a man everyone wants dead" (*The Venom Business*); "The perfect heist, planned by computer, in a luxury hotel off the coast of Spain" (*Odds On*). Yet, if considered from another angle, just like his later works, each story is about an affluent professional caught in an escalating—and increasingly preposterous—situation that can only be overcome through strategic thinking and quick decisions. It's intriguing to think about how this man, who never claimed to be a good writer and bragged about the simplicity of writing potboilers, went on to sell hundreds of millions of books and continue to outdo many competitors long after his death. He once told *American Film* magazine, "my desire is to have fresh problems" (McGilligan 15). This seems to have applied not only to his book projects but many elements of his life. "These products are, to a certain degree, excretions. I don't want to play with them once they're out" (Sauter 28).

In his half-century as a professional author, Crichton sparked many controversies on problems ranging from genetically manipulating dinosaur DNA to treating women equally in the workplace, to global warming, to nanotechnology. But perhaps his greatest product was Michael Crichton, the MD who went to Hollywood, who used to be Jeffery Hudson, the award-winning medical writer, who used to be John Lange, the lighting-quick writer of disposable pulps that were reissued half a century later to eagerly awaiting fans.

Works Cited

Alter, Alexandra. "Deciphering Michael Crichton's Clues." *Wall Street Journal - Eastern Edition* 18 Nov. 2011: D4.

Barnes, Fred. *Rebel-in-Chief: Inside the Bold and Controversial Presidency of George W. Bush.* New York: Crown Forum, 2006.

Blair, Sean. "Obituary: Michael Crichton: Artist of Science." *Engineering & Technology* 3.20 (2008): 92.

Chambers, Andrea. "Author-Director Michael Crichton Is a Master of Multimedia Monkey Business." *People Weekly,* 16 Feb. 1981: 94–98.

Denby, David. "Dim Sun." *New York,* 2 Aug. 1993: 50–51.

Hamming, Jeanne. "Nationalism, Masculinity, and the Politics of Climate Change in the Novels of Kim Stanley Robinson and Michael Crichton." *Extrapolation* (University Of Texas at Brownsville) 54.1 (2013): 21-45. Academic Search Complete. Web. 1 Nov. 2013.

Heller, Zoe. "The Admirable Crichton." *Conversations with Michael Crichton.* Ed. Robert Golla. Jackson: UP of Mississippi, 2011. 62–75.

McGilligan, Patrick. "Ready When You Are, Dr. Crichton." *Conversations with Michael Crichton.* Ed. Robert Golla. Jackson: UP of Mississippi, 2011. 14–21.

Minzesheimer, Bob. "Science inspired his fiction." *USA Today,* 6 Nov. 2008: Academic Search Complete. Web. 1 Nov. 2013.

Rezek, John and David Sheff. "*Playboy* Interview: Michael Crichton." *Conversations with Michael Crichton.* Ed. Robert Golla. Jackson: UP of Mississippi, 2011. 142–164.

Rose, B. "Hollywood Gets a New Man". *Conversations with Michael Crichton.* Ed. Robert Golla. Jackson: UP of Mississippi, 2011. 7–13.

Rose, Charlie. "An Interview with Michael Crichton/1995." *Conversations with Michael Crichton.* Ed. Robert Golla. Jackson: UP of Mississippi, 2011: 102–118.

_____. "An Interview with Michael Crichton/1996." *Conversations with Michael Crichton.* Ed. Robert Golla. Jackson: UP of Mississippi, 2011: 119–141.

_____. "An Interview with Michael Crichton/1999." *Conversations with Michael Crichton*. Ed. Robert Golla. Jackson: UP of Mississippi, 2011: 165–190.

Schott, Webster. "The Andromeda Strain." *The New York Times Book Review*. 8 Jun.1969: 4.

Shenker, Isreal. "Michael Crichton (Rhymes with Frighten)." *Conversations with Michael Crichton*. Ed. Robert Golla. Jackson: UP of Mississippi, 2011: 3–6.

Skolnick, Andrew A. "Jurassic Park." *Journal of the American Medical Association* 270.10 (September 1993): 1252–1254.

Students & Leaders Program. "Reflections on Careers in Entertainment." *Conversations with Michael Crichton*. Ed. Robert Golla. Jackson: UP of Mississippi, 2011. 207–223.

Terry, Valerie S. and Edward Schiappa. "Disclosing Antifeminism in Michael Crichton's Postfeminist Disclosure." *Journal of Communication Inquiry* 23.1 (1999): 68–89.

Trembley, Elizabeth A. *Michael Crichton: A Critical Companion. Critical Companions to Popular Contemporary Writers*. Westport, CT: Greenwood Press, 1996.

Warga, Wayne. "Fact, Fiction Intertwined by Crichton". *Conversations with Michael Crichton*. Ed. Robert Golla. Jackson: UP of Mississippi, 2011. 22–26.

James Patterson: An Uncertain Legacy _____

Philip L. Simpson

James Patterson (b. 1947), the creator of the fictional African American D.C. cop and forensic psychologist Alex Cross, is the most prolific and highest-earning contemporary American writer. Since publishing his first thriller, *The Thomas Berryman Number* (1976), Patterson has gone on to publish ninety-eight books to date. Following his first novel, he published *Season of the Machete* (1977), a psychological thriller; *The Jericho Commandment* (1979), a revenge thriller; *Virgin* (1980), a religious thriller (later rewritten by Patterson as *Cradle and All* [2000]); *Black Market* (1986), a finance thriller; and *The Midnight Club* (1988), a psychological thriller. His break-through blockbuster novel, *Along Came a Spider* (1993), introduced Alex Cross to the world, inaugurated Patterson's tradition of giving his Cross novels titles derived from nursery rhymes, and—aided by a then-innovative television advertising campaign run by Patterson himself—sold five million copies. Since 1996, he has published as many as ten books per year. Alex Cross, Patterson's most famous character, has featured in twenty more novels since *Along Came a Spider*. Patterson is also the author of the popular Women's Murder Club crime thriller series, beginning with the publication of *First to Die* (2001). The characters that constitute the Women's Murder Club reside in San Francisco and include Lindsey Boxer, a homicide detective; Yuki Castellano, a district attorney; Cindy Thomas, a reporter; and Claire Washburn, chief medical examiner. Not content to write only Alex Cross and Women's Murder Club thrillers, Patterson early in his career began branching out from the thriller genre that made his name into other genres, including science fiction, children's and young adult books, historical novels, romance, sports, and non-fiction. To date, three films and six television movie adaptations of his novels have been released. Two of the films, *Kiss the Girls* (1997) and *Along Came a Spider* (2001), starred veteran actor Morgan Freeman as Alex

Cross. *Alex Cross* (2012), a re-launch or reboot of the franchise and largely based on Patterson's novel *Cross* (2006), starred Tyler Perry. According to *Contemporary Authors Online*, *Roses are Red* (2000) has been adapted for film, *First to Die* has been adapted as a mini-series for NBC television, and the Women's Murder Club series has been made into a pilot for ABC.

The Alex Cross series, aka "the Nursery Rhyme Adventures," is Patterson's most well-known contribution to the thriller genre. Many of the novels are titled after lines from nursery rhymes, giving them an aura of "faux-naif grotesquerie," in Brian Stableford's memorable phrase, which has undoubtedly contributed to their popular appeal with thriller readers. Cross, a widowed cop with a doctorate in forensic psychology, has three children. He lives in Washington, D.C., with two of the children and his paternal grandmother. He works with the FBI as a profiler. In his various outings, Cross has faced adversaries such as "The Butcher," whose real name is Michael Sullivan, a prolific serial killer/rapist; "Casanova," whose real name is Nick Ruskin, a detective who also abducts and kills young women as part of his "harem;" "The DC Audience Killer," really an incestuous brother and sister couple and former patients of Cross' who, as their collective name suggests, like to kill their victims in front of audiences; Jimmy "Hats" Galati, a mob killer who murdered Cross' first wife, Maria; "The Mastermind," FBI Agent Kyle Craig, once Cross' friend before becoming one of his formidable enemies; Gary Soneji, the villain of *Along Came a Spider*, who kidnaps two young girls and bedevils Cross throughout several subsequent novels; "The Tiger," the leader of a gang of African teenage boys; "The Weasel," a British Army colonel, who becomes a serial killer and murderer of Cross' love interest; "The Wolf," an alias for several individuals, all of whom are Russian mobsters and former KGB agents; and "Zeus," whose real name is Theodore Vance, husband of the US President and killer of young women, including Cross' niece. As this partial list of Cross' ever-growing record of antagonists demonstrates, Patterson deliberately contrasts the decency of Cross, his love interests, and his family against the depravity of each book's villains. Of this juxtaposition,

Patterson says: "I am personally not terribly interested in the bad stuff that goes on. I'm very interested in the Cross family. I like the notion of good struggling in the middle of this maelstrom we're going to throw around them" (Zaleki 53).

The depiction of women and African American characters in the Cross series deserves special mention. To some readers, a disproportionate number of women—including Cross' first wife, a few assorted love interests, and family members—meet violent ends in these stories, a development that leads Patricia Holt, among others, to criticize Patterson as a practitioner of "the Female Dismemberment and Mutilation School of Mystery Writing" (D10). To this, Patterson would no doubt reply by pointing to the number of prominent female characters in his novels, including the four female protagonists of the Women's Murder Club series. He also says he "grew up in a house full of women. . . . My best friends tended to be women. I like the way they talk, the fact that a lot of subjects weave in and out of conversations. Sometimes men are a little more of a straight line" (Womack). Besides disengaging from the politics of femicide as depicted in his novels, Patterson also tends to decentralize race in the Cross series, another interesting authorial strategy for a series, which has a black man as its protagonist. Patterson intentionally created an African American hero because, as he tells Lewis Burke Frumkes, "I didn't think there were many." He also based Cross' close family on Patterson's memories of a female African American cook, who, after marital troubles, moved in with his family when he was a child. However, Patterson (perhaps deliberately, so as not to harm sales one way or another) does not specifically dwell upon Cross' race as a significant issue with which the profiler must contend either personally or professionally. Earni Young says, "Alex Cross occasionally encounters cases where his race becomes an issue, but it is never THE issue of the book" (28). Rather, Patterson chooses to focus on making Cross an endearing character, whose appeal cuts across racial lines as he solves the various criminal cases in which he becomes involved.

Patterson is truly a one-man publishing industry. He enjoys, through his publisher Little, Brown & Co., a support staff of editors, assistants, and managers dedicated solely to him. A former advertising executive with the agency J. Walter Thompson/North America, where he created campaigns for Kodak, Burger King, and Toys 'R' Us, among other companies, he has used that experience to run the advertising campaigns for his own novels. He shows his business savvy in other ways, particularly in his partnering with collaborators to create a "James Patterson brand." His brand, according to Patterson, is "trust that's established between something and a group of people—just trust. What I would like the trust to be is that, if you pick up a James Patterson novel, you won't be able to put it down" (Zaleski 53).

To perpetuate this brand, he hires other writers to turn his detailed sixty-to-seventy page story treatments and outlines into novels to help him sustain his massive output. While other thriller writers, such as Clive Cussler and Tom Clancy, have also worked with collaborators, Patterson in his typical style has done so with unapologetic fervor. Writers who have co-authored with Patterson include Gabrielle Charbonnet, Hal Friedman, Leopoldo Gout, Andrew Gross, Peter de Jonge, Michael Ledwidge, Peter Kim, NaRae Lee, Maxine Paetro, Howard Roughan, and Ned Rust. His collaborators typically turn in pages to him every two weeks, at which time he reviews, rewrites, and, if necessary, coaches his writers to amp up the suspense, twist the twists tighter, make the characters more compelling, and generally get the story back on track. Of his partnering with collaborators on series, such as the Women's Murder Club, at which some literary purists have looked askance, he says:

> My short answer to the question as to why work with other people is Gilbert and Sullivan, Rodgers and Hammerstein, Woodward and Bernstein, Lennon and McCartney and it goes on . . . There is a lot to be said for collaboration and it should be seen as just another way to do things as it is in other forms of writing, such as for television, where it is standard practice (Wroe).

Working with these collaborators, Patterson has been able to publish bestselling novels at a dizzying rate for many years now. He has become a fabulously wealthy man as a result.

Topping the 2012 Forbes list of wealthiest authors, with an annual income of $94 million (beating the next wealthiest writer on the list, Stephen King, by over $50 million), Patterson has sold more books than Stephen King (no slouch himself in number of books published), John Grisham, and Dan Brown combined. An average year of income for Patterson is somewhere in the neighborhood of $80 million (Blum). Patterson also holds the Guinness record for author with the largest number of *New York Times* #1 bestsellers on the list simultaneously (five every year since 2005) as well as the most *New York Times* hardcover bestsellers (sixty-three so far). He is, by most counts, the world's top-selling author. It is estimated that he has earned well over one billion in gross income (Wroe). According to his official website, one in four novels in the suspense/thriller genre in 2011 was written by Patterson. Since 2006, according to Jonathan Mahler, one out of every seventeen novels purchased in the United States was written by Patterson. He has sold approximately three hundred million copies of his books.

Additionally, as more consumers buy e-books, Patterson has become an outspoken advocate of the enduring value of libraries and bookstores in the digital reader era. In an interview with *CBS This Morning*, Patterson pledged to donate one million dollars to American independent bookstores (on the condition the bookstores are viable and contain a children's section) and explained his donation in this way:

> We're making this big transition right now to e-books, and that's fine and good and terrific and wonderful. But we're not doing it in an organized, sane, civilized way, so what's happening right now is a lot of bookstores are disappearing, a lot of libraries are disappearing or they're not being funded. School libraries are not being funded as well. This is not a good thing ("James Patterson Pledges").

Reacting to a recent statement from youth pop culture icon, Justin Bieber, that Bieber is just not that into reading and writing, Patterson explains why bookstores, and reading itself, are of such value, especially to younger people:

> This country needs readers. It needs people opening their minds up. It needs people capable of going to higher education and succeeding. This country needs people who can look at the world in different ways, have a broader perspective on things and be more compassionate. That concerns me and I'm in a position to nudge people and to help the discussion get going (Miller).

To fight against cultural "Bieberism," Patterson has established a diversity of scholarships, book donation programs, book awards (such as the Page-Turner Awards, which he funds himself), web sites, and many other initiatives that promote reading to young people.

At the center of this spectacular publishing phenomenon is a hard-working man, who writes seven days a week in the early mornings and late afternoons. Of course, an admirable work ethic and top book sales do not insulate him against his many critics, one of whom refers to him as "Mr. Sleaze Fiction himself" (Zaleski 48). In a more temperate voice, David Lazarus writes of *Roses Are Red* that Patterson's short chapters, while compelling, "do not allow for much depth, though, which prevents *Roses Are Red* from getting too far into the psychological makeup of the story's characters" (RV-6). Patterson readily acknowledges, as if to disarm his many critics with self-effacing candor, that he is not the best prose writer. He elaborates: "I'm not a writer's writer. I'm not a craftsman. I could be, and that would be a one-book-a-year operation" (Blum). So what, then is his strength, from his perspective? According to Patterson: "In my case I've always been a good storyteller. I'm very good at plot and characterization but there are better stylists" (Edge). Storytelling, to Patterson, is the "one thing that matters. There are a lot of ways to write good books. You can have *The Corrections*, which is very complicated sociology, or James Joyce, where the allusions and the writing are stunning. But my work is just pure storytelling" (Blum). He admits that "thousands of people hate my stuff, [but] millions of people like it" (Wroe).

In fact, Patterson takes pride in writing prose that is decidedly non-literary, where the language exists simply as a means to plot rather than an end in itself. Joan G. Kotker argues that "even [Patterson's] earliest work shows more emphasis on plot than character, always the sign of an author who is interested above all in the tale rather than in the telling" (5). Key to Patterson's effect on the reader is the emotional experience his tales provide. Through creating strong, decent characters, such as Alex Cross, and then pitting them against evil foes, Patterson guarantees reader engagement with character and plot.

Patterson's lean style is further accessible to readers who otherwise would not read much fiction, popular or otherwise. In this sense, his style has been compared to that of Jeffrey Deaver, another thriller writer best known for creating the character of Lincoln Rhyme, a quadriplegic detective introduced in *The Bone Collector* (1997). Jeff Zaleski describes Patterson's style in this way: "Patterson's novels are sleek entertainment machines, the Porsches of commercial fiction, expertly engineered and lightning fast" (54). His sentences and paragraphs are short, his plots straightforward and linear. Description and exposition are limited, practically non-existent. His short, two-to-four page chapters are entirely dedicated to the principle of getting the reader to turn the pages as quickly as possible, all the better to advance the slickly streamlined plot. He uses detailed outlines to keep track of all the plot twists and turns, the better to save himself time-wasting detours during the writing process. One of his many co-authors, Andrew Gross, describes what he learned about the art of best-selling storytelling from Patterson:

> I learned about pace: the kind of *24*-like pace, when a story is meant to be devoured in a sitting or two. When multiple chapters drive you from one to another before you even look up. Especially in the opening fifty pages and at the end. . . I learned the importance of making your lead character someone who readers love. . . And how to make your bad guys bad. . . In sum, I learned how to write for one's audience, not the people you want them to be (168).

Another co-author, Mark Sullivan, adds the following about Patterson's formula for reader engagement: "Exposition was severely limited. Each chapter . . . had to deepen a character, advance the plot, or turn the tale on its head. You began every scene with the end in mind; and the end had better blow the reader's mind or it would be revised and tossed" (64). As Gross and Sullivan make clear, Patterson has relentlessly honed his style into the service of commercialism, a move guaranteed to raise the hackles of many critics—but it has also guaranteed a huge audience, one that has elevated Patterson to the financial pinnacle of the fiction publishing world.

Probably the most important key to Patterson's success with readers of thrillers is his focus on a swiftly moving plot and emotionally engaging characters. Of his approach to writing, he says, "I didn't study it. A lot of it is emotional with me. You have to care. So many thrillers don't work because you don't care about the characters or the situation. . . . when someone condescends to the genre you can smell it straight away" (Wroe). This earnest desire to write stories that connect emotionally to readers is also something that he insists upon with his collaborators. The end result is a body of fiction that connects with millions, much to the delight of Patterson's publisher, but offends or otherwise disconcerts critics who value what they would call "high art" over Patterson's brand of commercialism. As Lev Grossman puts it, "[Patterson] will never get respect from the literati. Most reviewers ignore him. In a culture that values high style over storytelling, pretty prose over popularity and pulse-pounding plots, he's at the extreme wrong end of the spectrum, and he knows it." Typical is the response of James Yates, who calls Patterson's output "literary junk food" and calls Patterson "a corporation all to himself . . . He's going to keep churning out his works . . . People are going to keep buying them. But at the same time, actual writers are going to be doing the same thing. . . . The other writers will never match his sales numbers, but the fact that their focus is primarily on creativity says it all." Yates' stance obviously privileges the time-honored portrait of the solitary writer toiling away on works of genius to be savored by an elitist audience over Patterson's "corporate" model, which Yates derides as assembly-line writing-by-committee, mass-producing fluff product for mindless consumption. In general, Patterson remains above such criticism, content to receive the rewards of his industry from his readers instead of waiting for critical plaudits and literary awards.

Unlike his next-richest rival Stephen King, who in spite of commercial success has been creeping over the years into some semblance of literary respectability (notwithstanding critic Harold Bloom's serial vociferous attacks on the literary deficits of King's work), Patterson seems not only cognizant of, but content with the reality that he will not be winning anytime soon the National Book Foundation's Medal of Distinguished Contribution to American Letters, as King did in 2003, or the O. Henry Award, as King did in 1996. Even King, who has suffered his own share of critical brickbats over the years before making his halting ascent to grudging respectability in some circles of the literary establishment, has criticized Patterson for formulaic writing. After accepting a Lifetime Achievement Award from the Canadian Booksellers' Association in 2007, King stated bluntly: "I don't like [Patterson], every book is the same" ("Stephen King Is No Fan"). Then in 2009, he slammed Patterson again, as an aside in a lengthier denunciation of *Twilight* author Stephanie Meyer's authorial skill, "as a terrible writer, but he's very successful" (Flood). Patterson's equanimity toward negative criticism of his work is evident in his response to King's verbal ripostes: "Recently Stephen King stated he doesn't have any respect for me. Doesn't make too much sense—I'm a good dad, a nice husband—my only crime is that I've sold millions of books. I'm . . . in terms of the books anyway, a Stephen King fan" ("James Patterson Responds"). In an interview with Lauren Schuker Blum, he says of King: "I read his stuff. I like breaking his balls by saying positive things about him. . . he's taken shots at me for years. It's fine, but my approach is to do the opposite with him—to heap praise. . . I like a lot of his earlier stuff better."

What makes this polite little feud between the United States' two most successful fiction writers more remarkable is how often the arbiters of critical acceptance, such as the aforementioned Harold

Bloom, have accused King of the same lack of originality and, by implication, creativity or skill that King attributes to Patterson. King, in other contexts, such as his acceptance speech for the Medal of Distinguished Contribution to American Letters, has made impassioned pleas for the reconsideration, if not the erasure, of the distinction between popular and literary fiction. Just because it is popular, King argues, does not mean that it's not also good. While King is certainly entitled to his critical appraisal of Patterson's work, it is striking to see King deploy the same kind of disparaging language against Patterson's work that has, over many years, been directed toward that of King. Patterson indirectly references, with only a tinge of passive aggressiveness, King's rise from the literary basement to a penthouse suite when speaking of King's recent bestseller *11/22/63*: "I think his latest book . . . is pretty good. It's done well and it's also closer to what he was writing fifteen years ago. But if he had written it fifteen years ago, the critics would have torn it up, said 'schlockmeister writes more schlock.' Instead, they ate it up" (Blum).

It should be noted that, for a formulaic "hack," Patterson engages in more daring stylistic experiments than he is given credit for. It could be argued that his minimalist style in itself, at least at first—before it paid such dividends—was taking a chance in a publishing market that awards its literary stars, such as a Thomas Pynchon, with prestige, if not fabulous wealth. His short chapters are modeled, he says, after those of Evan S. Connell and Jerzy Kosinski, two writers who have certainly received more credit as stylists than Patterson has.

He credits *Tristram Shandy* with inspiring him to break "the rules whenever I damn well felt like it. Mix first person and third person? Sure, if it helps the story. Sentence fragments? Hell, yes" ("By the Book"). Patterson routinely switches between first- and third-person narrative voices within the same novel, or introduces a different first-person narrator within the same novel, such as in *Cat and Mouse*. It also would have been far easier and less risky for the Patterson "brand" had he settled comfortably into writing cop thrillers, but his success writing in other genres (such as historical fiction, science fiction, and romance) proves his versatility.

He has also won his fair share of writing awards over the years. His first novel won the Edgar Award, given annually by the Mystery Writers of America to first-time writers, in 1977. Since then, he has won the Reader's Digest Readers' Choice Award for fiction in 2003, based on a nationwide poll; the Children's Choice Book Awards' Author of the Year for *Max (A Maximum Ride Novel)* in 2010, an award chosen exclusively by children. One begins to notice a theme with Patterson's writing awards—that they are selected by popular fiction readers, young and old alike, not by the critics.

To date, there have been a handful of scholarly examinations of Patterson's work and only one full-length critical study, which in itself attests to the degree to which this prolific and staggeringly popular writer has been ignored or disregarded by the literary establishment. One scholarly essay by Rhonda Harris Taylor uses the Women's Murder Club novel, *Second Chance* (2002), as a case study to illustrate Taylor's thesis that, in the post-9/11 twenty-first century, American mysteries and crime thrillers pit the detective against an antagonist "who seeks to disrupt . . . society's natural order through the misuse of vital information." In *Second Chance*, the serial killer targets law enforcement personnel or their families by using "information gathered via a classic strategy—personal networking—to select, stalk, and kill his victims" (Taylor). Thus, the villain is "extraordinarily clever at acquiring and manipulating information for . . . nefarious purposes," which makes *Second Chance*, among the other thrillers examined by Taylor, a parable for the post-9/11 era in which society "cannot tell from appearances who holds the dangerous information and has the evil intentions" (Taylor). Another academic essay by Christiana Gregoriou explores the criminal mind as portrayed by in the fourth Alex Cross novel, *Cat and Mouse* (1997) and how Patterson's stylistic choices present an impression of the serial killer, Gary Soneji, as a born criminal, rather than his having become one. Specifically, Patterson's third-person narration technique allows the reader sympathetic access into Soneji's thoughts, but simultaneously creates a certain distance through which the narrator (and the reader) avoid overt sympathy with the criminal perspective. In the passages given through Soneji's point of view, as Gregoriou notes, no "justifications for his actions are provided and no excuses given," which portrays the killer as not only remorseless, but taking childish joy in his criminal actions. Patterson's technique, then, allows him to create malevolent characters, such as Soneji, who present depraved contrasts to the human decency of Alex Cross.

Joan G. Kotker's book *James Patterson: A Critical Companion* unequivocally places Patterson's work within the realm of popular fiction, as distinguished from mainstream (or literary) fiction. According to Kotker, popular fiction is "intended for a mass audience . . . to meet the already-established expectations of a particular group. . . popular fiction is a comforting fiction in that it seldom challenges the reader's preconceptions of how the world works: . . . Readers leave these stories entertained and unchallenged in their basic conceptions." Mainstream fiction, however, "has no clearly defined audience with clearly defined expectations . . . [The audience] must be active readers, willing to participate in the story with the author by taking an active role in working out its meaning . . . mainstream fiction is without doubt the more difficult of these two fictions because of the demands it places on the reader" (8).

Kotker further identifies Patterson as, in spite of his forays into different genres, a mystery writer, in that this is the genre Patterson began with in *The Thomas Berryman Number* and returns to repeatedly. Kotker defines the mystery genre's basic conventions: "a serious crime, usually a murder, is committed; a detective, who may be either an amateur or a member of the police is brought in to investigate the crime; the focus of the story then shifts to the gathering of clues . . . the solution to the crime is announced; finally, the fate of the criminal is resolved in some manner" (9). Patterson's first published novel, Kotker says, follows this basic mystery formula. For Kotker, later novels, such as the Alex Cross stories, follow a variant on the mystery genre, known as the police procedural, what most would deem a subgenre of the detective story. Simply put, the police procedural focuses, presumably in a realistic or at least plausible manner, on the process of a professional police investigator (or police force) as he or she attempts to solve a crime or crimes. The earliest full-length study of the subgenre, George Dove's aptly titled *The Police Procedural* (1982), outlines the formulaic conventions that structure most procedurals, such as "The Tyranny of Time," meaning that these stories are built upon the "supposition that time is always working against the police detective" (113). Certainly *The Tyranny of Time* and other such procedural conventions can be identified in the DNA of Patterson's novels. Given that Patterson's work does not center on traditional police officers or detectives, however, Kotker's classification must be tweaked somewhat. Peter Messent prefers the label "police novel" to "police procedural," the better to "describe the variety of fictions focusing on crime and police work: novels of detection, thrillers, psychological and/or sociological novels, narratives reliant on Gothic effects, and so on" (177).

Identifying Thomas Harris' serial-killer novel *The Silence of the Lambs* (1988) as one such work that includes elements of the procedural, but also disrupts them to foil reader expectations, Messent provides an indirect connection to Patterson's thrillers, specifically *Along Came a Spider*, which Patterson and his publisher advertised none-too-subtly as the next *Silence of the Lambs* that readers were waiting for. Patterson's second Alex Cross novel, *Kiss the Girls*, with its storyline of women imprisoned by a serial killer, is even more clearly influenced by (or derivative of) the serial killer captivity narrative found in *The Silence of the Lambs*.

In conclusion, while the literary establishment has not embraced Patterson, and the scholarly analysis has just started, it is clear the reading public has. They reward him every year by buying his books more than those of any other author. In turn, Patterson reaches millions more readers every year than any other popular fiction writer, let alone the literary critics who refuse to review him in venues such as the *New York Times Book Review*. While Patterson's ultimate legacy is still uncertain, and the artistic or creative merit of his work is certainly debated (when it even rises to critical attention, that is), he has undoubtedly been awarded the status of most popular author by the general reading public.

Works Cited

Blum, Lauren Schuker. "James Patterson Explains Why His Books Sell Like Crazy." "Speakeasy." *The Wall Street Journal*. 30 Mar. 2012. Web. 4 Oct. 2013.

"By the Book: James Patterson." *The New York Times Book Review*. 25 Aug. 2013: 8(L). Literature Resource Center. Web. 17 Oct. 2013.

Dove, George N. *The Police Procedural*. Bowling Green, OH: Popular Press, 1982.

Edge, Simon. "James Patterson: The Best Seller Who Doesn't Write His Own Books." *Express*. 26 Feb. 2013. Web. 2 Oct. 2013.

Flood, Alison. "Twilight Author Stephanie Meyer 'Can't Write Worth a Darn,' Says Stephen King." *The Guardian*. 5 Feb. 2009. Web. 8 Oct. 2013.

Frumkes, Lewis Burke. "A Conversation with James Patterson." *Writer* (2000): 13. Academic Search Complete. Web. 17 Oct. 2013.

Gregoriou, Christiana. "Criminally Minded: The Stylistics of Justification in Contemporary American Crime Fiction." *Style* 37.2 (Summer 2003): 144–59. Literature Online. Web. 17 Oct. 2013.

Gross, Andrew. "The Patterson School of Writing." *Publishers Weekly*. 30 April 2007. 168.

Grossman, Lev. "The Man Who Can't Miss." *Time* (2006): 106–115. Academic Search Complete. Web. 17 Oct. 2013.

Holt, Patricia. "Thriller Built on Slice-and-Dice Female Victims." *San Francisco Chronicle*. 13 January 1995: D10.

"James Patterson." *Contemporary Authors Online*. Detroit: Gale, 2013. Literature Resource Center. Web. 17 Oct. 2013.

"James Patterson Pledges $1 Million to Help Independent Booksellers." *CBS This Morning*. 16 September 2013. Web. 9 Oct. 2013.

"James Patterson Responds to Stephen King's Attack." *Writer's Blog*. 5 July 2007. Web. 7 Oct. 2013.

Kotker, Joan G. *James Patterson: A Critical Companion*. Critical Companions to Popular Contemporary Writers. Westport, CT: Greenwood Press, 2004.

Lazarus, David. "Detectives and Sleuths Need Love Too." San Francisco Chronicle. 3 Dec. 2000: RV-6.

Messent, Peter. "The Police Novel." *A Companion to Crime Fiction*. Eds. Charles Rzepka & Lee Horsley. West Sussex, UK: Blackwell, 2010. 175–86.

Miller, Laura. "James Patterson: Quit Knocking Reading, Justin Bieber!" *Salon*. 19 September 2013. Web. 9 Oct. 2013.

Stableford, Brian. "James Patterson." *Guide to Literary Masters and Their Works*. Literary Reference Center Plus. January 2007. Web. 17 Oct. 2013.

"Stephen King Is No Fan of James Patterson." *Writer's Blog*. 18 June 2007. Web. 7 Oct. 2013.

Sullivan, Mark. "What I Learned from James Patterson." *Publishers Weekly*. 17 Dec. 2012.

Taylor, Rhonda Harris. "'It's About Who Controls the Information': Mystery Antagonists and Information Literacy." *Clues* 24.1: 7–18. Literature Online. Web. 17 Oct. 2013.

Womack, Steven. "James Patterson: Stretching the Boundaries of the Thriller." *BookPage*. 2000. Web. 17 Oct. 2013.

Wroe, Nicholas. "James Patterson: A Life in Writing." *The Guardian*. 10 May 2013. Web. 4 Oct. 2013.

Yates, James. "The Troubling Patterns of James Patterson." *Chicago Ex-Patriate*. 30 Sept. 2010. Web. 7 Oct. 2013.

Young, Earni. "Writing White." *Black Issues Book Review*. July–August 2004: 26-28.

Zaleski, Jeff. "The James Patterson Business." *Publishers Weekly*. 4 Nov. 2002: 43–55.

John Grisham: The Master of the Fast-Moving Legal Thriller _____

Susan J. Tyburski

Over the last two and a half decades, John Grisham's novels and films have had tremendous influence on American popular culture and our view of lawyers and the law. From the day his surprising bestseller, *The Firm*, exploded onto the publishing scene in 1991, readers have devoured Grisham's fast-moving "David and Goliath" tales of individual lawyers pitted against the Mafia, the FBI, big corporations, and mega law firms. Grisham explains, "[T]he American reading public and movie and television audiences have had an insatiable appetite for stories about lawyers, courtroom drama, law firms, and shenanigans" (Norton Jr. 14). Together with Scott Turow, author of the 1987 best seller *Presumed Innocent,* Grisham reinvigorated the legal thriller genre that had lapsed since the 1950's. Following the debut of these two authors, the publication of legal thrillers exploded, and this genre shows no signs of slowing down (Robinson 21).

Grisham's best-selling novels are rooted in his life experiences, both personal and legal. John Ray Grisham, Jr. was born on February 8, 1955 in Jonesboro, Arkansas. His father worked in construction; the family moved around throughout the Deep South, following the available jobs. Grisham's father worked long hours and instilled in his son the principle that "hard work brings rewards" (Wroe). Grisham describes his "father's family" as "a family of storytellers, and there were long dinners and lots of stories. As children, we absorbed them" (Norton Jr. 14). These narrative gifts developed into a lucrative inheritance.

Grisham attended Mississippi State University, where he majored in accounting. After graduating in 1977, he obtained a law degree from the University of Mississippi (aka "Ole Miss") in 1981. Grisham originally planned to be a tax lawyer; however, his plans quickly changed after taking a course on tax law. He "was stunned by its complexity and lunacy" and "barely passed the course" (Grisham, "Boxers, Briefs and Books"). Instead, Grisham opened his own law practice in Southaven, Mississippi, taking on criminal defense and personal injury cases and doing other general practice work as a "street lawyer." Grisham accepted low-fee "indigent" criminal defense cases, accumulating a lot of valuable trial experience, but not much income. In 1983, he was elected to a position in the Mississippi House of Representatives. The state legislature was in session from January through March each year and was filled with "great storytellers" (Grisham, "Boxers, Briefs and Books"). As Grisham absorbed these stories, he continued to practice law.

These varied experiences would eventually find their way into Grisham's books. For example, *The Firm*'s protagonist Mitch McDeere had an accounting background similar to Grisham and went to work in a tax firm. Many of Grisham's legal protagonists either express an aversion to tax law, like Jake Brigance in *Sycamore Row* (2013), or, ironically, begin their law practice in a grinding corporate financial practice in a mega firm, like David Zinc's bond underwriting for foreign multinational corporations in *The Litigators*. Grisham's work as a "street lawyer" serves as fodder for many of the caricatures in *The Litigators*. His experiences in practicing tort law, and in facing the temptations and challenges of the sudden accumulation of wealth, are on display in *The King of Torts*.

Grisham's most important experience led to the idea for his first story and inspired him to pursue writing this story in a disciplined way. In 1984, while hanging around the courthouse, Grisham watched a trial concerning a young female victim of assault and rape. His experience was life-changing:

> Her testimony was gut-wrenching, graphic, heartbreaking and riveting. Every juror was crying. I remember staring at the defendant and wishing I had a gun. And like that, a story was born (Grisham, "Boxers, Briefs and Books").

Grisham developed this story into his first novel, *A Time to Kill*, published in 1989. *A Time to Kill* is set in the fictional town of Clanton, Mississippi, and involves the defense of an African American father, Carl Lee Hailey, who shot and killed the white rednecks who tortured and raped his young daughter. The white lawyer who defends Hailey, Jake Brigance, and his young wife and daughter, are subjected to harassment, threats, and violence from the KKK. Grisham admits that Brigance is "his most autobiographical character," embodying his early aspirations to be "a real trial lawyer" (Neary). Like his later legal thrillers, this novel relies primarily on dialogue and action, including courtroom scenes that keep the story moving quickly. It also includes scenes of small town life in Mississippi, describing the type of community in the Deep South where Grisham grew up. Unfortunately, *A Time to Kill* did not immediately prove to be popular. When the initial printing of 5,000 failed to sell, the book went out of print.

After failing to achieve success with his first novel, Grisham educated himself by reading other best-selling thrillers. He studied the strategies and techniques of other successful popular writers and adapted them to his next novel. In *The Firm,* Grisham created the narrative blueprint he would follow in his legal thrillers for more than twenty years. As Grisham explains, "you've got to have the drama, you've got to have the issues, you've got to have the narrative that drive the story and turn the pages" (Neary).

A thriller primarily consists of an exciting plot involving a protagonist with whom readers can identify. This protagonist must solve some kind of mystery and extricate himself or herself from a difficult and increasingly threatening situation. The plot of a thriller moves rapidly, with surprising twists and turns, much like a roller coaster ride. In addition to a page-turning plot, readers must be able to identify, at least to some extent, with the protagonist and project themselves into the place of this character, in order to experience the "thrill" of the fictive "ride." The more "thrilling" the "ride" is, the more successful the thriller.

Legal thrillers revolve around legal arenas and legal actors, and often employ dramatic courtroom scenes. They offer glimpses into the mysterious and confusing world of the law and allow readers to experience that world vicariously through the legal protagonist. Because the primary focus is on an entertaining and fast-moving story, narratives are usually bare-bones, descriptions are kept to a minimum, and character development is limited. Like many writers of thrillers, Grisham employs fast-moving action and dialogue and a minimum of descriptive detail to keep his readers turning the pages, which Grisham readily admits is his primary objective (Ferranti 43).

Grisham's stories typically involve tales of individual lawyers doing battle with more sophisticated, insidious corporations and mega law firms. This narrative blueprint was initially created by Grisham in *The Firm*, where his legal protagonist, young Mitch McDeere, is seductively recruited from Harvard Law School by an elite tax firm in Memphis. Upon joining the firm, McDeere and his wife Abby are treated to a series of luxurious perks and benefits that seem too good to be true. Their suspicions are confirmed when McDeere is contacted by the FBI and learns that the firm's primary client is the Mafia, for whom the firm is laundering massive amounts of money. McDeere is then pressured by the FBI to become an informant. Having placed his protagonist in peril, under surveillance by both the Mafia and the FBI, Grisham's narrative takes a number of twists and turns before finally extracting his hero and young wife in a spectacular fashion. The lesson is that, against seemingly impossible odds, a clever lawyer can manipulate the system to achieve some semblance of justice and, often, enough money to allow the lawyer to sail away safely into the sunset.

Like a good trial lawyer, John Grisham is an engaging and charismatic story-teller. He typically uses a third-person omniscient point of view. While the reader primarily experiences the action through the viewpoint of the protagonist, Grisham often allows the reader to view portions of the developing story from other characters' perspectives as well, adding irony and suspense to the narrative as the reader often learns more than the characters about the developing situation. This literary technique can be seen in *The Firm*, which opens from the point of view of the mysterious "senior partner" reviewing Mitch McDeere's résumé. We alternatively experience the developing action through the eyes of Mitch; his wife, Abby; various insidious members of the Memphis firm; FBI agent Waye Torrance; and Mitch's assistant, Tammy. The effect of this technique is to present the reader with a series of distinct pieces of an evolving puzzle, which the reader works to assemble as he or she reads. Often a key missing piece—such as the details of Mitch's plan to evade both the Mafia and the FBI in *The Firm*—is withheld from the reader until the end of the novel, allowing a satisfying sense of closure when that missing piece falls into place.

This narrative formula, adapted from traditional mysteries and set in legal arenas, has proven to be immensely popular with both lawyers and non-lawyers. Non-lawyers enjoy the vicarious thrill of battling giant corporations, criminals, and the government through Grisham's novels, while lawyers enjoy Grisham's entertaining use of legal issues and settings, as well as his skewering of various members of the legal profession. Grisham has offered some interesting twists to this basic narrative technique over the years. In *The Pelican Brief* and *The Client*, Grisham makes rare use of female protagonists, although they both need to team up with a stronger male character to be successful.

While Grisham offers different twists on his basic story line with each legal thriller, key elements recur. The legal protagonists almost always end up "on the run," evading detection by the mega firm they work for, the FBI, a criminal mob, etc. This narrative device helps to maintain tension and keeps the reader turning pages. The ruthlessness and greed displayed by large corporations, and the lawyers that represent them, are contrasted with the struggles of small firms and solo practitioners who, while not perfect, ultimately are motivated by the desire to achieve some kind of justice. Grisham's legal fictions often involve the machinations of the elite and the wealthy; however, his portrayal of the rich and powerful reveals the ruthlessness and greed of their actions. The Mafia; big pharmaceutical companies; corporate polluters; mass tort lawyers; ambulance-chasing attorneys, who use aggressive television ads to lure new clients; corrupt judges; prosecutors and politicians; and the CIA all serve as easy targets for the legal schemes hatched by Grisham's sympathetic, underdog protagonists.

Especially in his early thrillers, Grisham's stories are generally populated by rough, largely undeveloped sketches of characters. For the sake of an expedient plot, Grisham, like other thriller writers, employs stereotypes to enable the reader to move as quickly as possible through the story without getting bogged down in details, or being tempted to linger over a descriptive or explanatory passage. As a result, Grisham's novels often serve to perpetuate stereotypes found in popular culture. For example, in *The Litigators*, women are portrayed as virtuous mothers-to-be, such as Paula Finley, the wife of the young protagonist; seductive manipulators, like DeeAnna Nuxhall; motherly helpers, such as secretary Rochelle Gibson; or cold, ruthless attorneys, like Nadine Karros. In *The Associate*, women hardly appear at all, unless they are providing a possible love interest (Olivia and Dale) for the protagonist, young lawyer Kyle McAvoy. With few exceptions, the women in Grisham's novels, when they appear at all, take backseat roles to more powerful and successful men.

Over time, Grisham has developed increasingly complex characters, moving beyond the facile stereotypes employed in his early novels; many of his protagonists have become increasingly morally ambiguous. In *The Brethren*, Grisham's tale revolves around a group of imprisoned judges who organize a scam involving the solicitation of homosexual men through a letter writing campaign. The judges, known as the "brethren" in prison, masquerade in their letters as gay young men looking for companionship. They use the responses to their solicitations to extort money from the men answering their pleas. As the scam proceeds, the brethren "hook" an up and coming politician, Aaron Lake, who is being maneuvered into the Presidency by the CIA director. When the brethren and their scam are discovered by the CIA, they succeed in negotiating their release in return for secrecy, while Aaron Lake succeeds in being elected President. This novel is perhaps Grisham's most cynical story; it does not contain a single character that is not corrupted in some way.

In a more recent novel, *The Racketeer,* Grisham's protagonist is a lawyer, Malcom Bannister, who was sentenced to ten years in prison after he accidentally laundered money. Bannister is Grisham's first African American protagonist. Bannister negotiates a deal with the FBI to reveal the murderer of a federal judge; as a result, his sentence is commuted, and he is given a new identity through the Witness Protection Program. The novel traces his machinations to expose the real killer and the murdered judge's corrupt dealings, as well as recover millions of dollars of gold stolen from the judge. These characters are fighting for personal survival and wealth, as opposed to justice; in addition, their tactics are downright criminal. Despite these moral failings, these later characters are drawn with enough sympathy to encourage readers to root for their success.

Since the success of *The Firm* in 1991, Grisham has published at least one book every year except one; he's been called the "unstoppable Energizer bunny of legal fiction" (Maslin). To date, Grisham has written twenty-one legal thrillers, as well as a non-fiction book about the death penalty (*The Innocent Man*), four non-legal novels (*Bleachers, Calico Joe, A Painted House, Skipping Christmas*), a young adult series (*Theodore Boone*), and a short story collection (*Ford County*). In the 1990s, Grisham was ranked the top-selling author of the decade, easily outselling second ranked author Stephen King (CNN). By 2012, he had sold 275 million books globally (CBS News), and they have been translated into forty languages (Wroe). Grisham's influence on popular culture became even more pervasive with the adaptation of seven of his legal thrillers into films: *The Firm* (1992), *The Pelican Brief* (1993), *The Client* (1994), *A Time to Kill* (1996), *The Chamber* (1996), *The Rainmaker* (1997) and *The Runaway Jury* (2003), as well as the production of an original screenplay, *The Gingerbread Man* (1998). (*John Grisham: The Official Website*). In addition, two of his novels were adapted for short-lived TV series: *The Client* in 1995 and *The Firm* in 2012 (NBC; *New York Daily News*). Most recently, a dramatic adaptation of his first novel, *A Time to Kill*, premiered off Broadway in October 2013 (Isherwood).

At their root, Grisham's stories are grounded in, and reflect, the values of the American heartland. This ethical grounding reveals the influence of Grisham's long involvement with the southern Baptist church. Grisham has described his mother as "a devout Christian" and identified his acceptance of Christ at the age of eight as "the most important event" of his life. When he was practicing law, Grisham declined a number of cases because of his "faith," including "divorce work because the laws are now such that divorce is too easy." Now that he is a best-selling author, Grisham refuses to "resort to gratuitous sex, profanity, or violence" (Ferranti 43).

While some conservative southern Baptist attitudes peek through from time to time, Grisham's politics, as espoused by many of his characters, demonstrate a markedly liberal bent. He describes himself as a "moderate Democrat" (Wroe), and his novels often champion the rights of the individual over the power of big corporations or the government. Grisham also deals with important social issues, such as racism (*A Time to Kill, Sycamore Road*), homelessness (*The Street Lawyer),* the death penalty (*The Chamber, The Confession*), and overcrowded prison conditions (*The Brethren*).

Grisham's legal thrillers trace and, to a great extent, shape the law narrative in American society over the last twenty-five years. Attorney Jennifer Rubin argues that, more than any other source, John Grisham's works have created a "romanticized, glamorized depiction of law" that pervades popular culture and "has helped nudge jurors and judges toward creative legal theories and colossally large awards" (56). Because of Grisham's wide-ranging influence in different media, including books, movies, television and theatre, Rubin believes that Grisham has "effectively tainted the American jury pool" by creating a bias towards plaintiffs' lawyers (57). Jurors' expectations of legal actors in the courtroom and their interpretations of witnesses and evidence that appear before them are shaped, in large part, by what they have been exposed to in the popular media. Because of Grisham's pervasive influence in American popular culture, it is likely that many jurors are familiar with his courtroom tales. To be effective, lawyers must be aware of this influence and either use it to their advantage, in the case of plaintiffs' attorneys, or work to counteract it, as in the case of defense attorneys (60).

Scholar Terry White has written that our fascination with legal thrillers lies with our desire for justice, the battle between good and evil, and the contradictions between "ideal justice" and "real justice" (xxii). Grisham's works reflect this dance and, increasingly, can be seen as morality plays. In *The King of Torts*, Grisham's protagonist leaves his job as an underpaid and overworked public defender and, thanks to a shady informant named __, experiences a rapid rise to wealth and fame as a mass tort lawyer. This rapid accumulation of easy wealth proves too tempting for __, who spends his money faster than he can earn it, takes too many risks, becomes involved in too many shady deals, and then experiences a painful fall from grace unusual for one of Grisham's protagonists. Grisham's own experiences in dealing with the rapid accumulation of wealth (Wroe) are evident on the pages of this novel.

In recent years, Grisham has moved beyond the legal thriller genre to write tales about baseball, small towns, and football in Italy (*Playing for Pizza*). He has also begun a light mystery series for young adults involving two busy lawyers' precocious only child, Theodore Boone, who lives in a small town and is obsessed with the law and the legal world. He helps to solve mysteries surrounding local cases (*Theodore Boone: Kid Lawyer, Theodore Boone: The Abduction, Theodore Boone: The Accused, Theodore Boone: The Activist*). The character of Boone serves to demystify the often confusing world of courtrooms and lawyers for young people, describing the law and the legal world through a young person's eyes and portraying lawyers as heroes and champions of those in need.

Despite these creative departures, Grisham continues to write engaging legal thrillers. His most recent novel, *Sycamore Row*, is a sequel to his first novel, *A Time to Kill*, and has been garnering generally good reviews (see, e.g., Anderson and Maslin). *Sycamore Row* returns to Grisham's first protagonist, young lawyer Jake Brigance of Clanton, Mississippi, and plunges him into a controversial litigation involving the probate of a holographic will—a handwritten will signed by a secret multi-millionaire the day before he commits suicide. This handwritten will specifically excludes his estranged children and grandchildren and leaves ninety percent of his fortune to his black housekeeper. The reasons for this will are shrouded in mystery, which swirls around the entertaining antics of the lawyers in and out of the courtroom as the dead man's children pursue a bitter court battle over the will's legitimacy. Like Grisham's earliest legal thrillers, the plot twists and turns as more and more secrets are revealed.

As critics have noted, *Sycamore Row* contains some of Grisham's most entertaining and intriguing characters, including disbarred, dissolute lawyer Lucien Wilbanks, hard drinking divorce attorney Harry Rex Vonner, Judge Reuben Attlee, and local sheriff Ozzie Walls (Anderson). The successful blending in *Sycamore Row* of a fast-moving plot with engaging characters and a shocking ending demonstrates that, even after twenty-five years of churning out legal thrillers, John Grisham can still deliver satisfying stories that keep us turning the pages late into the night. As his own talents continue to evolve, Grisham has built a legal thriller dynasty that will continue to influence public perception of lawyers and the law for years to come.

Works Cited

Anderson, Patrick. "*Sycamore Row* by John Grisham." *The Washington Post*. 20 Oct. 2013. Web. 28 Oct. 2013.

CBS News. "John Grisham: E-books will be half of my sales." *CBS This Morning*. 11 Apr. 2012. Web. 20 Oct. 2013.

CNN. "Grisham ranks as top-selling author of decade." *CNN Book News*. 31 Dec. 1999. Web. 20 Oct. 2013.

Ferranti, Jennifer. "Grisham's Law." *The Saturday Evening Post*. (March/April 1997): 42–43, 81–82.

Grisham, John. "Boxers, Briefs and Books." *The New York Times*. 5 Sept. 2010. Web. 20 Oct. 2013.

Isherwood, Charles. "Grisham's Tale Retold Onstage: 'Time to Kill' by Rupert Holmes, Comes to Broadway." *The New York Times*. 20 Oct. 2013. Web. 28 Oct. 2013.

John Grisham: The Official Site. Web. 20 Oct. 2013. < www.jgrisham. com/>.

Maslin, Janet. "More Vexing Challenges for That Mississippi Lawyer." *The New York Times*. 30 Oct. 2013. Web. 1 Nov. 2013.

NBC. *The Firm*. NBC.com. Web. 20 Oct. 2013.

Neary, Lyn. "'A Time to' Revisit Clanton, Miss., in John Grisham's Latest." *NPR Books*. 18 Oct. 2013. Web. 20 Oct. 2013.

New York Daily News. "Author John Grisham gets back into TV with NBC series inspired by *The Firm*." 21 Dec. 2011. *Daily News*. 20 Oct. 2013.

Norton Jr., Will. "Why John Grisham Teaches Sunday School." *Christianity Today*. 3 Oct. 1994.

Robinson, Marlyn. "Collins to Grisham: A Brief History of the Legal Thriller." 22 *Legal Studies Forum* 21 (1992). Web. 20 Oct. 2013.

Rubin, Jennifer. "John Grisham's Law: The Social and Economic Impact of a Pop Novelist." *Commentary*. (Jun. 2009): 56–60.

University of Mississippi Department of English. "John Grisham." *The Mississippi Writers Page*. 11 Nov. 2008. Web. 20 Oct. 2013.

White, Terry. "Introduction: The Legal Thriller and the Modern Courtroom Drama." *Justice Denoted: The Legal Thriller in American, British, and Continental Courtroom Literature*. Westport, CT: Praeger, 2003. xvii–xxv.

Wroe, Nicholas. "A Life in Writing: John Grisham." Culture: Books. *The Guardian*. 25 Nov. 2011. Web. 21 Oct. 2013.

In the Popular Tradition ————————————

Helen S. Garson

For a long time Tom Clancy insisted he writes political thrillers, totally rejecting the term "technothriller" that numerous critics have bestowed on his work. But perhaps in recognition of the inevitable, he has finally given in. When Larry King on his 22 August 1994 television show introduced him as a writer of technothrillers, Clancy made no protest. As for labeling his work, a case could be made for both the large designation—thriller—and its subheading—technothriller, and also for spy/espionage fiction. Properties of all these types are easily found in Clancy's writing. Additionally, some book sellers, such as the Book-of-the-Month Club, list his novels under a more expansive and general category: Mystery/ Suspense Fiction. This broad, all-encompassing term may be useful for libraries. However, it does little to help the reader distinguish the real differences between Clancy's work and the detective stories of Agatha Christie or the uncanny fiction of Stephen King, which are often placed alongside Clancy's in such indeterminate classifications.

When his first published book, *The Hunt for Red October*, appeared, reviewers found the technical aspects of the novel so impressive and unusual that it seemed that a word had to be coined to describe the type. Although nobody seems to be able to pinpoint the origin of the term "technothriller," Patrick Anderson of the *New York Times* gave that label to Clancy's work in 1988. In Anderson's review, Clancy became the "king" of such fiction. In that same year, Evan Thomas of *Newsweek* described Clancy as the "inventor" of the technothriller, although Clancy himself has said that Michael Crichton's *The Andromeda Strain* is the first technothriller. Nonetheless, Clancy is considered both inventor and king of the genre by many of the reviewers and critics who have interviewed him or written about his novels. The "king" has gained much more territory since the title was first bestowed on him by Anderson. Numerous technothriller books have been written by other novelists, often imitating him, but Clancy does not feel at all threatened by disciples. Within the decade following publication of *The Hunt for Red October*, similar novels became part of literary history. Publishers are eager to print technothrillers for a readership which has a large appetite for the type of fiction that Clancy has made popular. Still, among the crowds of technical writers, Clancy, from 1984 to 1995 the author of eight novels, continues to hold clear title to the crown.

SCIENCE FICTION

A few critics have suggested that Clancy is a science fiction (SF) writer, comparing his work to that of the legendary French novelist Jules Verne. Verne is the parent of technological fiction, although today his fiction is classified as SF. However, it is the technological aspect that has led to the comparison of his novels with Clancy's. Clancy, however, flatly rejects the idea that anything he has done is in the SF mode.

H. G. Wells, perhaps the most significant figure in SF writing, scornfully labeled Verne "a short-term technological popularizer" (Suvin 211). Because of Wells' description, there is some ambiguity about the use of the terms "technological" and "SF." Verne and those who followed his example used advanced technology but also worked with elements we associate with SF, for example, projection into the future. Even though Wells seems disdainful of Verne, he and other innovative and seminal science fiction writers did very much what Verne had with advanced technology, enhancing plots which would be unsuccessful without such technology.

The beginnings of SF go as far back as Plato and continue throughout the centuries with the work of Thomas More, Swift, William Blake, Verne, Wells, Asimov, and many other writers. Science fiction appeared as "fortunate island" stories, utopian and anti-utopian fiction, marvelous voyages, planetary novels, and political works. Although SF has changed throughout the centuries, certain key aspects hold. Science fiction is different from mimetic—imitative and observed forms—of literature in time, place, and character. It has any possible time—present, past, or future. There may be forms of religion and mythic situations, political philosophy and social structures, but they are outside the norm or the known. Although SF is a form of fantasy, within the limits set by the author the story is not ultimately impossible of fulfillment. It is "a realistic irreality, with humanized nonhumans" and "this-worldly Other Worlds" (Suvin:viii). However, supernatural elements of horror, that is, the gothic, are not part of SF.

Science fiction writers reject the ordinary world of reality, creating instead new and strange worlds. Such writers (and many scientists) assume that there are other worlds inhabited by other forms of life. Within the conventions of SF there is no requirement that the writer be positive or negative toward the characters or their worlds, no preconceived notion of success, failure, or achievement. The search is for the unknown and for knowledge that goes beyond learning about character, about who we are or the world we live in. Science fiction characters and their surroundings are imaginary; yet the writer treats them factually and writes of them scientifically, perhaps bringing everything about science into play. Thus, SF is concerned with scientific philosophy, its politics, its psychology, and its anthropology. There is scientific logic in SF, so that it cannot go beyond nature. Although the material may be unrecognizable and unfamiliar to the reader, it is never so estranged as to be impossible to comprehend.

Clancy and Science Fiction

Because other worlds do not enter into Clancy's novels, he sees no fantasy in his work. What he creates is "real" to him, and he insists on his obligation to readers to write about reality, possibility, and probability. No matter that much science fiction has elements of possibility and sometimes probability; Clancy repudiates any resemblance to his work. Yet, examples abound. Clancy writes of some submarine equipment and experimental aircraft as if they were real; yet they do not exist. Further, he suggests that the Russians have developed a system to eliminate U.S. reconnaissance satellites (SDI in *Cardinal*). He treats these as operational actualities, though most experts would quarrel with his interpretation.

In *Red Storm Rising*, the reader accepts as possible, perhaps "real" in an SF sense, the projection of time into a future when a third world war is under way. The novel is both futuristic and scientific. Without the use of every type of technological information superior to that of the enemy, the forces of democracy could not defeat those of totalitarianism, the Soviets. The fact that the enemy is the USSR makes the plot plausible and also acceptably realistic (in a non-SF sense), given the state of the cold war in 1987, when the novel was published. The combination of elements lends itself to at least a partial classification of SF.

From early on, reviewers have spoken of Clancy as prophetic, as one might of a SF writer. Clancy's novels, like SF and some technothrillers, appear prophetic about current and future possibilities of scientific technology. In addition, SF books often involve politics, as do Clancy's, which have a political agenda along with scientific technology and prophetic characteristics. What seems unlikely today in a Clancy book, a science fiction novel, a work of political intrigue, or a technothriller is the reality of tomorrow. What if, as in Verne, a vessel could survive underwater? What if, as in Clancy, satellites and an SDI system could affect future wars and even determine outcomes? There is, however, one major difference between Clancy and SF writers. In science fiction "destiny" is not on anyone's side, although it looms large in technological fiction such as Clancy's, and that is an important distinction between his work and true science fiction.

THE THRILLER

Critics, reviewers, writers, and teachers have difficulty pinning down the word "thriller." Often we use it interchangeably with the terms spy/espionage story because of the many overlapping characteristics. Just as the technothriller may be subsumed by that more general term "thriller," so too may the spy story. However, not all thrillers are either spy or technological novels. They may be both or neither. They are also murder, suspense, or psychological stories. Terminology sometimes can be slippery, and labels often indistinct.

Ralph Harper calls the thriller "crisis literature" (46), claiming that the crises always are about war. Other scholars, though, see additional subjects, often personal and with a variety of landscapes. The landscape may even be limited to the mind of a character. Thriller subjects may range from global situations (suspense thrillers, political thrillers) to individual disturbances (psychological thrillers), from an attack on a vast region to the murder of a person. Nevertheless, according to Harper, the basic issue in the thriller is "death and responsibility" (60). Hostile acts are planned and executed, bringing violence and death as the story is played out. Resolution follows, though not invariably in the form of retribution or punishment.

Scholars disagree about the function of language and the importance of characters in thrillers. Some criticize the simplicity of language and form and the lack of character development typical of most thrillers. As a result, they believe too much attention is given to plot and not enough to character. Yet, another scholarly view holds "that in a thriller 'too much character clutters up the plot.'"[1] Because of the differences it is useful to separate thrillers into categories of "entertainments" (popular fiction) and "high art." For thrillers by such writers as Graham Greene and John Le Carré, the classification "high art" applies because their interest is more in character than in plot, and in style more than suspense. Technothrillers by their very nature are popular fiction. Although at times the two types—popular fiction and high art—merge, generally they are separable.

Few thrillers are high art. Rather, most are popular entertainment and should be evaluated as such, with different measurements applied. Style is as changeable in the two types of thrillers as in unlike genres. Usually the most successful popular thriller style is simple and unsubtle. For the reader to be drawn into the story immediately there must be sufficient familiarity with language and form. Then too, thrillers have particular language patterns. The violent emotion, which is a vital characteristic, requires a flatness of tone with a dual function. It "underlines the violence" as well as serving to contain it (Aisenberg 48). In the most exciting thrillers, the sentences are short, the structures imitative of news reports, frequently with a brevity suggestive of news bites.

Characters in popular art are familiar to readers, and because of their lack of individuality they border on stereotypes. To make them interesting and provocative, yet still generic, the author must create memorable and attention-getting figures, with qualities that attract readers and hold their attention. For that reason thrillers usually have heroes (heroines less often) who are exceptional, even fantastic people with whom most readers want to identify. Brave, dedicated heroes (heroines) represent the reader against deceitful and vicious enemies. Like us, heroes are vulnerable, but, unlike us, they overcome all odds. Heroes have developed over a long period of time and have changed little in basic ways from classical mythical figures to medieval knights to nineteenth-century adventurers. In nineteenth-and early twentieth-century popular fiction the heroes of adventure/suspense/mystery fiction were not professional detectives, policemen, or spies. They were amateurs, perhaps dilettantes, caught up in a situation they previously knew nothing about. Few of them had training to engage in the activities that became their lot. However, the hero was always someone with multiple skills learned perhaps in wartime or in some branch of service. Until shortly before and after the time of World War II, professional agents or investigative figures were rarely depicted in fiction, but the growth of police departments and defense and undercover agencies throughout the century helped create a somewhat different type of hero. Modern warfare also played a part in making the hero an informed and knowledgeable professional. Nevertheless, the contemporary thriller hero still carries the marks of the traditional figure.

Thriller heroes rarely take on their tasks for money, even though they are paid for their activities. Some become involved for excitement, some to protect people, some to fulfill their sense of duty or social responsibility. But the major function of the thriller hero usually is the righting or prevention of wrongs, whether his country, a group, or an individual has been attacked or injured. The hero's role may change from novel to novel and even within the same novel. He may be either the hunter or the hunted. (Clancy's heroes fill both roles.) Whatever task he has, he is expected to perform honorably and loyally, even if he has to commit acts he may not approve of, be forced to play a deceptive game, or get involved in the deaths of innocent people. In one way or another, the hero is a vulnerable man. Guilt, as well as danger, is something he may always have to live with. No matter how he attempts to avoid danger, he is never free. Not only can he not escape his own fate, he may bring danger, pain, and suffering to those he loves.

Clancy and the Thriller

In a number of ways, Clancy's novels make a perfect fit as thriller, even though "technothriller" is a more exact term. Most of his novels have the large landscape of war that Harper considers a requirement for thrillers. His wars may not invariably be shooting wars, but wars they are. There is the cold war of *The Hunt for Red October*. The wars of terrorists are central to *Patriot Games* and *The Sum of All Fears*. Drug wars propel the action of *Clear and Present Danger,* and both drug wars and a shooting war are at the heart of *Without Remorse*. Economic war is related to actual warfare in *Debt of Honor*. Furthermore, Clancy's pages are brimming over with death and responsibility, elements that Harper considers essential. In all Clancy's work, violence in some form brings on death to large or small groups of people. Responsibility for hostile acts is always clear, so that the reader knows from the start where the blame lies, and it is never with "us"—the "good guys."

Clancy's novels, like most popular thrillers, have certainty in them. A single-minded philosophy puts the United States, its military, and preselected individuals in the good category and the opposition in the bad. No shades of gray are sketched in. Although Clancy's world is technologically complex, his "friendly forces" characters, as well as the private and public world they live in, are not. They are "our" people, knowable and dependable. We can count on them to bring about justice as we understand it.

The heroes of Clancy's fiction risk their lives in the manner of medieval knights, even though at first nothing signals their special qualities. They may prefer to stay at home in a safe environment, doing familiar, enjoyable work, but when duty requires something else, they do it bravely. Toland in *Red Storm Rising* is an example. Ryan, the major Clancy hero, may be terrified of flying, but he does it anyway, just as he automatically risks his life again and again in dangerous situations. Ryan behaves that way from the moment he is introduced in *Red October* and on through each successive novel. There are also examples of ordinary, decent men who do not seem at first to have any of the makings of a hero. Yet, when events test them, they become leaders of men and saviors of women. Edwards, the meteorologist in *Red Storm Rising*, is that type of man. He would rather die than be a James Bond who secretly thrills to the idea of "the tang of rape" (*Casino Royale:* 157). Clancy's heroes do not have such thoughts. They are men set apart from others, superior to those around them. Nevertheless, almost always they work within the establishment.

Jack Ryan, though individualized in memorable ways, comes through the traditional line of thriller novels and is an amalgam of traits of prior figures. Like sleuths and agents of early suspense fiction, Ryan has not chosen as his vocation any form of secret or investigative work, but it finds him. Although he differs from the low-key hero of some of the 1920s–30s Golden Age English detective, he does have a number of resemblances. (It is not surprising that we think of English figures, for both author and his hero show great affection for all things English.) The famed English writer Dorothy Sayers' Lord Peter Wimsey, for example, is rich, intelligent, well educated, a university graduate. He served and was injured in World War I, is an amateur sleuth but plays a role in government intelligence. Jack Ryan is also rich, well educated, successful even when he least expects it, a failure at nothing, a former marine, and involved in intelligence. In yet another bow to the English heroes, Clancy has the queen reward an exploit of Ryan's by dubbing him Sir Ryan.

When introduced in Clancy's first thriller, Ryan thinks of himself as an average citizen, a teacher/scholar. Of course the experienced thriller reader knows and expects him to be anything but average. With each book Ryan becomes more like the superstars of other thriller novels. He soon gives up his enjoyable teaching position to work for the CIA, and his exploits begin to rival those of any thriller hero. Not only does he place himself in harm's way but unwittingly does the same with his family. Family attachments also put him in greater danger. In *Patriot Games* when wife Caroline (Cathy) and daughter Sally are seriously injured by terrorists seeking vengeance on Ryan himself, he takes actions that he would not have followed had they not been attacked. Like other thriller heroes he refuses to let the law do all the work, and he throws himself into the center of action. He wins out, but there is a price, and over time, that is, over a ten-year series of novels, he changes. The quiet, cool-headed man of the first book becomes secretive, extremely active, and even explosive as he ages. With each novel we also see a more cynical Ryan, the result of his exposure to evil men and philosophy.

THE SPY NOVEL

Another applicable description of Clancy's work is "spy novel." Lest someone protest that Clancy is not a spy writer, we have only to consider LeRoy Panek's judgment that a work is a spy novel if there is a single spy in it. Furthermore, that view is bolstered by Marc Cerasini's essay in *The Tom Clancy Companion.* In writing about "the birth of a genre," Cerasini describes Clancy's fusion of "military fiction with near-future apocalyptic science fiction, touches of espionage fiction, and a large dose of social realism" (25). Those "touches of espionage fiction" in Clancy's work require consideration of the features of spy stories if we are to place it completely.

Critics assign different dates to the "first" or most important British spy novel, which is the true ancestor of American espionage fiction, even though occasionally someone will name the American James Fenimore Cooper's *The Spy* (1821) as the earliest example of the genre. Historians have said spying came about as early as the Middle Ages. Nevertheless, actual spies did not have the romantic aura that fiction conferred on them with the development of the spy novel in the nineteenth century. Scholars agree that spy stories are linked to the Industrial Revolution, which occurred in Great Britain and parts of Europe before the United States. As Britain became highly industrialized, its weaponry, naval power, and eventually its airplanes were seen as a threat, as well as a source of envy to foreign powers. Spying took on an important role in reality and in fiction.

Modern thriller/espionage writers (as well as detective story writers) are indebted to a number of nineteenth-and early twentieth-century authors who created the form. According to some scholars, the prolific novelist William LeQueux is said to have provided the major guidelines of the spy novel, in spite of the unreadability of most of his work. LeQueux's importance to the development of espionage fiction also comes through what Panek calls his "pseudo-histories." These resemble war prophecy novels and argue "for military preparedness" (8). Although LeQueux was writing at the turn of the nineteenth century, his indirect effect may be seen in later writers who in turn influenced Clancy. LeQueux's work also suffers from what Panek calls "the worst brand of Victorian sentiment" (9). Sentiment, however, is not unique to LeQueux. Inasmuch as he is hardly the only author whose novels become mired in embarrassing mawkishness, we can't trace that tendency in Clancy back to LeQueux alone.

Also among the forerunners of the modern spy novel is the work of E. Phillips Oppenheimer, which provided one particular type of motif we find in Clancy. That is Oppenheimer's variation on the war prophecy novel, "prediction of an averted war instead of an actual one" (Panek 18). Oppenheimer's spy fiction takes on issues common to both the war prophecy novel and the averted war novel, issues that Clancy makes use of also. Both novelists show concern about the sufficiency of defense, the strength and weaknesses of military preparedness, and secret weapons.

Most scholars agree that the first "good" spy fiction is a war prophecy novel, *The Riddle of the Sands,* written by Erskine Childers in 1903. Critic/ novelist Julian Symons states it is that novel which established a double standard for spying. Enemy spies have evil motives, whereas "we" have only worthy intentions (234). (Depending on who the novelist is, the "we" may differ. In *Riddle of the Sands* it is the British, and in most spy fiction by English or

---

162   Critical Insights

American writers, their compatriots are the worthy "we.") Symons claims that the duality of the moral problem—we are good, they are bad—existed only through the first few decades of the twentieth century, coming to an end with the work of Eric Ambler. His position is belied not only by a reading of Clancy's novels but also by an examination of the varieties of fiction of the years following World War II.

The most important writer for our consideration of the "development of the spy novel or the detective novel" (and for examination of Clancy's relationship to them) is John Buchan. "The modern novel of espionage simply would not have developed along the same lines without him" (Panek 39). Even today his novels continue to exert their influence on mystery—spy/thriller/adventure novels, and "in its best manifestations the spy novel returns to him" (Panek 66). Even novelist John Le Carré tips his hat to the great earlier writer by using a Buchan title in one of his own books.

Like thrillers, all spy fiction is not the same. Several literary historians have called attention to two clear divisions in the spy fiction genre. One is in the heroic, conservative, traditional camp. The other is realistic and ironic, in the mode of modern fiction. The first, as defined by Symons, supports "authority," asserting "that agents are fighting to protect something valuable." He describes the other type as "radical, critical of authority," with claims "that agents perpetuate, and even create, false barriers between 'us' and 'them'" (243). Other critics note that the traditional archetypal form has more violence, as well as more vitality and hope than the later one. The earlier type generally has a happy and conclusive ending, much like the novels of the Victorian Age. All loose ends are tied, all issues settled, if only temporarily. The realistic spy novel with its antiheroes, its darkness, and sense of despair is much closer in tone to modern and postmodern thought. Not surprisingly, the spy novel that utilizes traditional motifs (even with updated variations) is the one that is most successful commercially even though it is the other type that literary pundits find more meaningful.

Clancy and the Spy Novel

By the 1980s the time was right for Clancy's unique blending of modes, the uniquely modern and the traditional. In traditional ways his work bears multiple resemblances to Buchan's. Both Buchan's novels and Clancy's are realistic in their use of actual historical events, but both mix them with fabricated incidents. Buchan's chief character Richard Hannay is, like the later Jack Ryan, a series figure. The two, who look and sound like the typical English or American reader, are a meld of romantic and ordinary figure. Buchan's fiction is a form of "Victorian" schoolboy literature, that is, it focuses on adventure, morality, heroism, and friendship. These same characteristics, though updated, are central to Clancy's work. Also notable in Buchan's novels is "the absence of believable, complete women characters" (Panek 45). Though hardly a remarkable characteristic in any spy novels, it is another resemblance between Buchan and Clancy's fiction. Finally, one small link that seems appropriate to Buchan but somewhat entertaining in Clancy: Buchan's characters have memories of grouse shooting. Sir Jack Ryan also has such memories.

THE TECHNOTHRILLER

Critics combined the words technology and thriller into "technothriller" to give a more precise definition to another variation in genre. The term "thriller" by itself does not suggest the differences in technological fiction. Although there is much overlapping of characteristics, the technological novel has some distinctive traits of its own.

Technothrillers are not completely the product of the modern age but have become significant additions to popular literature with the phenomenal advance of technology in the second half of the twentieth century. Contemporary writers have made use of technology unknown before the Second World War. These technothriller novelists build their work around technology that is both current and projected or futuristic. Every manner of complex machines, usually real but sometimes imagined, is fodder for the work. The technothriller may focus on any area from ocean to outer space. It may concern all forms of nuclear weaponry, missiles, submarines, aircraft. Perhaps it foregrounds computers that reach beyond human ability to solve problems. Laboratories with scientists—biologists, chemists, physicists, archaeologists—study unknown and as yet unsolved questions of existence, DNA, germs, viruses, extinct species.

In addition to the resemblances of technothriller to thriller fiction, there is sometimes the reminder of SF, and not only in the futuristic element. Still, some important distinctions exist. Unlike SF, the technothriller world is earthbound although its machines go out into space. It is the world the reader knows, even if its complexities are baffling. It is not the estranged world of SF. Scholars point out that characters in technothrillers are usually less interesting than the technology. However, people in technothrillers are recognizable humans, different from the fantasized, imaginary, or robotics figures of SF.

Although people are necessary to put things into motion (the thriller aspect), the plot in a technothriller depends more on advanced technology than on human character. Technothrillers are often a form of military fiction, with players who are soldiers, sailors, pilots. The novel serves as a subordinate backdrop to display advancements and projections of weaponry and war. Actual war, possible war, or averted war is fought on the pages of the technothriller. However, war is not limited to mass destruction of a martial nature. There may be other kinds of war, perhaps a financial war, dependent on modern technology, which could destroy the world economy. The crises and solutions in most technothrillers are mechanical. People may make mistakes, but the focus of the plot is on the machinery not on human limitations. The "good" characters in technothrillers are clearly delineated, are on the "right" side and, in the military fiction, are superpatriots. Invariably, the cast of characters is large. Although there may be a single traditional hero, the wide scope of the playing field requires a great many people, so many in fact that often they seem as faceless as their machines.

Clancy and the Technothriller

No matter how much technology dominates his books, Clancy's basic formula comes from the thriller. The fact that he sees himself as a writer of political thrillers further emphasizes the point that the thriller model is the primary one he has followed. Yet, his fiction has some SF connections and is especially close to espionage novels in its inclusion of spies, and, as critic William Ryan calls them, "other mavens of espionage" (26). However, Clancy's enjoyment of gadgets, his early reading of SF stories, including those filled with gadgetry, his monitoring of scientific developments, his fascination with computers, his admiration for all things military, and his very strong sense of patriotism connect him to the technothriller.

Marc Cerasini provides some background for Clancy's work, by describing the fiction and films that preceded his novels. He tells of the changing attitudes of the second half of this century: "Traditional war novels, tales of personal heroism and self-sacrifice that reinforced higher values of social responsibility, the type of fiction characteristic of the years following the Second World War, were replaced with a fiction of cynicism and defeat" (7). Antiwar novels and movies became popular for a time, one result of the unpopularity of the Vietnam War. But, even during the war, SF writers were creating promilitary novels and cleverly disguised war films. Cerasini writes that "Star Wars" is really a "reincarnation" of "unabashedly patriotic films of the 1940s." Filmmaker George Lucas, claims Cerasini, made "the villains clear-cut fascists, the good guys honest and noble" (8). Similar films proved popular, and novels moved in the direction of technology and politics.

By the 1980s the time was ripe for the fiction of Clancy. All his novels employ technology, even *Patriot Games,* which the novelist considers a love story. Like the work of other technothriller writers, almost everything in Clancy's plots and their central episodes depends on advanced technology. For Clancy, like many other contemporary technothriller writers, that technology involves military matters. Because of that identification he has been described as "the novelist laureate of the military industrial complex" (R. Thomas 1).

His multiple characters are often flat and subordinate to the technology. Aside from his alter-ego character, Jack Ryan, and his other favorite, John Kelly (Clark), Clancy's people are types rather than individuals. Some reviewers also classify Ryan and Kelly that way, comments that anger the author greatly. He is exasperated by critics who describe his machines as more interesting, complex, and lifelike than his characterizations. He angrily defends his portrayal of characters. Even if he scoffs at the word "literature," and at critics, he wants to be known as a writer who understands everything about his creations. In his determination to make his people real, he provides family background, wives, children, a few friends. However, the same flatness of characterization pervasive in most technothriller writing holds for these. Rarely do the families come alive. The wives and children are too perfect, friends too understanding, invariably good-humored and supportive. But the humanizing element in his characters (and a quality that adds to suspense) is that they can occasionally make mistakes. They misread, or overlook, or make a poor judgment that leads to serious consequences. Still, the effect of such action is seen to propel plot, not to alter or develop character. The military and government agents in the author's drama do not change with success or failure.

CONCLUSION

All the many facets of Clancy's work may explain the esteem in which it is held by readers, and also the less praiseful attitudes of most literary critics. While Clancy is an innovative and exciting writer in modern technological ways, paradoxically he is at the same time a traditional one. It is not pejorative to call his work formula writing. The entertainment technothriller, thriller, spy story always adheres to formula in language, plot, images and symbols. We readers like the assurance of that familiarity, while at the same time we want something new added in character or situation or "filler." (The filler is sometimes called "unbound motifs," that is, absorbing and interesting information but unnecessary to the progression of the story.) The pleasure readers gain from formula writing is the repetition of something we have experienced and enjoyed before, but with the excitement of newness. It might be the new plot or setting, or more about the serial hero, of whom we know much, yet never enough. We want to be told what he eats, drinks, drives, wears, what he feels about the world in which he functions. And, with all that, in such entertainments there is the promise of a complex world made comprehensible.

In Clancy's novels political views are central and powerful. He stirs old and new fears of the Russian bear, the Red menace, creeping communism, Asians and Latins, all these personified through evil characters. The enemy is known wherever or whenever he or she appears. The reader's apprehensions and the writer's become one. They are voiced by Fleming Meeks, who tells us Clancy plays on our "deep-seated geopolitical fears" as he "spins scary scenarios of world chaos" (42). Works become popular when the reader shares or sympathizes with the point of view and feels a kinship to all or most of the values. Clancy brings about most of these responses in readers, who cannot wait for each new book to appear.

Then why the attacks of some reviewers on such popular material? To answer that, we might consider a comment made by Kingsley Amis about hostility to the James Bond novels of Ian Fleming. They, the critics, are angered, says Amis, by the "attraction of something one disapproves of" (x). But few readers disapprove. For most, the use of formula brings the reassurance of safety even as the real or fictional world explodes. Our various repressed needs and longings are served. Many of us have an unconscious desire for danger and excitement, perhaps even violence, though in reality most of us do everything to avoid involvement. Through thrillers/ spy novels we can cross the boundaries of actual life into the world of the forbidden or unattainable. In our escape into the fantasized world we find wish fulfillment. We can confront our foes, knowing someone else will act for us and win. Our hero—ourself—will live to fight another day. Then, as the poet A. E. Housman tells us, we'll "see the world as the world's not" and ourselves as "sterling lad[s]" ("Terence, This Is Stupid Stuff").

The experience is cathartic. Whether we can finally decide that there is a single label for Clancy's work doesn't matter. Rather it is our understanding of the ways the pieces of the puzzle fit together to make up the world of Clancy's fiction.

Note:

1. This is a line by Dilys Powell that Julian Symons quotes on p. 235 of Mortal Consequences.

Garson, Helen S. "1. About Tom Clancy." In *Tom Clancy: A Critical Companion*. Santa Barbara, CA: Greenwood, 1996. http://ebooks.abc-clio.com/reader.aspx?isbn=9780313008375&id=20005D80-1. Reprinted with permission.

The Life of Robin Cook _____

Lorena Laura Stookey

The publication of *The Year of the Intern* in 1972 signaled the beginning of Dr. Robin Cook's long and successful career as a premonitory voice in popular culture. Writing from the authority of his position within the medical profession, Cook has secured a reputation as today's foremost practitioner of the contemporary fiction genre known as the medical thriller. To date, Cook has written seventeen novels. Fifteen of these books, most of them best-sellers, offer cautionary and suspenseful tales of conspiracy and intrigue set within the worlds of medicine or medical research. While Cook's fiction is written primarily to entertain his many avid readers, his novels, as a review of *Vital Signs* in *Publishers Weekly* aptly noted, are also "designed, in part, to keep the public aware of both the technological possibilities of modern medicine and the ensuing ethical problems" (Steinberg, 1990, 55).

Cook's career as writer of the medical thriller runs parallel to the recent growth of public interest in the field of medicine itself. For Cook's readers, a friendly and familiar figure once known as "Doc" (the bearer of the ubiquitous black bag) has faded into legend. The black bag has long since given way to medical technology, and the ancient art of healing has been broadly named—with obvious significance—the "health care industry." An industry indeed, incorporating private insurance plans and Medicare and Medicaid, emergency rooms, specialty clinics, for-profit hospitals, and medical teaching facilities. Pharmaceutical companies are part of the health care industry, as are the laboratories where medical research is conducted. Preventive medicine is an important concern within the burgeoning industry, and numerous varieties of alternative medicine have also attracted public attention. In one form or another, the health care industry commands a significant portion of the nation's economy and work force. With the high costs of medicine ever continuing to rise, the industry itself has become the subject of a national debate.

It is in the context of this general debate that Cook's literary contributions have assumed a special relevance. Other physicians, notably William Carlos Williams, Oliver Sacks, and Richard Selzer, have written insightfully about the medical profession; in both stories and essays, these writing doctors have shared poignant moments—triumphant ones or painful ones—garnered from their wisdom and experience. This literature offers laypersons an opportunity to see a side of medicine that is otherwise not generally available to them. The same can be said for Robin Cook's suspense fiction, though it is written from a different angle. In setting out to surprise, shock, and entertain his reading audience, Cook makes use of the popular narrative genres to draw the attention of an exceedingly broad reading audience. The platform of the thriller novel lets him engage ideological issues in a highly dramatic fashion. He, too, reveals dimensions of the world of medicine that lie beyond most readers' direct experience—with the express intention of encouraging them to become involved in the debates being carried out in Congress and in the press. As he stated in a 1983 interview for *Health* magazine: "The public is more powerful now. We've lived through an age of consumerism. I believe that medicine is just as amenable to that kind of approach. I would like to see more consumerism in medicine. I think it's perhaps the only way to goad this enormous inertial mass known as medicine into changing itself" (Grossmann, 57). In choosing the medium of popular literature, Cook strives to democratize an interest that many people have hitherto thought to be arcane. His timely fiction appeals to a reading audience that has grown increasingly conscious of the major role that health care issues have come to play in public life.

Cook is deeply committed to situating his interest in medical policies and practices within the larger context of contemporary culture. He is, for example, especially concerned about the effects of marketplace motivations on the health care industry. Many of his novels therefore explore, from one perspective or another, questions of the economy of medicine. When medicine's economy intersects with that of the law, as it clearly does in instances of personal injury claims or malpractice litigation, Cook focuses his social critique on the law. His overviews of the workings of social institutions such as medicine and law dramatically reveal many of the ways in which the self-interests of these professions impinge upon the public welfare.

In addition to matters of economic interest, the novels consider numerous current social problems. Cook is attentive to women's issues: to women's positions in the health science workplace and to their treatment by the medical profession. He is concerned about society's widespread use of drugs and about the health threats posed by industrial pollution. He enjoys engaging the ethical problems that medicine's new technologies have inevitably raised—questions about genetic engineering, for example, or in vitro fertilization or experiments with fetal tissue. His first best-seller, *Coma*, raises the problematic issue of organ transplants, suggesting by means of its startling plot that clearly time has come for a drastic revision of social attitudes about the collection and use of human organs. Always carefully researched, the subjects of Cook's medical thrillers offer his readers much to ponder. Because he characteristically uses the technical terminology employed by members of the medical profession, his books are also instructive, providing his reading audience with an authentic vision of the world of contemporary medicine.

Born May 4, 1940, in New York City, Robert Brian (shortened to Robin) Cook spent his childhood years in Leonia, New Jersey, a community that receives mention in a couple of his books. His father, Edgar Lee Cook, was a commercial artist and businessman. His mother, Audrey (Koons) Cook, has apparently been a particularly significant figure in Cook's life—he appreciatively dedicated both *Outbreak* and *Harmful Intent* to her. Robin Cook has an older brother, Lee, and a younger sister, Laurie. *(Mortal Fear* is dedicated to Cook's siblings with a heartfelt expression of his esteem and affection.)

As a young child, the winsome Robin Cook modeled toddler's fashions, but his first great enthusiasm was for archaeology, the subject he knowledgeably explores in his third work of fiction, *Sphinx*. As its title indicates, he was especially fascinated by the wonders of ancient Egypt, and as a youth regularly visited the mummy rooms of Manhattan's Metropolitan Museum—where he was, in fact, inspired to commit to memory the names of the rulers of all the Egyptian dynasties. This early interest in the lore of Egypt has remained a lifelong passion, one that indeed received expression in the only one of Cook's seventeen novels to date that is not set within the world of medicine.

Readers of his books will readily note that Robin Cook's first and third novels are anomalous in respect to the rest of his fiction. The largely autobiographical first book, *The Year of the Intern*, is not a thriller, and *Sphinx*, which is unquestionably a suspense novel (one that even features a double conspiracy plot), is not a medical thriller. Appearing in the wake of the popular success and critical acclaim that attended the publication of his second novel, *Coma*, *Sphinx* spent seven weeks on the best-seller list and was also adapted for the screen. The movie, in whose production Cook took no part at all, was not the success that the movie version of *Coma* had been, and reviews of the novel itself were decidedly mixed. It is quite apparent that, after writing *Coma*, Cook used his newly acquired facility with the suspense genre to write a novel that paid homage to his fascination with mysteries of the past. After experimenting, however, with a thriller that featured black market intrigue in the smuggling of Egyptian antiquities, Cook chose to return to his fictional exploration of a variety of medical issues, and it is this specialized focus that has come to distinguish his work within the body of contemporary suspense literature.

Sphinx's plot is an intricate one, providing room for Cook to play with standard conventions of the suspense novel, and the book is of general interest to his readers in two other noteworthy respects. In the figure of its central character, Erica Baron, it offers an example of a strong female protagonist, and in its "lovingly detailed and sensuous descriptions of Cairo, Luxor, and Egypt's holy places" (Aldridge, 36), it captures an atmosphere of place that can be favorably compared with the realistic effects that the writer characteristically achieves in his representations of hospital settings. *Sphinx*'s ingenious plot, based on the notion that the undisturbed tomb of another Egyptian ruler, Seti I, actually lies hidden beneath the familiar tomb of King Tutankhamen, proved to be of timely interest to many readers, for the book was published around the time artifacts from Tutankhamen's tomb were on exhibition in the United States.

Although his obsession with archaeology predated his interest in medicine, the latter passion also emerged early in Robin Cook's life. Indeed, it was at age fifteen, after he had witnessed a football injury at Leonia High School, that he determined that he would become a doctor. Cook graduated from Connecticut's Wesleyan University with a B.A. in premed in 1962. He then attended Columbia University's College of Physicians and Surgeons, receiving an M.D. in 1966. (Cook's summer job during his years at Columbia was a particularly interesting one: traveling each summer to Monaco, he served as a lab assistant to Jacques Cousteau; readers can see a reference to Cook's scuba diving experiences in *Vital Signs*, where one character is devoured by an immense white shark while diving off Australia's Great Barrier Reef.) While Cook found his university experiences at Wesleyan immensely stimulating, he has frequently criticized the ways advanced medical education is organized, believing that medical schools have "a tendency to stay in the past" (Grossmann, 56). The critique of medicine that is sounded throughout his literary career therefore first began to take shape while he was still a medical student.

In 1966 Cook became a surgical resident at Queen's Hospital in Honolulu, Hawaii; he remained at this post until 1968, later using his own experiences there as the inspiration for his first book, the insightful study of the institution of medical residency entitled *The Year of the Intern*. Deeply disturbed by the exhausting regimen of residency (or internship, as it was then called), and thoughtfully concerned about the ways this form of apprenticeship might in fact be counterproductive as a tool for training doctors, Cook felt compelled to find a way to express his thoughts on the subject. The opportunity arose during his stint in the U.S. Navy, where he served from 1969 to 1971 (eventually becoming lieutenant commander). Assigned to the USS *Kamehameha*, a Polaris submarine, Cook actually wrote his first novel, as he says, "under the Pacific Ocean" *(The Year of the Intern*, hereafter cited as *TYOTI*). Asked by an interviewer for *Contemporary Authors* (hereafter cited as *CA*) whether he had ever given thought to writing a novel before seizing the opportunity he enjoyed aboard the submarine, Cook acknowledged that he had wanted to begin writing while he was still in medical school, but that he had not had time. Then, the opportunity presented itself, and, as Cook said, "I didn't really know if I was going to be able to write one, but I assumed that I was" (*CA*, 119).

Although this first book, published when Cook returned to civilian life, was very well received, it did not enjoy as wide a circulation as he had hoped. Cook had a message he wanted to deliver (in fact, in 1973, the year following the publication of *The Year of the Intern*, he summarized its sentiments in "My Turn," *Newsweek*'s regular guest opinion column), and he now needed to find a way to appeal to a broader reading audience. Readers of *The Year of the Intern* had certainly included people with a specialized interest in the practice of medicine (it was recommended reading for both established doctors and doctors-to-be), but Cook was determined to write a novel that would catch the eye of the general public. With this ambition in mind, he set out to discover the secrets of successful popular fiction. Hoping to produce a best-seller himself, he spent six months in 1975 reading and analyzing best-sellers (over one hundred of them, in fact). Cook's reading suggested to him that the mystery-thriller genre would be likely to "capture the interest of the largest number of people" (*World Authors*, 183), and he therefore decided to write one, drawing upon his own special expertise through the use of a medical setting. The result of Cook's efforts was *Coma*, a best-seller that was also made into a successful motion picture.

"Learning to write a best-seller ," Cook later told *People* magazine, was "like teaching yourself to wire a house" (Jennes, 65). Having successfully published his first novel, he was unaware, until he wrote *Coma*, of how truly difficult it generally is to break into the highly competitive popular market. In fact, reflecting upon the earlier publication of *The Year of the Intern*, he commented to *Health* magazine's John Grossmann: "If I had known then what I know now—that the chances of a first-time author getting published are about as good as winning the state lottery—I don't think I would have attempted the book. I thought you simply wrote a book, sent it in, three weeks later it was in the bookstores, people ran and bought it, and then you went on the Johnny Carson show. I was very lucky" (Grossmann, 56). If Cook was lucky with *The Year of the Intern*, by the time he was ready to seek a publisher for *Coma* he had found a narrative formula that was probably guaranteed to win him success. His setting was marvelously authentic, his subject matter explosive, and, as Charles J. Keffer of *Best Sellers* observed, "I do not think anyone can beat the suspense and the story line developed throughout this novel. It is so close to the truth that one has to reinvestigate the title page to be sure that it really did say 'A novel by Robin Cook'" (*Contemporary Literary Criticism*, 131). *Coma* found readers of the thriller genre ready to embrace the possibilities of medical intrigue.

Before he was drafted into the navy, Cook had served his medical internship in general surgery. When he returned to civilian life, he decided to specialize in eye surgery, and therefore took up a residency in ophthalmology at the Massachusetts Eye and Ear Infirmary (an institution affiliated with Harvard Medical School). Cook was a resident there from 1971 to 1975. When his residency was completed, he opened a private practice near Boston and also joined the teaching staff at Massachusetts Eye and Ear. (Later, when he decided to commit more time to writing, he took a leave of absence from his Harvard teaching appointment.) Readers might be interested to note that two of Cook's villainous doctors, *Outbreak*'s Ralph Hempston and *Blindsight*'s Jordan Scheffield, are themselves ophthalmologists. Additionally, the medicine of the eye is featured in a couple of Cook's thriller plots. *Blindsight*'s central action is concerned with the great demand for cornea transplants, and, in *Mortal Fear*, where unsuspecting victims are administered a dose of a sinister "death hormone," the deadly substance is cunningly introduced into patients' bodies through the mucous membrane of their eyes. In Cook's most recent novel, *Contagion*, the central character is an opthalmologist who has been driven from private practice by a profit-oriented medical corporation.

Remarkably, Robin Cook wrote his second, third, and fourth novels while both maintaining his private practice and serving on the staff at the Massachusetts Eye and Ear Infirmary. Cook acknowledges that he writes rapidly (*The Year of the Intern* and *Coma* were reputedly drafted in six weeks and *Sphinx* in ninety days), but it is also likely that the disciplined habits he acquired while studying and practicing medicine have in fact served him well as a writer. When asked by an interviewer for *Contemporary Authors* whether it was difficult to establish a writing routine while practicing medicine full time, Cook answered that in his experience the two activities seemed to complement one another. "Medicine," he stated, "is a very episodic type of phenomenon where every fifteen minutes or so you're being faced with another problem to solve; you're making decisions, interacting with people all the time. Writing is just the opposite. You're sitting in your own room surrounded by your own objects, by yourself, for protracted periods of time. In a way I think the two things are compatible" (*CA*, 119).

After the publication of *Brain*, Cook decided to take an extended leave of absence from the active practice of medicine, and it now appears that he no longer intends to return to his original occupation. He has busied himself in the meantime with the prodigious task of researching and writing thirteen additional medical thrillers, and he remains an outspoken advocate for medical reform. His favorite reading, he recently informed the editor of *Reader's Digest Condensed Books*, remains the *New England Journal of Medicine*.

Cook's reading habits and longtime interest in all manner of medical issues keep him well abreast of new developments in his field, and he delights in opportunities to speculate about future trends in his profession. Indeed, in a 1989 interview for *Omni*, Cook had some startling predictions to make:

> Although we're going to see dramatic improvements in transplantation during the next ten or fifteen years, genetic manipulation is going to make organ transplants seem terribly old-fashioned. It will also cause most of modern medicine, perhaps even doctors, to become obsolete. The real physicians, in fact, will likely be genetic engineers.

I also believe that viruses are going to be useful in the genetic-engineering revolution. We're going to see a change in our perception of viruses. We'll no longer view them as some sort of inimical enemy. They may be much more helpful than we realize (Bryant, 22).

These intriguing predictions notwithstanding, Cook knows that issues surrounding organ transplants, viruses, and genetic engineering all lend themselves to suspenseful treatment in the hands of the writer of medical thrillers, and thus takes up these matters in *Coma, Outbreak,* and *Mutation.* He also has some thoughtful observations to make about cancer treatment, a subject he explores in both *Fever* and *Terminal.* As he told John Grossmann, "I think the major problem in cancer research is the system: The drug firms want the cure for cancer to be a white powder they can patent. I think the solution will come through prevention and an immunological approach, which are less likely to have that kind of economic impact. This is where I'd like to see the research concentrated" (Grossmann, 57).

Besides keeping up with developments within his field and conceiving plots for chilling thrillers, Cook enjoys refurbishing and decorating houses or apartments. He maintains homes in Boston and Naples, Florida, and has recently redecorated an apartment in New York City's Trump Tower. His current interest in architecture and decor is in fact given expression in a recent novel, *Acceptable Risk.* There his protagonist discovers that she too is fascinated by old buildings and by the creative challenges inherent in tackling problems of renovation and artful decoration. When he is not busy pursuing one of his many creative inclinations, Cook enjoys playing tennis, skiing, or organizing a pickup game of basketball at Columbia University's medical school gym (which is now called the Robin Cook Gymnasium in honor of the benefactor who arranged for its complete renovation). Basketball, as it turns out, is also an interest that Cook has found means to incorporate in his fiction. In a truly fascinating way, his perceptive study of the social conventions that inform playground basketball in New York's inner city plays an important role in *Contagion,* his latest thriller.

Twice married, Cook has no children. His first wife was a young Scandinavian woman whom he had met while working with Jacques Cousteau in Europe. They were married in 1968 and divorced only a few months later. A relationship that "was more romantic than practical" (Jennes, 65), as Cook later revealed to Gail Jennes, it came to an end just before he was drafted. In 1979 Cook married Barbara Ellen Mougin, an actress and model who served as the inspiration for his characterization of Denise Sanger, a central figure in his fourth novel, *Brain*. An end to this marriage, which was apparently a very happy one for several years, is seemingly signaled on the acknowledgments page of *Mortal Fear*, where Cook thanks the many friends who offered him support during "difficult" times.

To date, two of Robin Cook's novels, *Coma* and *Sphinx*, have been made into large screen motion pictures, and three others, *Mortal Fear, Outbreak* (renamed *Virus*), and *Terminal* have been specifically produced for television audiences. His fiction has been translated into Spanish, and many of his books are available on audiocassettes. Cook, a widely recognized figure within the contemporary literary scene, serves on *The American Heritage College Dictionary*'s select Usage Panel.

Robin Cook's Autobiographical First Novel

The Year of the Intern, written before Robin Cook determined that he would learn how to write a thriller novel, is intended to be an exposé of the "adverse environment" (*TYOTI*, 2) that he sees as a condition of the institution of medical internship. The novel is thus passionately earnest, indeed polemical, in its tone, and it is clear that when Cook wrote it, he had hopes that his poignant account of the ways the internship experience works to demoralize and harden idealistic young doctors might excite members of his profession to institute a change. Cook was, in this respect, somewhat disappointed, for although he was invited to be a keynote speaker at a subsequent conference on medical education, the book "didn't cause any particular movement to look into these things" (*CA*, 119). In Cook's opinion, the medical internship unfortunately remains a "kind of a hazing year" (*CA*, 119). Later on in his writing career, when he chose to master the possibilities of the suspense genre, Cook found a very different means to voice an exposé.

Dedicated to "the ideal of medicine we all held the year we entered medical school," Cook's first novel recounts the disillusioning experiences of one Dr. Peters (interestingly, a first name is never offered), intern at a community teaching hospital in Hawaii. It is the only one of Cook's seventeen novels to date to employ a first person narrative voice. The central character (generally called the protagonist) addresses the reader with an intimacy that is appropriate to the story he has to tell. The novel, which begins on the fifteenth day of Dr. Peters' internship, is divided into three sections that correspond to the different medical rotations that comprise the surgical intern's hospital assignments over the course of a year. Thus the first section, "General Surgery," relates Peters' initial experiences as an acting physician. The second section, called "Emergency Room," begins on the 172nd day of his internship, and the third section, "General Surgery: Private Teaching Service," takes up Peters' story on his 307th day of service. A concluding section, "Leaving," summarizes Dr. Peters' feelings on the 365th day, as he happily passes his responsibilities on to another beginning intern, the eager and idealistic Dr. Straus. And thus, as the book's ending suggests, the grueling, exhausting, and enervating cycle of medical internship will begin anew. The question that hangs in the air almost seems to answer itself: will Dr. Straus, after his year of internship has passed, emerge with his hopes and his high ideals intact?

The Year of the Intern marks Cook's first use of the episodic structure of plot development that he employs with such notable success within his suspense fiction. In this first novel, where plot is mainly a recounting of a series of unrelated events (events that Cook describes as "a synthesis of my own experiences and those of my fellow interns" [*TYOTI*, 2]), there is admittedly little occasion for the writer to demonstrate the skill that will later be his hallmark. Nonetheless, the story convincingly portrays the gradual transformation of an empathetic young doctor into something of a cynic, and in the closing pages of the book this change is emphatically registered upon the reader through Cook's use of a shrewd plotting device: with a wonderfully delicate touch, he repeats the moving scene with which his novel opened. This time, however, he places Dr. Peters in the position of detached observer of an event that less than a year earlier he had himself experienced with a great deal of pain and confusion. By the end of his internship, Dr. Peters has forgotten the immense trepidation he had felt the first time he "had been faced with the sole responsibility for pronouncing death" (*TYOTI*, 5).

Readers are first introduced to Dr. Peters as he is summoned in the middle of the night to confirm the death of an elderly patient. Although Peters has obviously witnessed death before, he has never before been responsible for making the "judgment call" (5). Stricken by the burden of this new responsibility and uncertain of what he should do, Dr. Peters wavers: "He was dead. Or…was he?" In touching detail, Cook depicts Peters' moments of uncertainty:

I took out my stethoscope slowly, postponing the decision, and finally settled the pieces into my ears while I held the diaphragm on the old man's heart.…I couldn't hear the heart—yet couldn't I, almost? Muffled and far away?…My overheated imagination kept giving me the vital, normal beat of life. And then I realized it was my own heart echoing in my ears. Pulling the stethoscope away, I tried again for pulses, at the wrists, groin, and neck. All was quiet, yet an eerie feeling said he was alive, that he was going to wake up and I was going to be a fool. How could he be dead when I had talked with him a few hours ago? I hated being where I was. Who was I to say whether he was alive or dead? Who was I? (*TYOTI*, 5–6)

Dr. Peters applies his stethoscope again, and finally says, "He's dead, I guess" (*TYOTI*, 6), but there is more for him to do. He must now call the next of kin, and this presents him with a new set of anxieties, as he tries to determine what he should say: "I tried to think of some neutral word, one to convey the fact without the meaning. 'Dead,' 'demise'…no, 'passed away.' " When an experienced nurse appears and asks him to sign the death certificate, Peters wonders aloud when the old man died; the nurse's scornful reply takes him by surprise: "He died when you pronounced him dead, Doctor" (*TYOTI*, 7). Not sure even yet that the man is really and truly dead, Peters fights the urge to go back and check the pulse once again.

This poignant (and sympathetically comical) scene—wherein the young doctor confronts mortality and most reluctantly admits it, awkwardly yielding to its horrendous finality—is echoed in the concluding chapter. On this occasion the experience is Dr. Straus', and Peters' response takes a measure of the changes he has undergone in his year as intern. Peters is packing his belongings when Straus phones him:

"Well, what's the current crisis?" I asked.

"An old lady died. About eighty-five years old."

There was a pause. I didn't say anything, expecting to be told more about the problem. Straus' breathing could be heard on the other end of the line, but he apparently had nothing to add (*TYOTI*, 198).

As the telephone conversation continues, punctuated with many hesitations on Straus' end, it becomes quite apparent to the reader (though not to Peters) that Straus is suffering uncertainties very similar to those that earlier confounded Peters. Straus does not know what to say to the family or how to handle the necessary paperwork. Indeed, he seems to need someone else to confirm the death, but Peters refuses to help him out. Thus Straus is left to undergo alone the intern's traditional rites of initiation, and Peters, for whom a full-fledged "medical practice was at last within sight" (*TYOTI*, 189) wonders whether he should purchase a Mercedes or a Porsche. (He knows that the Cadillac is a favorite car with surgeons, but this conspicuous status symbol is not—at least not yet—quite to his taste.)

Offering the first of Robin Cook's highly authentic depictions of life within a hospital setting, *The Year of the Intern* examines hospital politics, outlining the hierarchical order that defines staff members' relations to one another. It emphasizes the competition that exists among the interns—all striving to catch the attention of the hospital's most important doctors. It portrays occasional incompetence in medicine, often the result (at least in cases involving interns) of exhaustion or confusion. The novel takes a measure of the psychological wear and tear that naturally occurs when people witness others' suffering or death, and it even notes the various physical discomforts that are a doctor's lot: for example, the irritation of being unable to scratch an itch within the operating room's sterile conditions. The hospital setting brings with it associated problems, those of dealing with drug companies or handling insurance claims. All of these details and others (debates, for instance, about the relative advantages and disadvantages of Medicare) are significant to Cook, who is interested in capturing as realistic a portrait as possible of both the intern's typical experience and the general flavor of hospital life. (Before submitting his manuscript for publication, he asked eight other young doctors to read it and confirm his observations.) Indeed, for the reader who is curious about the inner workings of the medical profession, *The Year of the Intern* provides an excellent introduction. Gail Jennes describes the work as the "rather sour tale of the harsh life led by doctors in training" (Jennes, 65), but *World Authors* notes the book's importance, claiming that "it can be seen as part of a growing protest against the processes of depersonalization built into medical training" (*World Authors*, 182).

Stookey, Lorena L. "The Life of Robin Cook." In *Robin Cook: A Critical Companion*. Santa Barbara, CA: Greenwood, 1996. http://ebooks.abc-clio.com/reader.aspx?isbn=9781573566537&id=GR9578-1. Reprinted with permission.

RESOURCES

Works in the American Thriller Genre _____

Dan Brown

Digital Fortress, 1998

Angels & Demons, 2000

Deception Point, 2001

The Da Vinci Code, 2003

The Lost Symbol, 2009

Inferno, 2013

Lee Child

Die Trying, 1997

Tripwire, 1999

Running Blind, 2000

Echo Burning, 2001

Without Fail, 2002

Persuader, 2003

The Enemy, 2004

One Shot, 2005

The Hard Way, 2006

Bad Luck and Trouble, 2007

Nothing to Lose, 2008

Gone Tomorrow, 2009

61 Hours, 2010

Worth Dying For, 2010

The Affair, 2011

A Wanted Man, 2012

Never Go Back, 2013

Tom Clancy

The Hunt for Red October, 1984

Red Storm Rising, 1986

Patriot Games, 1987

The Cardinal of the Kremlin, 1988

Clear and Present Danger, 1989

The Sum of All Fears, 1991

Without Remorse, 1993

Debt of Honor, 1994

Executive Orders, 1996

Rainbow Six, 1998

The Bear and the Dragon, 2000

Red Rabbit, 2002

The Teeth of the Tiger, 2003

Against All Enemies, 2011

Robin Cook

Year of the Intern, 1972

Coma, 1977

Sphinx, 1979

Brain, 1981

Fever, 1982

Godplayer, 1983

Mindbend, 1985

Outbreak, 1987

Mortal Fear, 1988

Mutation, 1989

Harmful Intent, 1990

Vital Signs, 1991

Blindsight, 1992

Terminal, 1993

Fatal Cure, 1994

Acceptable Risk, 1994

Contagion, 1995

Chromosome 6, 1997

Invasion, 1997

Toxin, 1998

Vector, 1999

Abduction, 2000

Shock, 2001

Seizure, 2003

Marker, 2005

Crisis, 2006

Foreign Body, 2008

Intervention, 2009

Michael Crichton

The Andromeda Strain, 1969

The Terminal Man, 1972

The Great Train Robbery, 1975

Eaters of the Dead, 1976

Congo, 1980

Sphere, 1987

Jurassic Park, 1990

Rising Sun, 1992

Disclosure, 1994

The Lost World, 1995

Airframe, 1996

Timeline, 1999

Prey, 2002

State of Fear, 2004

Next, 2006

Clive Cussler

The Mediterranean Caper, 1973

Iceberg, 1975

Raise the Titanic, 1976

Vixen 03, 1978

Night Probe, 1981

Pacific Vortex, 1983

Deep Six, 1984

Cyclops, 1986

Treasure, 1988

Dragon, 1990

Sahara, 1992

Inca Gold, 1994

Shock Wave, 1996

Flood Tide, 1997

Atlantis Found, 1999

Valhalla Rising, 2001

Trojan Odyssey, 2003

John Grisham

A Time to Kill, 1989

The Firm, 1991

The Pelican Brief, 1992

The Client, 1993

The Chamber, 1994

The Rainmaker, 1995

The Runaway Jury, 1996

The Partner, 1997

The Street Lawyer, 1998

The Testament, 1999

The Brethren, 2000

A Painted House, 2001

The Summons, 2002

The King of Torts, 2003
The Last Juror, 2004
The Broker, 2005
The Appeal, 2008
The Associate, 2009
The Confession, 2010
The Litigators, 2011
The Racketeer, 2012
Sycamore Row, 2013

Thomas Harris

Black Sunday, 1975
Red Dragon, 1981
The Silence of the Lambs, 1988
Hannibal, 1999
Hannibal Rising, 2006

James Patterson

Along Came a Spider, 1993
Kiss the Girls, 1995
Hide and Seek, 1996
Jack & Jill, 1996
Cat and Mouse, 1997
When the Wind Blows, 1998
Pop Goes the Weasel, 1999
Roses are Red, 2000
1st to Die, 2001
Violets Are Blue, 2001
2nd Chance, 2002
Four Blind Mice, 2002
The Lake House, 2003
The Big Bad Wolf, 2003

3rd Degree, 2004

London Bridges, 2004

Mary, Mary, 2005

Cross, 2006

Double Cross, 2007

Cross Country, 2008

I, Alex Cross, 2009

Cross Fire, 2010

Kill Alex Cross, 2011

Merry Christmas, Alex Cross, 2012

Alex Cross, Run, 2013

Cross My Heart, 2013

Bibliography

Anderson, Patrick. *The Triumph of the Thriller: How Cops, Crooks, and Cannibals Captured Popular Fiction.* New York: Random House, 2007.

Bloom, Clive. *Bestsellers: Popular Fiction Since 1900.* New York: Palgrave Macmillan, 2002.

Branton, Matthew. *Writing a Bestselling Thriller.* London: Hodder Education, 2012.

Brown, Jeffrey A. *Dangerous Curves: Action Heroines, Gender, Fetishism, and Popular Culture.* Jackson, MI: UP of Mississippi, 2011.

Caweli, John G. *Adventure, Mystery, and Romance: Formula Stories as Art and Popular Culture.* Chicago: U of Chicago P, 1976.

Cobley, Paul. *The American Thriller: Generic Innovation and Social Change in the 1970s.* New York: Palgrave Macmillan, 2000.

DeAndrea, William L. *Encyclopedia Mysteriosa: A Comprehensive Guide to the Art of Detection in Print, Film, Radio, and Television.* New York: Prentice Hall, 1994.

Grafton, Sue, ed. *Writing Mysteries: A Handbook by the Mystery Writers of America.* Cincinnati, OH: Writer's Digest Books, 2002.

Harper, Ralph. *The World of the Thriller.* Cleveland, OH: Case Western Reserve University Press, 1969.

Haycraft, Howard. *Murder for Pleasure: The Life and Times of the Detective Story.* New York: D. Appleton-Century Company, 1941.

Hilfer, Tony. *The Crime Novel: A Deviant Genre.* Austin, TX: University of Texas Press, 1990.

James, P. D. *Talking About Detective Fiction.* New York: Vintage Books, 2009.

Kotker, Joan G. *Dean Koontz: A Critical Companion.* Westport: Greenwood Press, 1996.

Mansfield-Kelley, Deane and Lois A. Marchino, eds. *The Longman Anthology of Detective Fiction.* New York: Pearson, 2005.

Martin, Brett. *Difficult Men—Behind the Scenes of a Creative Revolution: From* TheSopranos *and* The Wire *to* Mad Men *and* Breaking Bad. New York: Penguin Books, 2013.

Meehan, Paul. *Tech-Noir: The Fusion of Science Fiction and Film Noir.* Jefferson: McFarland, 2008.

Mortimer, John, ed. *The Oxford Book of Villains*. Oxford, UK: Oxford UP, 1992.

Noel, Mary. *Villains Galore: The Heyday of the Popular Story Weekly*. New York: Macmillan, 1954.

Palmer, Jerry. *Thrillers: Genesis and Structure of a Popular Genre*. New York: St. Martin's Press, 1979.

Peach, Linda. *Masquerade, Crime and Fiction: Criminal Deceptions*. New York: Palgrave Macmillan, 2006.

Penzler, Otto, Chris Steinbrunner, & Marvin Lachman, eds. *Detectionary: A Biographical Dictionary of Leading Characters in Detective and Mystery Fiction, including Famous and Little-Known Sleuths, Their Helpers, Rogues both Heroic and Sinister, and Some of Their Most Memorable Adventures, as Recounted in Novels, Short Stories, and Films*. New York: Overlook Press, 1977.

Renner, Jodie. *Writing a Killer Thriller: An Editor's Guide to Writing Compelling Fiction*. Jacksonville: Cobalt Books, 2012.

Rzepka, Charles J. *Detective Fiction*. Malden, MA: Polty Press, 2005.

Sampson, Robert. *Yesterday's Faces: A Study of Series Characters in the Early Pulp Magazines—Volume I, Glory Figures*. Bowling Green, OH: Bowling Green U Popular U, 1983.

Sims, Michael, ed. *The Penguin Book of Gaslight Crime*. New York: Penguin Books, 2009.

Steinbrunner, Chris and Otto Penzler, eds. *Encyclopedia of Mystery and Detection*. New York: McGraw-Hill, 1976.

Stone, Nancy-Stephanie. *A Reader's Guide to the Spy and Thriller Novel*. New York: G.K. Hall, 1997.

Stookey, Lorena Laura. *Robin Cook: A Critical Companion*. Westport: Greenwood Press, 1996.

Symons, Julian. *Bloody Murder—From the Detective Story to the Crime Novel: A History*. New York: Viking, 1985.

Trembley, Elizabeth A. *Michael Crichton: A Critical Companion*. Westport, CT: Greenwood Press, 1996.

Watson, Colin. *Snobbery with Violence: Crime Stories and Their Audience*. New York: St. Martin's Press, 1971.

Weinman, Sarah, ed. *Troubled Daughters, Twisted Wives: Stories from the Trailblazers of Domestic Suspense*. New York: Penguin Books, 2013.

About the Editor ⎯⎯⎯⎯⎯⎯⎯⎯⎯⎯⎯⎯⎯⎯

Gary Hoppenstand is a professor in the Department of English at Michigan State University. As a graduate student, he studied with Professor Ray Browne, one of the most important scholars involved in the creation of popular culture studies at the university level. Hoppenstand's major research areas are genre and formula studies in fiction and film. He has published numerous books and articles and has won many awards for his teaching and research. Currently, he is serving as associate dean of undergraduate academic affairs in the College of Arts and Letters at Michigan State University.

Contributors _____

Abby Bentham is a PhD candidate at the University of Salford. Her research interests range from literary studies to film and television, and she has published on subjects as diverse as Dickens and *Dexter*. Abby is particularly interested in representations of the psychopath, and her thesis charts the literary trajectory of this figure from the late nineteenth century to the present day. Her latest project, which looks at spectatorship and surveillance in the *Saw* films, will be published in an edited collection on the franchise in 2014.

Elizabeth Blakesley holds an MLS degree and an MA in comparative literature from Indiana University. Her BA is in English and Spanish from the University of Dayton. Blakesley currently serves as the associate dean of libraries at Washington State University. Blakesley is also adjunct associate professor at the University of Maryland University College, where she has taught information literacy courses online since 2001. In addition to a number of articles on instruction, assessment, and leadership topics, Blakesley is the author of *Great Women Mystery Writers,* 2nd ed. (Greenwood 2006); co-author of *Literary Research and American Modernism, 1915–1949* (Scarecrow 2008); and co-editor of *Information Literacy Instruction Handbook* (ACRL, 2008). She reviews mystery and suspense novels for *Library Journal* and is an active member of the Mystery/Detective Fiction Area of the Popular Culture Association.

John A. Dowell's work and thought have appeared on Detroit's WXYZ-TV, in *Grue* magazine, in the *Encyclopedia of American Popular Beliefs and Superstition*, in *Salon*, and in the *Journal of Popular Film and Television*. In addition to playing bass for a variety of musical venues, Dowell has sold a number of scripts, screenplays, and video treatments for cold, hard cash. He has also chaired the Midwest Popular Culture Association/ American Culture Association panels for the Humor Area and the Horror/ Science Fiction/Fantasy Area for over a decade. Dowell is currently the technology literacy specialist for the Undergraduate University Division's Learning Resources Center at Michigan State University. When he isn't helping students discover effective gizmo/software tech, he likes to work on their brainpan wetware by lecturing and work-shopping various rhetorical techniques for presenting their innovative ideas with convincing authority. With backgrounds in anthropology, sociology, and folk studies from Western Kentucky University, and American popular culture studies from Bowling Green State University, he is currently co-editing a book on his dissertation topic, sLaughter (the nexus of simultaneous humor and horror), titled *Sidesplitting: sLaughter in Popular Cinema*. It promises to tear you a new one.

Kristopher Mecholsky is a member of the faculty at Louisiana State University and a scholar of American literature and culture, crime narratives, adaptation, film, and science and literature. He earned his bachelor's degree in physics and English from the Catholic University of America (2004), his master's in literature and language at Marymount University (2008), and his doctorate in English at LSU (2012). His book on James M. Cain (co-authored with David Madden) was published in 2011 through Scarecrow Press. He has written on Douglas Sirk and has articles forthcoming on Sherlock Holmes (through the Victorian journal *The OScholars*) and on Martin Scorsese's *Shutter Island* (for an edited collection published by McFarland). He is also a contributing columnist for the University of Texas at Austin's online television journal, *Flow*.

Ayoola Onatade is a freelance crime fiction critic and blogger. She received her bachelor of arts in social science from the University of Westminster and a masters degree in reading modernity (specifically, postcolonial and postmodern English literature) from London South Bank University in 2001. She has written a number of articles on different aspects of crime fiction and has also given papers on the subject, mainly at the annual St Hilda's Crime and Mystery Conference, Oxford. She blogs at *Shotsmag Confidential* (wwwshotsmagcouk.blogspot.com) and writes articles and interviews at *Shotsmag* (www.shotsmag.co.uk), an online crime fiction e-zine. She has been a regular contributor to *Crimespree Magazine* since 2007 and is an occasional contributor to *Mystery Journal International*. She was a contributor to *British Crime Writing: An Encyclopaedia* (2008), edited by Barry Forshaw. She has also moderated and taken part in panels at Crimefest and Bouchercon. A member of the Crime Writers Association of Great Britain (CWA) and Sisters in Crime (SinC), she currently chairs the CWA Short Story Dagger Judging Panel and also helps judge the Historical Writers Association (HWA)/Goldsboro Crown Award for debut historical fiction. Her research interests include historical and crime fiction.

Chris Richardson's research explores representations of crime in contemporary popular culture. His PhD in Media Studies (Western University, 2012) built on his bachelor of journalism degree (Ryerson University, 2007) and his master of arts degree in interdisciplinary studies of popular culture (Brock University, 2008) to explore how media professionals can improve the impact and accuracy of crime coverage by reassessing how they choose sources, establish metaphorical language, and reproduce popular crime narratives. Richardson is an executive member of the Popular Culture Association of Canada; a Faculty Advisor for Lambda Pi Eta, The National Communication Association's undergraduate honors society; and the founder and supervisor of the Young Harris College Media Studies Research Collective. His research has appeared in *Popular Music and Society*, *The Canadian Journal of Criminology and Criminal Justice*, and *The British Journal of Canadian Studies*. In 2012, he published *Habitus of the Hood* with Hans Skott-Myhre, interrogating intersections of street culture and popular media. Their next project is on social theory and drug dealing.

Garyn G. Roberts, PhD, is a college and university professor. He holds multiple literary and teaching awards. Roberts was born in northern Wisconsin, one hundred miles north of Plainfield, about a year after Ed Gein's atrocities were discovered. (When Gein's activities were discovered in November 1957, it was deer season in Wisconsin and Roberts' father was hunting. To this day, Roberts' mother recounts how frightened she was at home alone in the woods, a twenty-three-year-old newlywed, when the news from Plainfield broke.) Though he never met Robert Bloch in person, Roberts maintained a prolific, ongoing correspondence with Bloch (his dear friend) until Bloch's passing in 1994. Writing this essay, Roberts rediscovered how much original writing Bloch had done for him that has yet to be published. Someday…

Philip L. Simpson received his bachelor's and master's degrees in English from Eastern Illinois University in 1986 and 1989, respectively, and his doctorate in American literature from Southern Illinois University in 1996.

He serves as Provost of the Titusville Campus of Eastern Florida State College. Before that, he was a tenured professor of Communications and Humanities, as well as Department Chair of Liberal Arts, at the Palm Bay campus of Brevard Community College. He also served as President of the Popular Culture Association and Area Chair of Horror for the Association. He received the Association's Felicia Campbell Area Chair Award in 2006. He currently serves as Area Co-Chair of the Stephen King Area and the Association's Vampire in Literature, Culture, and Film Area, and he sits on the editorial board of the *Journal of Popular Culture*. His first book, *Psycho Paths: Tracking the Serial Killer through Contemporary American Film and Fiction*, was published in 2000 by Southern Illinois University Press; his second book, *Making Murder: The Fiction of Thomas Harris*, was published in 2010 by Praeger Press. He is the author of numerous other published essays on film, literature, popular culture, and horror.

Susan J. Tyburski practiced "street law" for twenty years before retiring to become a part-time hearings officer for the Colorado Department of Corrections. She teaches law and literature at the University of Denver, as well as literature and writing at Red Rocks Community College. She is currently working on a study of Polish crime fiction. Her research interests include the intersections of law, literature, and society.

Kate Watson completed a PhD on gender and crime fiction at Cardiff University in 2010 and is a lecturer in English at Cardiff Metropolitan University, UK. She has published several articles on crime fiction. Recent outputs include *Women Writing Crime Fiction, 1860-1880: Fourteen American, British and Australian Authors* (McFarland 2012); "Engendering Violence: Textual and Sexual Torture in Val McDermid's *The Mermaids Singing*" in *Constructing Crime: Discourse and Cultural Representations of Crime and 'Deviance'* (Palgrave Macmillan 2012); and an entry on Ngaio Marsh in *100 British Crime Writers*, ed. Esme Miskimmin (Palgrave Macmillan 2013). Her article "The Imprint in Print: Tattoos, Women, and Crime Narratives" has been accepted for *Mystery, Magnified: An Investigation into Contemporary and Classic Detective Fiction*, ed. Casey Cothran and Mercy Cannon (to be published in 2014). Her second book is *A Reader's Guide to Essential Criticism: Crime and Detective Fiction* (Palgrave Macmillan), scheduled for publication in 2015.

Index _____
